Human Rights and Islam

ELGAR STUDIES IN HUMAN RIGHTS

Discourse on human rights has grown ever more visible and essential, with human rights principles being discussed and scrutinized on both the international and national stage. This series brings together high-quality works of scholarship in the field of human rights, primarily in law, but particularly those with a critical or analytical edge, or those taking innovative and interdisciplinary approaches. Books in the series also address concerns at the intersection of human rights and other fields, such as trade, the environment, international investment and religion, thus contributing to the depth and breadth of scholarship so vital to understanding the complicated matters at stake.

Titles in the series include:

Refugees, Regionalism and Responsibility
Penelope Mathew and Tristan Harley

Expanding Human Rights
21st Century Norms and Governance
Edited by Alison Brysk and Michael Stohl

The Legal Protection of Refugees with Disabilities
Forgotten and Invisible?
Mary Crock, Laura Smith-Khan, Ron McCallum and Ben Saul

Contracting Human Rights
Crisis, Accountability, and Opportunity
Edited by Alison Brysk and Michael Stohl

Using Human Rights to Counter Terrorism
Edited by Manfred Nowak and Anne Charbord

Human Rights and Islam
An Introduction to Key Debates between Islamic Law and International Human Rights Law
Abdullah Saeed

Human Rights and Islam

An Introduction to Key Debates between Islamic Law and International Human Rights Law

Abdullah Saeed

Sultan of Oman Professor of Arab and Islamic Studies, University of Melbourne, Australia, and Advisor to the Studies in Interreligious Relations in Plural Societies Programme, RSIS, Nanyang Technological University, Singapore

ELGAR STUDIES IN HUMAN RIGHTS

Edward Elgar PUBLISHING

Cheltenham, UK • Northampton, MA, USA

Published by
Edward Elgar Publishing Limited
The Lypiatts
15 Lansdown Road
Cheltenham
Glos GL50 2JA
UK

Edward Elgar Publishing, Inc.
William Pratt House
9 Dewey Court
Northampton
Massachusetts 01060
USA

A catalogue record for this book
is available from the British Library

Library of Congress Control Number: 2017959499

This book is available electronically in the **Elgar**online
Law subject collection
DOI 10.4337/9781784716585

Printed on elemental chlorine free (ECF)
recycled paper containing 30% Post-Consumer Waste

ISBN 978 1 78471 657 8 (cased)
ISBN 978 1 78471 658 5 (eBook)

Typeset by Columns Design XML Ltd, Reading
Printed and bound in the USA

Contents

Introduction

Despite common perceptions to the contrary, there is a dynamic human rights discourse in Muslim thought today. However, there is no consensus among scholars on the question of whether Islam and human rights are compatible. Some Muslim thinkers have embraced the notion of human rights, taking the position that they are basically compatible with Islam. Other scholars argue that contemporary notions of human rights are fundamentally at odds with Islam. Still others see tensions between the two traditions, but believe that they are in no way incompatible with each other. This "harmonistic perspective"[1] acknowledges that although there are differences between Islam and international human rights discourse that can lead to conflicts and tension, "there are concepts, doctrines and tools of interpretation … that can be used to harmonise the two".[2] Of these approaches, this book is concerned primarily with the harmonistic perspective; in other words, the view that Islam can be reconciled with human rights.

The idea of "rights" is not new to Islam. In fact, the concept of a "right" (or in Arabic, *haqq)* can be found in classical and modern Islamic scholarship. The most important sources of rights and obligations in Islam are the Qur'an and the Sunnah (the traditions of the Prophet Muhammad). This means that rights come from a "religious-moral framework where the omission of a duty/right is subject to religious sanction and its commission results in the acquisition of virtue".[3] While, based on this view, God grants rights to human beings, it is human authorities who realise and enforce them in communities. Thus, over time, different Islamic theological and legal schools have developed bodies of jurisprudence and scholarship on rights that have come to different conclusions about what a right is and how it can be conferred.[4] The idea of "human rights" comes under this wider discourse on "rights" in Islamic tradition.

More recently, since the 1980s, the amount of scholarship on the relationship between Islam and human rights has increased.[5] There are a number of reasons for this. Human rights are an influential discourse in political, legal, and sometimes even economic circles today, and "as members of the international community … Muslim-majority states have not been immune to the influence of these norms and the debates on their implementation".[6] The number of civil society groups within Muslim-majority states has also grown, which has brought even greater awareness of human rights to many Muslim communities. Thus, "Muslim governments, activists and scholars are … increasingly interested in the question of whether and how human rights norms should be implemented in Muslim-majority states."[7]

In recent years a number of scholars have emerged who are working to overcome the idea of the "incompatibility" of Islam and international human rights. Some scholars argue that among Muslims, the view that human rights and Islam are incompatible does not actually come from opposition to the concept of human rights itself. Instead, it reflects "a disappointment and protest towards Western hegemony and consequently any ideology that is apparently championed by the Western nations".[8] Alternatively, it might originate from a perception that the West has double standards when it comes to human rights because it reacts differently to abuses under Muslim-majority, compared to non-Muslim, regimes.[9] However, there are also legitimate faith-based objections to the idea of human rights. Michael Freeman points out that, for a religious Muslim, submitting to any authority other than the divine law is problematic from the perspective of personal piety.[10] Abdullahi An-Na'im, a prominent Muslim human rights scholar, argues that if adherents of religions (including Islam) are excluded from the human rights conversation, they are unlikely to accept the universal applicability of human rights.[11]

Focusing on the area of law, Mashood Baderin has argued that international human rights law and Islamic law can be reconciled. However, to achieve compatibility, a number of barriers must first be surmounted. These include Western perspectives of Islamic law as "essentially [a] defective legal system",[12] as well as "hardline interpretations of the *Shari'ah*".[13] However, Baderin believes the two systems are not antithetical, particularly if human rights can be "convincingly established from within … Islamic law rather than … as a concept alien to [it]".[14] Baderin draws on principles from the Islamic legal tradition such as *maslaha* (public welfare),[15] which I discuss further in Chapter 1. Baderin also finds support in modern legal ideas such as the doctrine of the "margin of appreciation"[16] put forward by the European Court of Human Rights. This doctrine refers to "an area of discretion left to the national authority" in international law.[17] According to Baderin, this doctrine might allow for the harmonisation of different societies' "justifiable moral values", by "striking a balance between a right guaranteed [by international treaty] ... and a permitted derogation"[18] that allows variation at the state level.[19]

As I have written previously,[20] at the core of many discussions about the compatibility of Islam and international human rights norms is the question of the role of the classical Islamic legal tradition in our contemporary context. In my view, scholars who hold more closely to classical interpretations of Islamic law tend to conclude that modern human rights norms are incompatible with Islamic tradition.[21] In contrast, scholars who allow more room in interpretation and see Islamic law as flexible and able to evolve are more open to the human rights discourse.[22]

These latter scholars perceive that Islamic law offers many values, concepts, and moral principles that can be adapted to construct human rights principles.[23] For example, An-Na'im argues that Islamic law can be reformed from within to conform to international human rights principles using a reverse process of *naskh* (the abrogation of certain rulings of the Qur'an by others). In this he follows the view of Sudanese scholar Mahmoud Mohamed Taha (d. 1985). An-Na'im suggests that those parts of the Qur'an that seem to be incompatible with international human rights—almost entirely from the later Medinan phase of the Prophet's life—could be set aside in favour of the earlier Meccan part.[24]

Other scholars propose an approach that draws on the concept of *maqasid al-shari'a* (purposes of the Shari'a or Islamic law). The *maqasid* approach focuses on identifying the essential goals or objectives of the Shari'a, such as the promotion of human welfare and the prevention of harm, which can be used to approach contemporary issues. The *maqasid* approach, in its more systematic form, is often traced back to the fourteenth-century Andalusian jurist Abu Ishaq al-Shatibi (d. 790/1388), who believed that God's original intention when revealing the Shari'a was to protect the religious and ordinary interests of human beings.[25] Modern scholars have seen in the *maqasid* perspective a "holistic approach for realising the appropriate and benevolent scope of Islamic law".[26]

A key issue that arises in the debate on Islam and human rights is whether Islamic law can accommodate a conception of rights similar to that found in the international human rights discourse. Those commentators who argue that Islamic law and international human rights law are fundamentally incompatible often suggest that Islamic law comes from a duties-based paradigm where duties are emphasised over rights.[27] Others, however, argue that giving effect to human rights necessarily imposes certain duties, whether on the state or individuals.[28] Still others suggest that more recognition of the duties arising from human rights can only be beneficial for international human rights law.[29]

The discourse on whether Islam and human rights are compatible is a critically important one. It is related to the broader concern about whether human rights are indeed universal and has important ramifications for those in the Muslim world who do not experience the freedoms and entitlements that other people around the world take for granted.[30] Islam is a pervasive influence legally, socially, and culturally in Muslim states; thus, as I have argued elsewhere, "the relationship between Islam and human rights needs to be clarified for human rights norms to be accepted and implemented in the Muslim world".[31]

In my view, international human rights law, as articulated by instruments such as the Universal Declaration of Human Rights, can be harmonised with Islamic law. The goal, as I see it, is not necessarily to develop an alternative "Islamic" rights framework but to foster participation in the global discourse. However, it is important for Muslims to have the opportunity to re-frame universal rights in such a way that reflects the contexts and values that are most relevant to them. This way of conceptualising the human rights discourse is probably important for many religious traditions, not just for Islam. It is crucial for people of different religious traditions and cultures to be able to conceptualise human rights in ways that are meaningful to them.

The theologian and former UN Special Rapporteur on freedom of religion or belief Heiner Bielefeldt argues that human rights should not be seen as a "yardstick" for measuring cultures and religions generally.[32] Nor, indeed, are they an all-encompassing "way of life", nor even "the highest manifestation of ethical spirit in human history".[33] However, because they rely on the idea that human beings deserve equal respect, they affirm the principle of human dignity, which has roots in many cultures and religious traditions.[34] For this reason, they have the potential for "significant influence on the self-perception of societies and cultural or religious communities in a way that extends beyond law and politics".[35] In my view, this approach will lead to the promotion of human rights in any religious community, including in Muslim communities across the globe.

ABOUT THIS BOOK

This book is written to introduce some of the key debates surrounding the compatibility of Islamic law (or Shari'a) and human rights and how Muslims today are responding to those debates with a view to reconciling the human rights discourse with Islamic norms and values. Given the range of topics it covers, it is not practical to deal with each topic in great depth or to discuss how this reconciliation might work in relation to every right this book covers. However, the topics covered provide the student and the general reader with a sense of how both international human rights law and Islamic law deal with each issue, the challenges they are facing in dealing with the issue, and some suggestions for reconciliation between the two. The book is expected to be accessible for the student and the general reader. As it proposes ways by which tensions can be addressed, readers will also be exposed to the potential that exists within Islamic tradition for the generation of new ideas in this space.

Specifically, the book aims to:

- Identify and reflect on some of the key issues in the discourse on Islam and human rights;
- Explain briefly the emergence and development of human rights and Islamic law within their respective historical contexts and highlight key influences and sources of authority;
- Highlight the plurality of approaches, responses, and understandings of human rights among Muslims and Muslim-majority states;
- Critically assess some arguments which suggest that Islam and international human rights are fundamentally incompatible;
- Discuss some Muslim-majority states' engagement with the international human rights system and the contributions of Muslim states towards the development of alternative human rights systems; and
- Reflect on the contemporary challenges that Muslim-majority and "secular" states are experiencing when promoting and protecting human rights.

The book consists of eleven chapters, each of which contains a "case" or "extract" to assist readers and students to think through a core issue related to the topic of the chapter.

The first two chapters establish a conceptual framework understanding international human rights law and Islamic law, and the perspectives on human rights that have emerged in each tradition. Chapter 1 describes the most important Islamic textual sources of authority and presents an overview of Islam's legal framework, including the tools and methodologies that are regularly used in legal reasoning. Chapter 2 addresses the fundamental question: what are human rights? It also provides an overview of the development of the international human rights discourse, from its inception in the context of natural law theories to its codification in the aftermath of the Second World War.

Chapters 3 and 4 consider two key developments in the discourse on Islam and international human rights. Chapter 3 focuses on the efforts made by Muslims to engage with the international human rights system and reflects on the "Islamic" human rights instruments that have been developed in recent years as alternatives to international human rights instruments. Chapter 4 considers the controversial argument put forward by Samuel Huntington that differences between "civilisations" would be a fundamental source of conflict in the future. Arguments such as Huntington's, including some from Muslims, have had important ramifications for the discourse on human rights, with some arguing that Islamic conceptions of rights are fundamentally different to modern conceptions and therefore irreconcilable with them.

Chapters 5 and 6 shift the discussion to the state context, and consider how modern nation states—both Muslim-majority and "secular" states—are responding to the challenges of religion, governance, and the protection of all citizens' human rights. Chapter 5 asks whether there is one particular model that is best for realising human rights. If this is the case, is it possible that "Islamic" models of governance can promote and protect human rights? This chapter also considers the beneficial elements of democracy as a system of governance and whether Islamic norms and democracy are in fact compatible. Chapter 6 also looks at governance, but explores a number of different frameworks for managing the relationship between religion and the state. It reflects on how these impact the practice of human rights and religious freedom in various states.

The final five chapters of the book focus on substantive areas of rights. Each chapter presents an overview of a right or set of rights as conceptualised under international human rights law, including key elements of the right and the main instruments and provisions that elaborate it. The chapters then set out Islamic conceptions of the rights, emphasising areas of common ground and key challenges or tensions. Each chapter concludes with a brief assessment of the compatibility of Islamic and international law in that area, and potential strategies for moving the discourse forward. The substantive rights that are addressed in this book are those that are commonly cited in discussions about Islam and human rights and are arguably areas where the greatest challenges exist in finding common points between the two traditions. These rights or sets of rights include: the rights of women and non-discrimination (Chapter 7); the rights of the child (Chapter 8); freedom of expression (Chapter 9); freedom of religion (Chapter 10); and the regulations governing armed conflict (Chapter 11).

I would like thank a number of my colleagues who acted as research assistants for this project. In particular, Rowan Gould, Patricia Prentice and Adis Duderija and many others who read the draft of the chapters and contributed immensely to polish the arguments and content of the book.

NOTES

1. See Mashood A. Baderin, "Islam and the Realization of Human Rights in the Muslim World: A Reflection on Two Essential Approaches and Two Divergent Perspectives", *Muslim World Journal of Human Rights* 4(1) (2007): 12.
2. See Abdullah Saeed, "Review Article" in *Islam and Human Rights*, Abdullah Saeed (ed.) (Cheltenham, UK and Northampton, MA, USA: Edward Elgar Publishing, 2012).
3. Ebrahim Moosa, "The Dilemma of Islamic Rights Schemes", *Journal of Law and Religion* 15(1/2) (2000–2001): 193.
4. Moosa, "The Dilemma of Islamic Rights Schemes", 194.
5. Ann Elizabeth Mayer, "The Islam and Human Rights Nexus: Shifting Dimensions", *Muslim World Journal of Human Rights* 4(1) (2007): 2.
6. Saeed, "Review Article".
7. Ibid.
8. Farrukh B. Hakeem, M.R. Haberfeld, and Arvind Verma, *Policing Muslim Communities: Comparative International Context* (New York: Springer, 2012), 45–6.
9. Hakeem, Haberfeld, and Verma, *Policing Muslim Communities*, 46. See also Abdullahi A. An-Na'im, *Toward an Islamic Reformation: Civil Liberties, Human Rights, and International Law* (Syracuse, NY: Syracuse University Press, 1990), 159.
10. Michael Freeman, "The Problem of Secularism in Human Rights Theory", *Human Rights Quarterly* 26 (2004): 377.
11. Abdullahi A. An-Na'im, "The Interdependence of Religion, Secularism, and Human Rights", *Common Knowledge* 11(1) (2005): 61.
12. Mashood A. Baderin, *International Human Rights and Islamic Law* (Oxford: Oxford University Press, 2005), 11.
13. Ibid.
14. Ibid, 6.
15. Ibid.
16. Ibid.
17. Wing-wah Mary Wong, "The Sunday Times Case: Freedom of Expression versus English Contempt-of-Court Law in the European Court of Human Rights", *New York University Journal of International Law and Politics* 17 (1984): 58.
18. Baderin, *International Human Rights*, 231. See Yourow, H.C., *The Margin of Appreciation Doctrine in the Dynamics of European Human Rights Jurisprudence* (1996) p. 13, citing Wong, W.M., ibid., 35 at 58.
19. Baderin, *International Human Rights*, 6.
20. Saeed, "Review Article".
21. Ibid.
22. Ibid.
23. Hakeem, Haberfeld, and Verma, *Policing Muslim Communities*, 45.
24. An-Na'im, *Toward an Islamic Reformation, 52–7.*
25. Wael B. Hallaq, *A History of Islamic Legal Theories: An Introduction to Sunni uṣul al-fiqh*, (Cambridge: Cambridge University Press, 1997), 168.
26. Hakeem, Haberfeld, and Verma, *Policing Muslim Communities*, 49.
27. Jack Donnelly, "Human Rights and Human Dignity: An Analytic Critique of Non-Western Conceptions of Human Rights", *American Political Science Review* 76(2) (1982): 306–7.

28. Mashood A. Baderin, "Human Rights and Islamic Law: The Myth of Discord", *European Human Rights Law Review* 2 (2005): 174–5.
29. Jason Morgan-Foster, "Third Generation Rights: What Islamic Law Can Teach the International Human Rights Movement", *Yale Human Rights and Development Law Journal* 8 (2005): 115–16.
30. Baderin, "Islam and the Realization of Human Rights", 1.
31. Saeed, "Review Article".
32. Heiner Bielefeldt, "Muslim Voices in the Human Rights Debate", *Human Rights Quarterly* 17(4) (1995): 588.
33. Ibid.
34. Ibid, 589.
35. Ibid, 588.

1. Human rights and Islamic legal sources

Muslim thinkers and scholars who argue for an Islamic conception of human rights, in general, agree that it is essential for a connection between international human rights and Islamic values to be established if the human rights discourse is to gain widespread support among Muslims. For many Muslims, an Islamic conception of human rights should be based on the authoritative texts of Islam, namely, the Qur'an and the traditions of the Prophet Muhammad (d. 11/632), as well as the principles of Islamic law, as there is a close connection between Muslim discourses on human rights and Islamic law. Therefore, it is important for us to commence our journey exploring Islam and human rights with a brief look at the most important sources of Islamic law and at least some understanding of what Islamic law is. With this in mind, this chapter will first set out the most important Islamic textual sources and legal tools that can be used in this pursuit, briefly recounting some of the history of their development and exploring their potential in developing an Islamic conception of human rights.

THE SOURCES OF ISLAMIC LAW

The Qur'an

While Muslims consider the Qur'an to be the Word of God, it is not a legal code. Instead, the Qur'an describes itself as "guidance for humankind" (Q. 2:185). According to Muslim belief, the Qur'an was revealed by God to the Prophet Muhammad over a period stretching from 610 to 632 CE, while he lived in Mecca and Medina. These revelations became the foundation for the Prophet's practical and ethical teachings and guidance. Importantly, the particular guidance and teaching that the Qur'an provided to the Prophet and his followers were closely connected to the context of the seventh century CE. Moreover, as the community's situation changed, so did the Qur'an's instructions.

The society into which the Qur'an was revealed had a different understanding of individual and collective rights to that which exists in many parts of the world today. But despite such differences, I argue that much of the guidance provided in the Qur'an can be applied to our context today. There are only a few verses that are clearly not applicable to the contemporary period. I do not believe that these verses pose an obstacle to the construction of an Islamic human rights discourse. Throughout this book I will highlight some of the verses that appear problematic, as well as those that offer clear pathways towards a conception of human rights that can operate in an Islamic framework.

The most significant such pathway is the Qur'an's insistence on recognising the dignity of the human person. The Qur'an says, "We created human beings in the finest state." (Q. 95:4) The Qur'an also declares that: "We have honoured the children of Adam" (Q 17:70) and, in describing Adam's creation, "I breathed from My Spirit into him." (Q. 38:72) Thus, a unique dignity was granted through God's very act of the creation of Adam, and in particular His breathing into him of His Spirit. Since all of humanity is, according Muslim belief, descended from Adam, every human being possesses this God-given dignity.[1]

In contemporary Muslim scholarship on human rights, it is quite common to find references to these Qur'anic verses, with scholars highlighting the similarities that certain human rights have to the message of the Qur'an. Since God is the primary authority in Islam and the Qur'an is, for Muslims, the very Word of God, to cite the Qur'an in support of a particular human right gives this position great legitimacy. However, this can work both ways. It is equally possible to reject certain rights while drawing on the Qur'an for justification. Qur'anic verses can and have been interpreted towards a variety of ends.

In my view, if the context of any given verse is given proper consideration, the Qur'an can be of great help in developing an Islamic human rights discourse. This is not simply a matter of trying to read certain meanings into relevant Qur'anic texts to support a particular right. Such texts need to be read within the broader framework of the values and norms that the Qur'an contains. It is important to consider how any given text was understood in the early centuries of Islam; how it is understood today; and how this may or may not be applied to contemporary issues. The interpretation of such texts will, of course, vary from period to period, but I agree with Fazlur Rahman that it is always possible to find meaning that remains as a core value, transcending time and place.[2] It is these core values that can be drawn upon to argue in support of particular human rights within an Islamic framework.

Hadith or Traditions of the Prophet

The second important authority in Islam that can be used in developing a meaningful Islamic human rights discourse is the "traditions" of the Prophet, known as the hadith. The hadith are the documentation of the Prophet's example or normative behaviour. An example of hadith relevant to the discourse on human rights are the reports of the Prophet's famous Farewell Sermon, delivered in 10/632:

> O People, just as you regard this month, this day, this city as sacred, so regard the life and property of every Muslim as a sacred trust.
>
> Return the goods entrusted to you to their rightful owners. Hurt no one so that no one may hurt you.
>
> O People, it is true that you have certain rights with regard to your women, but they also have rights over you.
>
> Treat your women well and be kind to them, for they are your partners and committed helpers.
>
> All humankind is from Adam and Eve; an Arab has no superiority over a non-Arab and a non-Arab has no superiority over an Arab; a white has no superiority over a black and a black has no superiority over a white, except by piety and good action.[3]

Even though the Prophet lived in the early part of the seventh century CE in Mecca and Medina, his practice and teachings still have relevance to the contemporary period and need to be taken seriously. Given the sheer number of relevant hadith texts and their importance in Islamic legal tradition, it is impossible not to refer to hadith when developing an Islamic conception of human rights based on the practice of the Prophet. Indeed, some Muslim scholars argue that there are a wide range of hadith texts that are extremely relevant to contemporary thinking on human rights. The problem then arises: on what basis can Muslims differentiate between hadith texts that support human rights, and those that may not?

A key issue to be aware of when discussing hadith is that of historical authenticity. While Muslims consider the Qur'anic text to be historically reliable because it was compiled very soon after the Prophet died, the recording of hadith occurred differently. The first generation of Muslims were not particularly keen on putting together a reliable collection of hadith for future generations. This unfortunately resulted in a proliferation of unreliable hadith among the second and third generations of Muslims and beyond. When political conflict was rife among early

Muslims in the post-prophetic period, hadith were deliberately manipulated and in some cases entirely created in the service of political and ideological ends. Many hadith on the same subject thus may have contradictory messages. Sometimes, understanding the context may help to determine the true message of the hadith in question, but in other cases these contradictions cannot be overcome. Moreover, while the Qur'an quickly became a closed text, the hadith corpus was never a single, fixed document. Rather, they were proliferate and unregulated, and the reports that emerged contained both true prophetic example and inauthentic material.

To address the issue of authenticity, some scholars made it their project to scrutinise the chain of transmission of every hadith in public circulation. Through this analysis, these scholars were able to put together a number of hadith collections that Muslims deemed (to varying degrees) "reliable". Such collections began to emerge in the second century of Islam, continuing into the third and fourth centuries. Eventually, six major hadith collections came to be considered canonical, and remain so today for Sunni Muslims. However, the problem of contradiction continues to exist. Even when referring to the most "authentic" reports, it is still possible to find contradictory material within the hadith sources.

Traditional hadith scholarship relied heavily on the practice of scrutinising the chains of transmission to determine authenticity, but in contemporary Islamic scholarship there is a tendency to question this dependence. Following this view, those hadith that create difficulties for a contemporary human rights discourse might be subjected to further critical analysis. This might include interpreting them in light of their social and historical context, as well as the more traditional scrutiny of their chains of transmission. When a greater awareness of context is reached, it is possible to conclude that some of these hadith are simply no longer applicable in their literal form; alternatively, they might have a deeper message that transcends the literal meaning.

Ijma' (Consensus)

Apart from its two primary sources—the Qur'an and hadith—Islamic legal tradition deploys other tools that are also relevant here. One of these is *ijma'* or the consensus of the community (usually understood to be that of the jurists), which is considered a secondary source of law. Like many other issues or concepts within Islam, there are different ways of conceptualising "consensus", and there is no final agreement on what consensus means. However, what is clear is that consensus concerns initial disagreement and diversity of views around a particular issue, and then a collectively agreed upon position developing over time. The source of authority on which it appears to be based is Q. 4:59, which states: "You who believe, obey God and the Messenger, and those in authority among you. If you are in dispute over any matter, refer it to God and the Messenger." A hadith attributed to the Prophet also states, "My community will never agree on an error."[4]

The actual process of consensus therefore involves arriving at a collectively acceptable position after a process of discussion and debate. Such debates may take place over decades or even centuries, but when consensus is achieved, it carries a very high degree of authority. Some examples of consensus that have remained authoritative since the time of the Prophet include the importance of the five daily prayers, the practice of *zakat* (the obligatory alms tax), and the belief that the Qur'an is revelation from God.

In relation to human rights, Muslim scholars in the past came to a consensus on the idea that in certain cases human beings could be bought and sold. This notion of slavery was accepted in the Islamic legal tradition and was practised by Muslim societies up until the modern period. However, almost all Muslim scholars now argue that this consensus does not have any authority today. In fact, slavery in the sense of buying and selling human beings was abolished in all Muslim societies, where it was practised, in the twentieth century. This means that even though there may have been consensus on certain issues in the past, such consensus can be challenged in the modern period because of the significant differences between the context of the modern period and of the past.

Qiyas (Analogical Reasoning)

The final tool that is used to derive Islamic law is analogy or *qiyas*. Analogical reasoning has always been important in Islamic legal tradition. In fact, a large number of rules that are part of what we call Islamic law today were actually developed using analogy, based on the Qur'an and hadith. Given that there are very few texts in the Qur'an that are specifically related to matters of law, and the limitations in using hadith (discussed above), *qiyas* was regularly deployed to expand and apply what was textually available to a wider range of situations and circumstances.[5] As an example, Q. 2:219 clearly prohibits the consumption of wine. The rationale behind this prohibition, according to many jurists, is the effect of alcohol on the mind. Based on this rationale, any product that produces the same effects, such as narcotics, can be considered prohibited by analogy, thus expanding the scope of the rule.[6]

Without analogical reasoning, Islamic law as we know it probably would not have developed. It is because of analogy that we have such a comprehensive system of rules, regulations and laws in classical Islamic legal sources for addressing most aspects of life. However as people living in the twenty-first century, we may not necessarily agree with all the precepts that Muslim jurists developed during the early period of Islam. The twenty-first century is a very different time compared to the pre-modern period, and thus calls for different understandings, particularly in the area of rights. This is where analogical reasoning is crucial today: it is possible to use analogy to broaden our understanding of an Islamic conception of human rights and to develop new ideas or positions in relation to particular human rights.

THE SHARI'A OR ISLAMIC LAW

I will now turn to an overview of the development of Islamic law—the Shari'a—with particular emphasis on the features of that development which lend themselves to the modern discourse on human rights.

Meaning and Historical Development

'Shari'a' is the term usually associated with the idea of "Islamic law". The term occurs once in the Qur'an, where it designates a divinely appointed path: "Now we have set you on a clear religious path (*shari'a*), so follow it." (Q. 45:18) The term is linguistically associated with notions of "the way" or "the road". From this, the Shari'a is considered to be the path set out by God for Muslims to follow in order to achieve salvation. It refers to the totality of the guidance contained in the Qur'an and Sunna (the normative example of Prophet Muhammad).

Although Shari'a is the term most commonly associated with Islamic law, it is important to distinguish between Shari'a and *fiqh*. The word *fiqh* originally meant "understanding" or "discernment" in a general sense, and it occurs in the Qur'an and hadith with that meaning.[7] With the development of separate disciplines of law, theology, and asceticism in the second/eighth and third/ninth centuries, *fiqh* came to refer only to legal knowledge. Gradually, Shari'a and *fiqh* also came to be differentiated. "Shari'a" came to refer to the totality of God's law in its perfect state, whereas "*fiqh*" referred to specific rulings obtained by interpreting the primary texts of the Qur'an and hadith using the tools referred to above.[8] Thus, for Muslims, while the source of the Shari'a is God, *fiqh* comes from human effort. Despite these differences, in the modern period (and also throughout this book), "Islamic law" and "Shari'a" are often used synonymously.

It is important to emphasise that Shari'a or "Islamic law" is not a unified body of law. Within it there are many schools of legal thought and, on any particular legal or moral issue, there may be a wide range of divergent views. On the one hand, this makes the task of determining whether human rights norms and Islamic law can be reconciled more difficult; on the other, it also allows considerable scope for finding compatibilities.

The Historical Development of the Shari'a: Four Key Stages

As I have written elsewhere,[9] the early development of the Shari'a (or Islamic law) can be divided into four stages. The first stage was the period when the Qur'an was revealed. At this time the Qur'an set down laws related to the individual (such as prayers and fasting) and for society more broadly (such as marriage, commercial transactions, and criminal law). All of these laws reoriented society towards a new, universal set of norms
that transcended the previous pre-Islamic focus on kinship and tribal allegiance.[10]

The laws of the Qur'an were not arbitrary—they aimed to realise certain ideals. These included the creation of a just and compassionate society, as well as instilling personal morality and God-consciousness.[11] By "laws" I refer both to specific rulings as well as more general principles and values. The Qur'an often prescribes conduct but is silent on the details, such as for the prayer and the *zakat* alms-tax.[12]

The second stage occurred after the Prophet's death. Islamic law was being developed by the Prophet's Companions utilising *ijtihad* (individual reasoning). Islam was spreading outside Arabia and coming into contact with other cultures. The Muslim community had to "navigate an uncharted path for which the Qur'an provided little guidance".[13]

The Companions were able to guide the Muslim community in situations where the Qur'an or the Sunna did not provide a specific answer. Alongside the development and use of *ijtihad*, a type of consultation also existed in the development of law, especially during the time of the first four caliphs, known among Sunni Muslims as "Rightly Guided". Historical reports point to the existence of a consultative body that could debate points of law and enact new rulings at the time.

The third stage begins with the time of the Successors (the second generation of Muslims), which spanned roughly the Umayyad caliphate from 41/661 to 132/750, up to the early years of the Abbasid caliphate. At this time, some changes took place which affected the trajectory of

Islamic legal development. The Umayyads instituted dynastic rule and ended the form of consultation which had existed under the Rashidun (Rightly Guided) caliphs. Also, "law" was increasingly being developed by individual jurists in various key regions of the expanding Muslim caliphate. These jurists continued to practise *ijtihad*, and their efforts and creativity had a significant impact on the form and content of Islamic law. Their debates, teaching, and opinions are considered part of the raw material for Islamic law.

During this period, the practice of the Prophet and the Companions began to be emphasised as a fundamental source of law. In addition, two distinct approaches towards law and legal theory began to emerge: that of the "people of reason/opinion", often called "rationalists", and that of the "people of hadith", or "traditionists".[14] While the former emphasised the importance of reason, without neglecting the texts, the latter tended to base their opinions largely on texts (specifically, the Qur'an and hadith).[15] These two approaches struggled for hermeneutic primacy. This struggle was exemplified in the *Mihna* (inquisition), from 218/833 until 234/848.[16] The Mihna was a critical struggle between the traditionists (led by the hadith scholar Ahmad b. Hanbal (d. 241/855)) and the rationalists (led by a group of rationalist theologians, known as Mu'tazilis, and some Abbasid caliphs). Debate over the status of the Qur'an and whether it was "created" or not led to a much broader debate on the place of human reason in the interpretation of the divinely revealed texts and, by extension, the role of reason in deducing the law. This intellectual struggle ebbed and flowed throughout the early history of Islam, until the fourth/tenth century saw what Wael Hallaq has termed "the great synthesis". This was in essence a compromise between traditionism and rationalism: "It was the midpoint between the two movements that constituted the normative position of the majority; and it was from this centrist position that Sunnism, the religious and legal ideology of the majority of Muslims, was to emerge".[17]

The combining of the two dominant approaches culminated in the idea "that human reasoning must play a significant role in the law, but can in no way transcend the dictates of revelation".[18]

The final stage of the early development of Islamic law can be described as the rise of the jurists. The evolution of their authority meant that the jurists formed a separate source of legal authority to the caliph, creating a kind of separation of powers. As Hallaq explains:

> Those men in possession of a greater store of knowledge grew more influential than others less learned, gaining in the process—by the sheer

> virtuousness of their knowledge—an authority that began to challenge the legal (but not political) authority of the caliphs.[19]

This period began around 150/767 and continued into the third/ninth century. At that time, the major schools of law (the Sunni schools, Hanafi, Maliki, Shafi'i, and Hanbali, and the Shi'i Ja'fari school) began to emerge. Once established, these schools began to exercise great authority over the interpretation and application of Islamic law, and the view eventually emerged that somehow the venerated founders of the schools had completed all the necessary tasks of legal analysis and defined all the major intellectual structures of the law. As a result, new ways of looking at the text and constructing or interpreting law were discouraged to some extent in favour of faithfully following what these earlier scholars had done.

ISLAMIC LEGAL CONCEPTS AND STRATEGIES TO ENGAGE WITH INTERNATIONAL HUMAN RIGHTS NORMS

Since Shari'a (or Islamic law) forms such a central part of Muslim discourses on human rights today, it is important to identify resources from within this tradition that can be used to engage with international human rights norms. There are many concepts and tools that could be used for this purpose, but in this chapter I will identify those that I believe are the most important in this endeavour. In the second half of the book I will explore how Muslim thinkers and scholars are using such resources to harmonise international human rights law and Islamic law.

Human Rights as Binding by Agreement

It is possible to conceive of human rights norms as arising out of international law, and thus binding on all states by agreement. This way of thinking about human rights does not require us to subscribe to particular philosophical justifications, but sees them as an important part of the current legal and political landscape. Muslim-majority states function within a framework of international law and relations that have been established by the international community. Although it is theoretically possible for states to disconnect or isolate themselves from other states, in practice this would be extremely costly politically and economically, to say the least. An important tenet of Islamic law is the requirement to honour one's agreements. All Muslim-majority countries are member states of the United Nations, and a number of important Muslim jurists have stated the view that the United Nations Charter represents a binding international agreement for Muslim States. In addition, since at least the 1980s, human rights language has been incorporated into trade agreements by major powers such as the United States and European Union.[20] Today, most important trading countries sometimes include human rights provisions in their preferential trade agreements. Some of these are binding.[21] Thus Muslim-majority states must function and interact within a global environment where human rights are strongly valued and considered an important part of the international legal and political framework.

Taking into Consideration the Principle of *Darura* (Necessity)

A key principle that is highly relevant is that of necessity (*darura*). This Islamic legal concept allows Muslims to depart from an established legal ruling in exceptional circumstances, as long as the result does not go against the fundamental objectives of the Shari'a. The principle of *darura* can be invoked in a situation where applying the original legal ruling may result in loss or damage to one of the "five fundamentals": protection of a person's religion, life, lineage, reason, or property.[22] In such cases, this legal concept of necessity can be used to remove the hardship or risk to the person.[23]

A related concept is "need" (*haja*). *Haja* is defined in Islamic jurisprudence as "those things which put the Muslim in a difficulty, if not fulfilled, even if he/she can do without".[24] The concept of *haja* therefore allows the removal of a difficulty that is causing a person hardship.[25] *Haja* is different from *darura* because with *haja* a person's life is not threatened or in danger from the impediment (nor are any of the five fundamentals at stake); however, without removing the difficulty, the person will face significant hardship.[26] When a *haja* affects a whole society, the need becomes a "universal need" (*haja 'amma*).[27] When it becomes such a universal need, then it becomes very similar to necessity.

Both of these concepts are very useful for helping Muslims respond to the international human rights discourse today. Where difficulties or tensions arise in the areas of certain rights, the concepts of necessity and need can be used as a justification for modifying certain traditional legal rulings because of compelling circumstances.

Reliance on *Hikma* (Rationale and Wisdom)

Another way to address difficulties between Islamic law and international human rights law is to apply the concept of *hikma*, where the rationale and wisdom behind a Qur'anic or prophetic prescription is taken into account. For instance, as discussed further in Chapter 7, many scholars argue that the rationale behind the Qur'an allowing the practice of polygyny was to ensure justice and protection for vulnerable members of the Muslim community; namely widows and orphans. If Q. 4:3, the verse that sanctions polygyny, is taken *literally*, without any deeper understanding, it stands in tension with those provisions of human rights law that affirm equality between men and women, particularly in the context of marriage. However, by taking into account the *hikma* of the verse, the apparent difficulties can be resolved to some extent.

Contextualisation of Relevant Texts

One approach that is useful for addressing tensions between Islamic law and international human rights law is to contextualise, where feasible, those verses of the Qur'an or traditions of the Prophet (hadith) that appear to conflict with international human rights standards. By contextualising these texts, scholars may consider a text's original purpose, and how this might be applied in today's context.

However, it is important to keep in mind that contextualising a text is not simply a matter of reading into the text a predetermined meaning. Rather, it is a principled approach that not only takes the linguistic meaning of the text seriously but goes further, and gives consideration to the original context in which the Qur'anic revelation occurred in the early seventh century CE. This includes its political, social, economic, intellectual, and religious context, and the values, norms, and institutions that existed in that society and have a bearing on the particular issue being explored. Through analysis, the interpreter can determine how the text was understood among the first generation of Muslims and in the early periods of Islamic history, as well as within the context of that time.

Once this has been determined, the interpreter will then relate this understanding to the present context. This involves analysing all the relevant aspects of the contemporary context, including its social, political, cultural, economic or intellectual elements, and comparing and contrasting this to the original context of the text. This process will lead to a relevant interpretation of the text, without sacrificing its ultimate objective and fundamental message. Consideration also needs to be given to the concerns and needs of the time; common sense; the sensibilities of the broader religious community; and the fundamental values and practices that the Qur'an and Prophet Muhammad emphasised.

Keeping an Eye on the Mutable and Immutable

When contextualising texts of the Qur'an or hadith that are associated with human rights, Muslim scholars often discuss whether a particular ruling or decision associated with a text is changeable or unchangeable (or, in other words, mutable or immutable). Many Muslims would argue that if a ruling is considered so important or fundamental to Islamic law it should not be modified or changed in light of international human rights law and, in such cases, Muslim scholars should not give in to demands made by the international human rights community. While Muslim scholars have explored the idea of mutable and immutable in Islamic law for many centuries, using different terminology and language, it still remains an important concern for Muslims today when engaging with international human rights norms.

Although there is no universally agreed upon definition of what is considered mutable or immutable, it is possible to list categories of rulings that Muslims, in general, consider to be immutable. For example, the fundamental beliefs of Muslims: belief in one God, the prophets, the Scriptures and life after death; the fundamental pillars of Islam: the five daily prayers, fasting, zakat and pilgrimage; and those matters that are clearly made permissible or prohibited in the Qur'an or traditions of the Prophet, such as theft (prohibited) or buying and selling (permitted). These are all considered immutable, and the belief is that no Muslim has the authority to go against them. Beyond this, there may also be other immutables, although they may not have the broad universal agreement that these kinds of fundamentals enjoy.

In the area of human rights, most of the difficulties Muslims experience are not about such universally agreed upon immutables, but about legal rulings where there is less agreement. These rulings often come from a particular scholar's independent reasoning (*ijtihad*) or may even be the standard position of a particular school of law. In such cases there is room to check whether the ruling is in fact a universally agreed upon immutable or not. For example, in the case of gender equality, there is no universally agreed upon position among Muslims that opposing (or supporting) gender equality is a fundamental value in Islam. Similarly, in the case of Muslim men being able to marry more than one woman, there is no universally agreed upon position which suggests that this is something Muslim men *must* do. Thus, there is room for Muslim scholars to explore whether such rulings can be rethought in light of our contemporary context and brought in line with contemporary human rights concerns and standards. This gives Muslim scholars significant flexibility to creatively engage with international human rights law; contribute new ideas to this engagement; and to perhaps develop relevant new 'Islamic' understandings.

The issue of immutability is particularly important when we examine the engagement of Muslim-majority states with the international human rights treaty regime. The vast majority of states' objections to particular rights, which can be seen in the reservations made against various articles of the treaties, are by and large not related to immutable issues, as we will see in Chapters 7 to 11.

CONCLUSION

This chapter has provided a brief overview of the most important sources of Islamic law for any discussion on Islam and human rights today. In developing arguments in favour of human rights or even against human rights, Muslims have relied on these sources as well as methods of interpretation that have been developed over many centuries. While texts can be read in very different ways, what is important is to highlight that within Islamic tradition, there are a large number of texts, ideas, views and interpretations, as well as principles and strategies that provide room for exploring and perhaps even rethinking some of the legal rulings that may have relevance to the kind of concerns articulated in this book. As I will argue, these can be used successfully to develop an Islamic understanding of human rights that is not in conflict with internationally accepted standards and norms. An understanding of these views, principles and strategies is extremely important for engaging successfully in the discourse on Islam and human rights.

* * *

LOOKING AT AN ISSUE CLOSELY: THE CASE OF "RIGHTS" IN THE HADITH

The second most important textual authority in Islam after the Qur'an is the collected traditions of the Prophet, known as hadith. Below a number of hadith that support the notion of rights in general or specific substantive rights. In any attempt to provide an Islamic conception of human rights that may form a basis for reconciliation with international human rights law, it is often important to cite the necessary texts from the Qur'an and the traditions of the Prophet. As we can see below, there are resources in these traditions that can be helpful when developing Islamic arguments in favour of human rights.

- One of the Companions of the Prophet, Salman said: "Your Lord has a right over you; and your soul has a right over you; and your family has a right over you; so you should give all those who have a right over you their rights." The Prophet said, "Salman has spoken the truth."[28]
- The Prophet said: "Whoever has oppressed another person concerning his reputation or anything else, he should beg him to forgive him before the Day of Resurrection when there will be no money [to compensate for wrong deeds]; if he has good deeds, those good deeds will be taken from him according to the oppression he has committed, and if he has no good deeds, the sins of the oppressed person will be loaded onto him."[29]
- The Prophet said: "On the Day of Judgment, [all] rights will be given to those to whom they are due."[30]
- When a funeral procession passed by the Prophet, and he stood up, it was said to him, "It is a Jew." The Prophet said, "Was he not a soul?"[31]
- The Prophet said, "Certainly, I witnessed a pact [of justice] in the house of Abd Allah b. Jud'an which, if I were called to it now in the time of Islam, I would respond. Make such alliances in order to return rights to their people, that no oppressor should have power over the oppressed."[32] This hadith is regarding the Hilf al-Fudul [Pact of the Virtuous], a pact of justice made by the people of Mecca, including the young Prophet Muhammad, in which they pledged to respect the principles of justice and intervene to support the oppressed, no matter what their tribal affiliation.
- The Prophet said: "Five are the rights of a Muslim over his brother: returning the greeting of peace; visiting the sick; following the funeral processions; accepting invitations; and saying "God have mercy on you" when someone sneezes.[33]
- The Prophet said during his Farewell Sermon: "Verily, your blood, your property and your honour are sacred to one another, like the sanctity of this day of yours, in this month of yours and in this city of yours."[34]

- The Prophet said: "Guard [the right of] the two weak ones: the slave and the woman."[35]
- The Prophet said, "He is not from my nation who does not honour our elders, nor have mercy on our young ones, nor recognize the rights of our scholars."[36]

Apart from the traditions of the Prophet, there are also views expressed by Muslim jurists on issues that are relevant to the human rights discourse today. Below I provide two such views:

- Abu Bakr al-Sarakhsi (d. 483/1090), a leading Hanafi jurist of the eleventh century CE, said: "When God the Exalted created humanity to carry His Trust *(amana)*, He dignified them with reason (*'aql*) and sacred inviolability (*dhimma*) in order to be responsible for fulfilling the rights (*huquq*) of God placed over them. Then He granted them sanctity (*'isma*), freedom (*hurriyya*), and property rights, so that they might endure, and be able to carry out the Trust. Hence, this freedom, sanctity, and right of property are established [as a property] of a person at the time they are born. Those capable of discernment (*mumayyiz*) and those who are not are equal in this regard, and likewise sacred inviolability is established at birth whether they are of sound mind or not."[37]
- Muhammad al-Shaybani (d. 189/805), an eminent early Hanafi jurist, said: "The basic principle (*asl*) is that it is an obligation upon the leader of the Muslims to support those who reside in our country under a covenant of protection (*al-musta'manun*). They must be given recourse against anyone who oppresses them, just as it is an obligation to fulfil the rights of non-Muslim citizens."[38]

NOTES

1. See Abdullah al-Ahsan, "Law, Religion and Human Dignity in the Muslim World Today: An Examination of OIC's Cairo Declaration of Human Rights", *Journal of Law and Religion* 24(2) (2008–09): 569.
2. See Fazlur Rahman, *Islam and Modernity: Transformation of an Intellectual Tradition* (Chicago: University of Chicago Press, 1984), 6–7.
3. The Prophet Muhammad, "Prophet Muhammad's Last Sermon" (Islam The Modern Religion). Available http://www.themodernreligion.com/prophet/prophet-lastsermon.htm (last accessed 4 December 2017).
4. Ibn Majah, *Sunan Ibn Majah*, Kitab al-fitan, bab al-sawad al-a'ẓam, No. 3950; Tirmidhi, *Jami' al-Tirmidhi*, Kitab al-fitan, No. 2167.
5. Abdullah Saeed, *Islamic Thought: An Introduction* (Abingdon, UK: Routledge, 2006), 49.
6. Saeed, *Islamic Thought*, 49.
7. See Q. 7:179.

8. Saeed, *Islamic Thought*, 44.
9. Ibid, 46–7.
10. See Wael B. Hallaq, *The Origins and Evolution of Islamic Law* (Cambridge: Cambridge University Press, 2005), 22.
11. Saeed, *Islamic Thought*, 46.
12. Ibid.
13. Hallaq, *Origins*, 33.
14. Saeed, *Islamic Thought*, 47.
15. Ibid.
16. Hallaq, *Origins*, 124.
17. Ibid 125.
18. Ibid 148.
19. Ibid 77.
20. Susan Ariel Aaronson and Jean Pierre Chauffour, "The Wedding of Trade and Human Rights: Marriage of Convenience or Permanent Match?" (2011) WTO 15 February 2011. Available https://www.wto.org/english/res_e/publications_e/wtr11_forum_e/wtr11_15feb11_e.htm#feedback (last accessed 28 November 2017).
21. Ibid.
22. Mansour Z. Al-Mutairi, "Necessity in Islamic Law" (1997). Thesis submitted to the University of Edinburgh for the Degree of Doctor of Philosophy. January 1997, 171–2.
23. Ibid.
24. European Council for Fatwa and Research's Resolution on "Permissibility of Conventional Mortgage under Necessity". Fourth Ordinary Session [27–31 October, 1999]. Available http://eshaykh.com/halal_haram/permissibility-of-conventional-mortgage-under-necessity (last accessed 4 December 2017).
25. Al-Mutairi, "Necessity in Islamic Law", 17.
26. Ibid 66.
27. Rationale for the Fatwa on Mortgage (2001), 4.
28. Al-Bukhari, *Sahih al-Bukhari*, Kitab al-sawm, No. 1968.
29. Al-Bukhari, *Sahih al-Bukhari*, Kitab al-mazalim, No. 2449.
30. Muslim, *Sahih Muslim*, Kitab al-birr wa-l-sila wa-l-adab, No. 2582.
31. Al-Bukhari, *Sahih al-Bukhari*, Kitab al-jana'iz, Nos. 1312–13; Muslim, *Sahih Muslim*, Kitab al-jana'iz, No. 961.
32. Abu Muhammad Qasim b. Thabit al-Saraqusti, *al-Dala'il fi gharib al-hadith*, ed. Muhammad al-Qannas (Riyadh: Maktabat al-Ubaykan, 1421), 2:487, No. 265; Abu Bakr al-Bayhaqi, *al-Sunan al-Kubra*, ed. Muhammad Ata (Beirut: Dar al-Kutub al-Ilmiyya, 1424/2003), 6:596, Kitab al-wasaya, No. 13080.
33. Al-Bukhari, *Sahih al-Bukhari*, Kitab al-jana'iz, No. 1240.
34. Al-Bukhari, *Sahih al-Bukhari*, Kitab al-hajj, No. 1739; idem, Kitab al-hudud, No. 6785; Muslim, *Sahih Muslim*, Kitab al-qasama, No. 1679.
35. Abu al-Qasim b. Asakir, *Tarikh Madinat Dimashq*, ed. Amr al-Amrawi (Cairo: Dar al-Fikr, 1415/1995), 52:38, No. 6086. In another narration, the Prophet said: "Fear God [regarding the rights of] the two weak ones: the orphan and the woman." Abu Ja'far al-Tabari, *Jami' al-bayan an tafsir ay al-Qur'an*, ed. Ahmad Shakir (Beirut: Mu'assasat al-Risala, 1420/2000), 7:561, sub Q. 4:5.
36. Ahmad b. Hanbal, *Musnad*, eds, Shu'ayb al-Arna'ut and Adil Murshid et al. (Beirut: Mu'assasat al-Risala, 1421/2001), 37:416, Hadith Ubada b. al-Samit, No. 22755.
37. Abu Bakr al-Sarakhsi, *Kitab al-Usul* (Beirut: Dar al-Maʿrifa, n.d.), 2:334, Fasl fi bayan taqsim al-alama.
38. Abu Bakr al-Sarakhsi, *Sharh al-siyar al-kabir*, (n.p.: al-Sharika al-Sharqiyya li-l-I'lanat, 1971), 1853, Bab ma yajib min al-nusra li-l-musta'manin wa-ahl al-dhimma.

2. Development of human rights and some basic conceptions

INTRODUCTION

A human right is that which every human being is entitled to on the simple basis that they are human beings. In human rights theory, rights stem from "the inherent dignity of the human person".[1] This is an obvious and seemingly ordinary statement to make. However, it may only appear ordinary because the human rights discourse is so much a part of our contemporary way of thinking. Ideas such as equality and non-discrimination, which centre on the fundamental status of human beings, are incredibly familiar today. But as Brian Orend argues, the idea that we all share "a basic level of equal moral worth" is a modern one.[2] Even as recently as two centuries ago, many thinkers and politicians could not conceive that human rights could belong equally to all human beings. For example, while the Constitution of the United States emphasised in written word that all people should be treated equally, in practice discrimination was still rife. Equal rights were simply not granted to groups such as African Americans, indigenous Americans, women, and other minorities. Equality was conceptualised in an extremely narrow fashion. However, in the twenty-first century, it is clear that there has been a shift in how equality is defined—to an idea that is far more inclusive.

In the twentieth and twenty-first centuries, a discourse emerged that argued for an all-encompassing or universal understanding of human rights: a discourse which insists that all human beings are equal, and that equality is not a privilege, but a right. This notion of universality is critically important and underlies the idea that all human beings, regardless of wealth, ethnicity, religion, sex, or gender, are equal and all share the same entitlements..

This chapter provides an overview of the development of modern human rights. For many scholars, what we understand as "human rights" today emerged from natural law theories, which argued that human beings possessed a set of "natural" or inalienable rights by their very nature. From there, the idea of rights was further shaped by the European

Enlightenment before eventually being codified in the aftermath of the Second World War in the treaties of the United Nations. While this is a widely accepted history, not all scholars accept that human rights developed in this manner, and in the coming chapters other histories and theories about the origins of human rights will be briefly referred to when relevant. This chapter will also consider the question of whether human rights are universal, or whether they are culturally determined and may be applied differently according to the cultural setting.

HUMAN RIGHTS DEFINED

The notion of a right is usually associated with a corresponding claim. As Brian Orend puts it, "[t]here is considerable consensus … that a right can be defined, at least initially, as a justified claim or entitlement. A right is a justified claim on someone, or on some institution, for something which one is owed."[3] Thus, when a right holder claims a right, they are stating that they are entitled to be treated in a particular way by other people or by social institutions. Importantly, however, as Orend notes, a right may exist even if no one claims it. A right is an entitlement to make a claim, so even if a person does not deliberately or explicitly claim a right, it still exists.[4]

As Jack Donnelly notes, rights are distinct from benefits, duties or privileges.[5] Moreover, rights cannot be considered properties of persons. They are, essentially, reasons for treating people in a certain way.[6] This contrasts with the position put forward by some early thinkers on the topic, such as the philosopher John Locke (d. 1704), who considered rights to be the property of a person. Rights, for some early thinkers like Locke, were a non-visible part of human beings just like a soul was.[7]

Rights can be moral, legal or both. A legal right exists in law and if one does not abide by the law then there are legal means of redress.[8] Therefore, if someone violates a legal right, the legal system offers a means to recover or address that which has been violated. Moral rights, on the other hand, are not legally enshrined rights but rather a collectively understood set of values, shared by a particular community or larger society. Orend argues that moral rights exist either within "social moralities" (referring to a "practiced code of conduct within a given society")[9] or within a "critical or justified morality" (referring to "a complex and well-defined theoretical system of morals").[10] For example, honesty might be a shared moral value within a community. This would give rise to the expectation that each member of the community holds a moral right to expect honest interaction. There is nothing that binds people to behave in an honest way, in terms of the law, but there may exist a recognised moral imperative, which then functions as a moral right. Human rights are a combination of both legal and moral rights.[11]

Finally, human rights are not bestowed by a particular institution, nor are they a result of membership of a particular class or social sphere. They are not conferred by governments or earned by anything that a person can do or refrain from doing. They are naturally inherent to human beings, and they cannot be separated or taken away by another. Human rights are therefore inalienable: to be human means to have human rights. Donnelly therefore argues that to strip someone of their human rights ultimately means to destroy that person's humanity.[12]

A HISTORICAL ACCOUNT OF INTERNATIONAL HUMAN RIGHTS

Some scholars argue that the international human rights discourse emerged originally from Western traditions of thought. For example, human rights theorist Jack Donnelly argues that "[a]s a matter of historical fact, the concept of human rights is an artifact of modern Western civilization".[13] For these scholars, the notion of human rights is a specifically Western contribution. They may acknowledge that other traditions have also developed ideas about human dignity, but the discourse that exists today is specifically derived from particular contributions made by Western thinkers.

There are also scholars who acknowledge the contributions of other traditions and thinkers to the discourse. These scholars, while accepting that modern ideas about international human rights may have largely unfolded from Western thought, suggest its fundamental principles have precedents in other traditions and cultures and in religion (both Western and non-Western). As Micheline Ishay notes, "[s]keptics over the achievements of Western civilization are correct to point out that current notions of morality cannot be associated solely with European history".[14] The values of justice, fairness, freedom of conscience, religious tolerance, and protection of life and property have all been part of the thinking of all major world religions, cultures and civilisations. Again, as Ishay explains:

> Indeed, views represented within the first cluster of [the] [U]niversal [D]eclaration [of Human Rights], such as proportionate punishments, judicial fairness, freedom of conscience, religious toleration, the right to life and the security of

> persons, among other conceptions one may associate with "liberty" or toleration, were not unknown in ancient texts.[15]

Non-Western cultures and traditions have also had an impact on modern human rights instruments, in particular the Universal Declaration of Human Rights (UDHR), as we will see below. As John Betton points out, "to argue that the [UDHR] is simply a product of western values is to ignore the contributions of Asian and Latin American countries to the document".[16] Further, other scholars have pointed to the presence of values shared with Buddhist, Muslim, and Confucian civilisations in the document.[17]

THE INFLUENCE OF THE ENLIGHTENMENT ON INTERNATIONAL HUMAN RIGHTS

The European Enlightenment paved the way, to a large extent, for the idea of human rights we have today. Indeed, as Ishay notes, "the legacy of the European Enlightenment for our current understanding of human rights supersedes other influences".[18] This period saw a radical shift away from using religion as a primary framework for understanding the world. Beginning with the scientific revolution of the sixteenth and seventeenth centuries, the Enlightenment was a period of dramatic change in the fields of science, philosophy, society and politics.[19] The medieval worldview of the previous centuries was swept aside, and the new ways of thinking directly challenged existing hierarchies of power, such as monarchy and the Church.[20] New social orders were established on the basis of Enlightenment ideals, such as freedom and equality for all, which were based upon the principles of human reason, instead of divine command.[21] At the same time, new scientific knowledge challenged ancient conceptions of the world. During this period, human rights were gradually separated from any divine or theological origin.

NATURAL LAW

The English philosopher John Locke is one of the most well-known theorists to discuss the idea of "natural rights". In his *Second Treatise on Government*, Locke refers to a "state of nature" prior to society or government.[22] Locke argued that even in this state, every person has certain rights, including the right to life and property. Thus, when individuals come together to form a society, the key objective is to secure or protect those natural rights.[23] However, the extent to which individuals can protect their own rights is limited. Society therefore fulfils the purpose of maintaining these rights through a government and its institutions, which are established in order to achieve this.[24] For Locke, society is thus founded on the need to preserve the natural rights of human beings, and government is the instrument that protects and, if necessary, enforces these rights.

This Lockean framework is called classical liberalism and it represented a radical break from the ideas of government and rule that had existed until Locke's time. In particular, it challenged the prevailing view that a government's authority and right to rule derived from a divine mandate. As described by the Levin Institute, this new framework:

> helped foster a new way of thinking about individuals, governments, and the rights that link the two. Previously, heads of state claimed to rule by divine right, tracing their authority through genealogy to the ultimate source ... [a] divine being. This was as true for Roman emperors as it was [for] Chinese and Japanese emperors. The theory of divine right was most forcefully asserted during the Renaissance by monarchs across Europe, most notoriously James I of England (1566–1625) and Louis XIV of France (1638–1715).[25]

Locke's ideas became very influential. His ideas about the nature of rights and the purpose of government were key influences on the subsequent American Declaration of Independence (1776) and first United States Constitution (1787).[26] The Declaration of Independence states, for example:

> We hold these truths to be self-evident, that all men are created equal, that they are endowed by their Creator with certain unalienable Rights, that among these are Life, Liberty and the pursuit of Happiness.—That to secure these rights, Governments are instituted among Men, deriving their just powers from the consent of the governed.[27]

Locke's legacy cemented the idea that rights were something inherent or inalienable to human beings because of their very nature. He also established that the purpose, and therefore ongoing legitimacy, of government was to secure and protect those rights.

Today, many scholars conclude that contemporary notions of rights developed from natural rights or that they are one and the same.[28] Both the American Declaration of Independence (1776) and the French Declaration of the Rights of Man and of the Citizen (1789) specifically refer to natural law and natural rights.[29] Some of these documents combine references to natural law and God to justify rights and their preservation. But despite these explicit references to God in the eighteenth century, during the nineteenth century a tension arose between the secular human rights discourse and the religious discourse of natural law and natural rights. Over time, the notion of God-given natural rights was marginalised in favour of secular human rights.[30]

During the twentieth century, attempts were made to establish an international human rights regime based on this secular notion of rights. While initial efforts in the wake of the First World War were unsuccessful,[31] the establishment of the United Nations was pivotal in the development of the international human rights discourse.

THE SECOND WORLD WAR

Perhaps the most significant factor in raising the profile of human rights and shaping the discourse we have today was the horrors of the Second World War. The atrocities of the death camps and the mass killings of minorities and vulnerable communities, including Jews, gypsies, and homosexuals, shocked the world. In the Nuremberg trials held after the war, Nazi officials were prosecuted for war crimes and crimes against humanity. After the war, the establishment of the United Nations in 1945 aimed to prevent future conflict and future atrocities against human rights.

The horrors of the Second World War shocked the international community to an extent that it had never experienced before, moving it to seek measures to ensure that human rights would be protected in the future. Thus even before the war had officially ended, allied states had already agreed that the post-war settlement should include "international commitment to the protection of human rights".[32] Although the United Nations was not specifically formed to deal with the question of human rights, it became clear that the issue could no longer be ignored. Calls emerged from developed and developing nations alike for human rights standards to be agreed to, and for states to be held accountable for abuses against their citizens.[33] Human rights thus became an important issue in global discourse. The preamble of the UN Charter affirmed the commitment of the international community "to save succeeding generations from the scourge of war, which twice in our lifetime has brought untold sorrow to mankind"[34] and reaffirmed its "faith in fundamental human rights, in the dignity and worth of the human person, in the equal rights of men and women and of nations large and small".[35] A Commission on Human Rights was established to draft a document that set out the meaning of the fundamental rights and freedoms proclaimed in the

Charter.[36] This process culminated in the Universal Declaration of Human Rights, adopted by all 56 members of the UN in 1948.[37]

THE UN CHARTER

In the process of drafting the UN Charter, the major powers actually resisted greater formal recognition of human rights. Great Britain was concerned that including human rights language in the UN Charter would cause unrest in its colonies and threaten its empire.[38] The Soviet Union similarly resisted the inclusion of human rights in the Charter, fearing that this would threaten its own state practices and governing policies. China and to a lesser extent the United States were more interested in human rights, but as Susan Waltz notes, "at mid-century it was small states and nongovernmental organisations rather than the great powers who were the most ardent and outspoken champions of human rights".[39]

In the end, the first proposals which emerged from the great powers' meeting at Dumbarton Oaks in the United States in 1944 only referred to human rights once.[40] Further proposals by other states, such as the Latin American states, Australia, New Zealand, and France, ultimately influenced the drafting of the UN Charter, and seven references to human rights were eventually included.[41] For example, Article 55 of the UN Charter now states:

> The United Nations shall promote:
>
> a. higher standards of living, full employment, in conditions of economic and social progress and development;
> b. the solutions of international economic social, health and related problems; and international cultural and educational cooperation; and
> c. universal respect for, and observance of, human rights and fundamental freedoms for all without distinction as to race, sex, language, or religion.[42]

The UN Charter is the first of a series of influential international documents to promote human rights that emerged in the aftermath of the Second World War. Three years later, in 1948, the UN adopted the most important human rights document of the twentieth century: the Universal Declaration of Human Rights (UDHR).

THE UNIVERSAL DECLARATION OF HUMAN RIGHTS

The UDHR was not the first international legal instrument to contain the idea of rights. The Geneva Conventions (first adopted in 1864) and several instruments of the International Labour Organization also formalised particular rights.[43] Various national documents had also already contained the language of rights, such as the US Declaration of Independence and the French Declaration on the Rights of Man (see above). However, as Betton emphasises, the UDHR was an extremely important achievement because it was the first document to establish the universality of human rights—namely, that all human beings have rights simply by virtue of being human.[44]

The idea of the universality of human rights presented a new way of approaching cultural difference. By insisting that human rights were generally indifferent to cultural or societal specificities, they could serve as a source of guidance or a standard for all nations and cultures in the recognition of a universally shared ideal: human dignity and equality. As Betton notes, the UDHR "established *global* rights to which all peoples could appeal"[45] that transcended particular practices in particular countries. For example, the right to be free from torture was recognised, even though some states claimed the practice was legitimate.

Although its implementation has been imperfect, as Betton argues, "the Universal Declaration's idea of universality is not premised on the imposition of values but rather on values toward which people may aspire".[46] The UDHR can therefore be thought of as the documentation of certain ideals that all human beings should move towards. Its full realisation is still a long way off. Nevertheless, it was crucially important to develop, document and promote such ideas so they could become normalised and hopefully, over time, fully implemented.

In order to promote the idea of universal rights, it was critical that the language of the UDHR was neutral, leaving aside any reference to specific religious, theological, or even cultural frameworks that could prove problematic. Such references were considered an obstacle to universality because there are a myriad of religious traditions around the world, with different and perhaps contradictory theological frameworks, languages, and symbolism. States such as the Soviet Union were radically atheistic, and religious language had no possible value there at all. It was therefore critically important for the drafters of the UDHR to use a language that transcended religious particularities, though they may have had their own religious beliefs.

However, the UDHR was not devoid of cultural or religious influence. At a personal level, many people with diverse backgrounds and even strong religious convictions, including Christians, Jews, Buddhists, Muslims, agnostics, and atheists, were involved in the drafting process. Indeed, many of the rights included in the UDHR could easily have been supported by biblical, Qur'anic, or other religious texts, though it was considered not useful to do so.

The UDHR was thus a genuine attempt by many people from diverse backgrounds to come to terms with the promotion of human dignity as a universal value. It was not a document that was imposed upon the people of the world by the great powers of the time, but rather a collective effort, with non-Western individuals and nations involved in all stages of its drafting. Former UN official Sashi Tharoor notes that several non-Western countries, notably India, China, Chile, Cuba, Lebanon, and Panama, "played an active and highly influential part" in drafting the UDHR.[47] Obtaining widespread international support, however, for a universal understanding of human dignity was a major challenge. As Ishay highlights:

> Conflicting political traditions across the centuries have elaborated different visions of human rights rooted in past social struggles. That historical legacy and current conflicting meanings of human rights are, despite the admirable efforts of the architects of the [UDHR], all reflected in the structure and the substance of this important UN document.[48]

Waltz has described the two-year process of intensive discussion and negotiation in which the delegates of many countries were closely involved, concluding that "it is difficult to imagine a more elaborate process" of consultation and debate.[49] While some have argued that the UDHR is essentially a propagation of Western values, the document that was finally adopted was the result of the efforts of many people, not the views of a particular political bloc or geographical location.

While the UDHR may not satisfy every person, culture or society around the world, it does ultimately represent an important compromise in the establishment of a universal standard of rights, centred on the dignity and fundamental equality of each and every human being. In this context, the UDHR must be considered a universal standard towards which all societies should and could aspire.

THE INTERNATIONAL COVENANTS AND OTHER UN HUMAN RIGHTS TREATIES

The UDHR, adopted by the UN General Assembly in 1948, is a non-binding instrument. There is no mechanism to enforce the rights specified in it. In order to take the initiative of human rights further, the UN Commission on Human Rights (UNCHR) proceeded to draft two additional covenants: the International Covenant on Civil and Political

Rights (ICCPR) and the International Covenant on Economic, Social, and Cultural Rights (ICESCR). Together, with the UDHR, they are referred to as the International Bill of Human Rights.

The covenants become binding under international law once a state has ratified them. By ratifying either or both of the covenants, states are essentially agreeing to put into place laws and other domestic measures to ensure that the provisions of the covenants are given legal effect.[50] This means that while the covenant sets out the state's obligations and duties under international law, it is the country's domestic legal system that "provides the principle legal protection of human rights".[51]

Each international covenant elaborates further the rights contained in the UDHR. As its name suggests, the ICCPR expands the civil and political rights contained in the first part of the UDHR. These include rights such as the right to life and freedom of speech and religion. The ICESCR likewise expands the economic, social and cultural rights contained in the second part of the UDHR, such as the right to education, food, health, and shelter. However, both covenants include two rights in common: the right to self-determination and the prohibition against discrimination.

There are several reasons why the UNCHR decided to elaborate on the UDHR in two separate instruments, rather than just drafting a single treaty. Civil and political rights are associated with a range of freedoms and legal protections that some commentators refer to as first-generation rights. This means they cover the original set of rights that human rights proponents emphasised. These rights are also achievable by states with (arguably) minimal cost and are therefore seen as affordable.[52] In contrast, economic, social and cultural rights are often considered "second-generation rights", as they began to be argued for in industrialised nations once many first-generation rights had been achieved. They are also considered by some to be costlier because they involve the allocation of material benefits, such as food, or the provision of services, such as education. These require the state to allocate sufficient economic resources to achieve them.

Later, other declarations and binding human rights treaties were also drafted to elaborate further on specific topics or rights included in the UDHR.[53] The other main UN human rights instruments include the Convention on the Elimination of All Forms of Discrimination against Women (1979); the Convention against Torture and Other Cruel, Inhuman or Degrading Treatment (1984); the Convention on the Rights of the Child (1989); the Convention on the Protection of the Rights of all Migrant Workers and Members of their Families (1990); the Convention for the Protection of All Persons from Enforced Disappearance (2006) and the Convention on the Rights of Persons with Disabilities (2006). Some of these treaties also establish individual or group complaint mechanisms where individuals or groups have the right to submit a complaint if they believe their rights under the treaty are not being guaranteed by the state.[54]

REGIONAL HUMAN RIGHTS PROTECTIONS

The efforts to create human rights protections through the mechanisms of the United Nations were not the only developments in the human rights discourse during this period. In the post-Second World War period, various regional intergovernmental bodies were also established that included in their mandates human rights provisions.[55] These included the Organization of American States (OAS) and Council of Europe (CoE), which also sought to "identify the individual rights and liberties which all governments should respect, and to establish mechanisms for both promoting States' adherence to their human rights obligations and for addressing serious breaches".[56] By the middle of the twentieth century, a European and American system had also been created alongside the UN to promote and protect human rights regionally through non-binding declarations, treaties and specific enforcement mechanisms. These included the European Commission of Human Rights (now defunct), the European Court of Human Rights and the Inter-American Commission on Human Rights.[57]

Subsequently, regional mechanisms were also extended to the African region, with the establishment of the African Commission on Human and Peoples' Rights in 1987 and the African Court on Human and Peoples' Rights in 2004. These two bodies "monitor State compliance with the African Charter on Human and Peoples' Rights".[58]

HUMAN RIGHTS RAPPORTEURS AND INDIVIDUAL EXPERTS

Another level of protection provided by both the UN and regional human rights systems comes from the individual experts appointed to monitor particular human rights. These experts—often termed special rapporteurs—are appointed as neutral/impartial experts to receive information from individuals and non-governmental organisations on human rights situations or abuses, visit states and report on specific human rights conditions.[59]

GENERATIONS OF RIGHTS

The idea of different generations of human rights is an interesting issue in the human rights discourse, and there is no consensus on whether the division between first and second generation rights is a legitimate one, not to mention whether human rights should be classified into "generations" at all.[60] Many human rights activists and theorists are uncomfortable with the idea that there are categories or hierarchies of rights, while other theorists only acknowledge civil and political rights, referring to economic and social rights as "desirable goals dressed up in the more powerful rhetoric of rights".[61]

To understand the conceptual basis of the UDHR and the influence of generations of rights on its structure, we can note that René Cassin, a key drafter of the UDHR, conceptualised the document based on four key values: dignity, liberty, equality, and brotherhood.[62] There are thirty articles in the UDHR, and the first twenty-seven essentially relate to these four ideals.[63] The last three articles of the UDHR (Articles 28 to 30) specify the circumstances and conditions under which the rights of individuals within the state can be achieved. The idea of dignity is addressed in the first two articles of the UDHR, which emphasise that human dignity is shared by all human beings, regardless of sex, ethnicity, race, or religion.[64] Liberty is covered in Articles 3 to 19, centring on "first-generation" rights or freedoms emphasised during the Enlightenment period. Equality is addressed in Articles 20 to 26, which includes rights relating to social and economic equality, as emphasised during the Industrial Revolution, or "second-generation" rights. The notion of universal brotherhood is covered in Articles 27 to 28, in what has been described as "third-generation" rights. Third-generation rights can be seen as a product of the postcolonial period, and they centre on ideas of national solidarity.[65] As Ishay explains, "in a sense, the sequence of the articles corresponds to the historical appearance of successive generations and visions of universal rights".[66]

Those theorists and activists that are uncomfortable with a "generational" approach to human rights argue that it is erroneous to use the term "generation" to describe human rights because it implies that "when a new generation comes to life, the previous one becomes outdated. In this scheme, the older generation is progressively set aside in favor of the new generation, which will eventually replace it."[67] Instead, they argue, when "new" generations of rights are identified they should be added to the body of human rights already recognised.[68] Other theorists argue that the UDHR was never meant to be "disaggregated" into lists of rights.[69]

Rather, it should be seen as "a coherent document where all the enumerated rights are indivisible, interrelated, and interdependent".[70] This coherence has been affirmed by subsequent General Assembly resolutions and other international agreements.[71] Finally, it is very difficult to resolve the contradiction between "referring to 'generations' of rights, while at the same time maintaining that human rights are inherent to human beings as such, i.e. that everyone is entitled to them by the mere fact of his or her birth".[72]

Even so, the notion that some rights should "predominate over others" has been evident in the human rights discourse until recent decades. Choices over which rights should take priority have been made on the basis of "different values, ideologies and economic interests in society", not to mention "various socio-political and cultural traditions".[73] Since the 1990s, however, efforts have been made to do away with competing notions of rights by emphasising the "indivisibility" of human rights. This means that:

> the major categories of human rights—particularly civil and political rights (CPR) and economic, social and cultural rights (ESCR)—are inherently complementary and equal in importance, and that any attempt to privilege one set of rights over another displaces their natural balance and compromises their effectiveness.[74]

This notion of rights is affirmed in the fifth paragraph of the *Vienna Declaration and Programme of Action* (1993), which describes the idea of the indivisibility of human rights that has continued to the present day:[75]

> All human rights are universal, indivisible and interdependent and interrelated. The international community must treat human rights globally in a fair and equal manner, on the same footing, and with the same emphasis. While the significance of national and regional particularities and various historical, cultural and religious backgrounds must be borne in mind, it is the duty of States, regardless of their political, economic and cultural systems, to promote and protect all human rights and fundamental freedoms.[76]

The practical effect of emphasising the indivisibility of human rights has meant that there is greater attention given to economic, social and cultural rights today.[77]

UNIVERSALITY VERSUS CULTURAL RELATIVISM

One of the most critical debates in the realm of human rights involves the question of whether human rights are universal or whether they are culturally contingent. The universality of human rights is a modern concept. As the world underwent radical change in response to certain intellectual currents, such as the Enlightenment or the ideals that underpinned the French Revolution, it became increasingly possible to imagine common elements across cultures, religions, and nations.

The universality of human rights is not accepted by everyone, however. Some thinkers argue that because the human rights discourse as we know it today emerged in a Western cultural and intellectual context, human rights are primarily a Western cultural construct and may not apply to other cultures. In other words, human rights are not necessarily universal. Such a position is usually described as "culturally relativist".

Heine Bielefeldt divides cultural relativist positions further into "left-wing" and "right-wing".[78] Although all reject the idea that human rights are self-evidently universal, they disagree about the implications and reasons for this. "Left-wing" relativists emphasise the fact that human rights, as a Western cultural construct, have no right to supersede other cultural traditions. Indeed, imposing them on other cultures can be understood as a form of cultural imperialism. As Douglas Donoho puts it, according to this view "foreign scrutiny challenging the legitimacy of culturally or politically accepted domestic practices at best constitutes intolerance and disrespect, and at worst, cultural imperialism and a violation of domestic sovereignty".[79]

For example, some Muslim opponents of human rights argue that because Islam has its own concepts of rights, freedoms, and duties, imposing Western ideas of rights on Muslims is problematic. Not only that, but it also violates the idea of religious freedom by limiting Muslim religious practices in favour of Western ideals.

"Right-wing" relativists, such as Samuel Huntington, also do not see human rights as universal. Huntington's ideas are examined in more detail in Chapter 4, but in brief, he believes that the world is composed of different civilisations with fundamentally different values.[80] Huntington argues that since human rights come from Western history they cannot be assumed to exist in other civilisations. Thus, attempting to spread the human rights discourse only causes resentment.[81]

Similarly, Jack Donnelly, another relativist, argues that other cultures may know about ideas of human dignity, but these should not be mistaken for human rights.[82] For Donnelly, the notion of human rights is an idea which arose from a particular Western context.[83] To argue uncritically that they are "universal" runs the risk of diluting the notion of human rights and the protections which they provide.[84]

The issue that arises with accepting a cultural relativist viewpoint, whether left- or right-wing, is that it can be used by repressive governments as a shield to justify domestic human rights abuses. Such governments argue that practices which would not be acceptable according to Western ideas of human rights are justifiable in the domestic context because of traditional cultural norms. For example, some Muslim-majority states justify punishments for apostasy or curtailing women's rights on the basis that Islamic culture and legal tradition have a differing standard to Western notions of human rights.

This phenomenon is not limited to Muslim states. For example, in the decades following the adoption of the UDHR in 1948, the main clash was over Western and Communist ideas of rights. During the Cold War, the Western world accused Communist states of violating the human rights of their citizens, and the Communist world accused Western states of violating economic and social rights. Although the Cold War is now over, the issue of the universal nature of rights has not gone away. More recently, in the 1990s, a number of Asian states made reference to "Asian values" to respond to international pressure regarding domestic political repression.

It is also possible to argue that the involvement of many countries from different backgrounds justifies the labelling of UDHR as "universal". A number of Muslim states participated in the formation of the UDHR. At the end of the Second World War non-Western countries, many of which were former victims of colonialism, also pushed for an international human rights declaration.[85] While Western states played their role, the "constructive input from Muslim states had a strong influence on the development of human rights instruments".[86]

Countries such as Pakistan, Saudi Arabia, Syria, Iraq, and Egypt all played a role in the lengthy process of negotiation. These Muslim-majority states often disagreed with each other, calling into question the idea that there is one "Islamic" culture, or that Islam necessarily opposes human rights. Although the Saudi delegate (who was a Syrian Christian), for example, made various objections to the wording of Article 18 on freedom of religion, they were not expressed on the basis of Islam, and his comments were in fact supported by a number of non-Muslim states.[87] Meanwhile, Pakistani delegate Muhammed Zafrullah Khan disagreed, arguing that the Qur'an supports freedom of religion.[88] In the end, no Muslim countries voted against Article 18.[89] Thus, as Ann Elizabeth Mayer argues, "to generalise about a supposed 'Islamic' hostility to the UDHR [at the time of its negotiation] is unwarranted".[90]

It is true that only a minority of Muslim-majority states were independent at the time of the drafting of the UDHR. However, the overwhelming majority of Muslim-majority countries today are parties to the major international human rights instruments: the UN Charter, the UDHR, the ICCPR, the ICESCR, and CEDAW. This suggests that they accept most, if not all, of the rights enumerated in them. The Organisation of Islamic Cooperation's (OIC) 1972 charter explicitly affirms the UN Charter and the human rights principles embedded within it:

> REAFFIRMING their commitment to the UN Charter and fundamental Human Rights, the purposes and principles of which provide the basis for fruitful cooperation amongst all people.

As discussed in Chapter 3, the form of various Islamic human rights instruments, including the 1990 Cairo Declaration of Human Rights in Islam (CDHRI), mirrors to some extent the UDHR, although with various caveats and exemptions. Again, this suggests that the idea of human rights, and the content of the majority of these rights, is supported by most Muslim-majority states.

Mayer relates the account of Iranian diplomat Fereydoun Hoveyda, who was an assistant to René Cassin during the UDHR's drafting. Hoveyda recalls that

> back in the 1940s, Muslim states were less inclined to find the UDHR religiously objectionable than to deem it problematic because of its unrealistic and utopian character. They found it hard to imagine that it could be implemented in their own countries, but they likewise did not see how one could expect Western countries to adhere to it.[91]

The idea that human rights are broadly universal is further strengthened by the fact that many citizens of states with poor human rights records are often in favour of human rights ideals. As Mayer notes, even

> Muslims who do not use the terminology of modern human rights often display attitudes revealing their belief in its foundational ideals, maintaining that justice, equality, and respect for human life and dignity are such central principles of Islam that a system that fails to honor these cannot be in conformity with Islamic requirements.[92]

This is particularly the case for political rights, as I have discussed in more depth in Chapter 4. Research does indicate that on social issues, such as the status of women, there is some truth to the idea that ideas about gender and women's rights may be different in predominantly Muslim populations to those commonly found in the West.[93] However, such difference is not uniform, and within Muslim-majority states there are many Muslims who do not support patriarchal, state-imposed restrictions on women. Even if these Muslims currently do not *appear* to be in the majority, their existence weakens the argument that there is a single "Islamic" culture which opposes "human rights".

It is arguably true that the foundation of the modern human rights discourse has evolved within specific cultural traditions. But as Xiaorong Li notes, "the recognition that culture has an ethical significance need not undermine the plausibility of universal moral values and ethical principles".[94] It is possible to accept that cultures are different, while continuing to advocate for human rights.

The Muslim scholar Abdullahi An-Na'im is an example of a scholar who adopts a nuanced position. An-Na'im recognises that the UDHR was drafted at a time when the vast majority of non-Western countries were still colonised, and thus in that way it was not "globally inclusive". However, he also argues that

> while initially limited by Western experience, the rights that have emerged since 1948 are broader in scope ... The Western origins and immediate antecedents of human rights have been overtaken by developments reflecting the experiences and expectations of other peoples of the world.[95]

To put it another way, even if we accept the view that the UDHR could have been more representative, the human rights instruments that have emerged after the UDHR, and those that have been ratified by the vast majority of Muslim-majority states, have an even stronger claim to legitimately reflecting the aspirations of people from all cultures.

Today, the debate over the universality of human rights tends to occur between the wealthy nations of the global "North" and the poorer states of the global "South", or between the nations of the West and Muslim-majority states.[96] Yet Louise Arbour, former High Commissioner for Human Rights, describes the debate as an unnecessary distraction:

> I am further concerned that we have unduly embroiled our normative discourse in unnecessary clashes of vision, created competing images, each incomplete and ineffective without the addition of the other: Are human rights universal or culturally specific? Are they collectively or individually held? Should we promote them, or protect them? Which is the more effective: technical cooperation or naming and shaming; country analysis or thematic debates? Which comes first: peace or justice; economic, social and cultural rights, or civil and political rights; development or democracy?
>
> Such questions serve, in practice, as little more than a series of diversions to the real task at hand. They become the theoretical playground within which we demonstrate our irrelevance and justify our inaction, whether that inaction is borne [*sic*] of indifference, shrewd calculation, or despair.[97]

CONCLUSION

The debate over whether human rights are universal or whether they are culturally contingent is important in the discourse on Islam and human rights. Although there are strong arguments for both sides, the debate continues. For many Muslims, it is easier to dismiss human rights if they are regarded as external cultural expectations or standards that are being imposed from "outside" (particularly from the West). The debate on universality also shapes how Muslim-majority states engage with the UN human rights treaties. It lies behind many of the reservations that have been made in response to specific articles, and whether these states accept the observations or recommendations of the treaty monitoring bodies. The idea that international human rights may not be universal appears to have led to the development of specific "Islamic" human rights instruments. This is a topic that will be examined in the following chapter.

* * *

LOOKING AT AN ISSUE CLOSELY: THE CONTRIBUTION OF MUSLIM-MAJORITY STATES TO THE DRAFTING OF THE UDHR

Ann Elizabeth Mayer, *Islam and Human Rights: Tradition and Politics* (Boulder, CO: Westview Press, 2012), pp. 22–4. Extract*

This case examines the contributions of Muslim-majority states to the drafting process of the Universal Declaration of Human Rights (UDHR). Perhaps contrary to popular perceptions, these states did play an active part in the drafting process and almost unanimously voted in favour of the final version of the declaration when it came before the General Assembly for adoption.

In Western accounts of the genesis of the UDHR, the objections and complaints made by the Saudi Arabian representative, Jamil Baroody, are often noted, leading to generalizations about "Islamic" challenges to human rights universality or "Islamic" hostility to the UDHR.[98] In fact,

---

* Ann Elizabeth Mayer, *Islam and Human Rights: Tradition and Politics* (Boulder, CO: Westview Press).

the record is more complicated. As it happens, Baroody was neither a Saudi nor a Muslim but a Syrian Christian. Baroody did oppose including a phrase on the freedom to change religion that was eventually to be guaranteed in Article 18 of the UDHR, which some observers have attributed to Islam, but he did not expressly invoke Islam as a reason for his opposition. Johannes Morsink notes that Baroody's objections to Article 18 included his assessment that the language concerning the freedom to *change* religion was superfluous and that it was inconsistent to provide for the right to *change* religion as part of the freedom of religion when there were no corresponding provisions guaranteeing the right to *change* positions in the provisions on freedom of thought and conscience.[99] Some other delegations supported Baroody's objections, and not all of these were from Muslim states.[100] Thus, using Baroody's remarks to generalize about a supposed "Islamic" hostility to the UDHR is unwarranted.

Afghanistan, Egypt, Iraq, Pakistan, and Syria joined Baroody in expressing some qualms about Article 18, but as Waltz observes, at one point Sir Muhammed Zafrullah Khan, speaking for the Pakistani delegation, insisted that the Qur'an itself supported freedom of religion.[101] Significantly, no Muslim countries actually voted against Article 18 when it was finally put to a vote, suggesting that whatever objections they did have were not deemed so important that they wanted to go on the record as opposing it.

As Waltz has noted, some objections were registered regarding UDHR Article 16 of the UDHR on marriage and the family. Among other things, this article provides that spouses are to have equal rights in marriage, that it should be entered into only with the free and full consent of both spouses, and that men and women have the right to marry and found a family "without any limitation due to race, nationality or religion". Elements in the article conflicted with Islamic family laws in force in many Muslim states. Egypt, Iraq, Saudi Arabia, and Syria were among those objecting to Article 16. The Egyptian delegate argued that religious restrictions on who could marry whom should be acceptable.[102] Among Baroody's proposals was that in lieu of being accorded equal rights, women should be entitled to "the full rights as defined in the marriage laws of their country"—a proposal that prompted a strong objection by the Pakistani delegate on the grounds that Baroody's wording "would enable countries with laws discriminating against women to continue to apply them".[103] Again, Muslim states were divided. Meanwhile, not all Western states concurred with Article 16; the United States, where laws criminalizing interracial marriage were still widely in force, objected to a proposal for prohibiting limitations on marriage that were based on race, nationality, or religion.[104] Significantly, such an objection, which showed that the United States was unwilling to accommodate one of the most basic human rights ideals, has been largely ignored in accounts of the discussions leading up to the UDHR.

Baroody did make what sounded like a resentful complaint that the authors of Article 16 were, for the most part, using standards recognized by Western civilization and ignoring "more ancient civilizations", and he challenged the right of the committee to "establish uniform standards for all the countries of the world" or to proclaim "the superiority of one civilization" over others.[105] This challenge, which anticipates aspects of the Asian values debates in the 1990s, seems to have had little resonance. No Muslim states voted against Article 16, nor did any specifically object that the idea of women's equality in marital matters conflicted with Islam. That is, delegates from Muslim states seem to have steered away from complaining that Article 16 was in conflict with Islamic law.

Although Baroody was prone to quarrel with several proposals, his was not an absolute rejectionist stance. Far from insisting that the UDHR would engender an irremediable clash of cultures, Baroody proposed that, although the declaration was "frequently at variance with the patterns of culture of Eastern states, that did not mean, however, that the declaration went counter to the latter, even if it did not conform to them".[106] Moreover, the special emphasis on Baroody's carping in the secondary literature does not paint a balanced picture, because Muslim states generally supported the consensus behind the UDHR. They, along with an array of small- to medium-sized states, stayed engaged in the drafting process in the Third Committee, which worked to finalize the text. In contrast, by that stage the major powers had largely ceased their involvement.[107]

When the UDHR as a whole was submitted to the General Assembly, no Muslim state cast a vote against it, and Saudi Arabia was alone among Muslim states in abstaining, being joined only by South Africa and some Eastern Bloc countries. All in all, it is inaccurate to claim that when the foundations of the modern UN human rights system were being laid, Muslim states stood out as foes of human rights universality.

NOTES

1. Jack Donnelly, "Human Rights and Human Dignity: An Analytic Critique of Non-Western Conceptions of Human Rights", *American Political Science Review* 76(2) (1982): 303.
2. Brian Orend, *Human Rights: Concept and Context* (Peterborough, ON: Broadview Press, 2002), 16.

3. Ibid, 17.
4. Ibid, 24.
5. Donnelly, "Human Rights and Human Dignity", 304.
6. Orend, *Human Rights: Concept and Context*, 18.
7. Ibid.
8. Ibid, 25.
9. Ibid, 24.
10. Ibid, 25.
11. Orend, *Human Rights*.
12. Donnelly, "Human Rights and Human Dignity", 306.
13. Ibid, 303.
14. Micheline Ishay, "What Are Human Rights? Six Historical Controversies", *Journal of Human Rights* 3(3) (2004): 361.
15. Ibid.
16. John Betton, "Human Rights, Globalism and Cultural Values: Universality and the Nation State", *International Journal of the Humanities* 4(3) (2006): 2.
17. Ibid.
18. Ishay, "What Are Human Rights?", 362.
19. William Bristow, "Enlightenment", *Stanford Encyclopedia of Philosophy* (Summer 2011 edition), Edward N. Zalta (ed.). Available http://plato.stanford.edu/entries/enlightenment/ (last accessed 5 December 2017).
20. Ibid.
21. Ibid.
22. The Levin Institute, "Origins of Human Rights", Globalization 101: A Project of SUNY–Levin Institute. Available http://www.globalization101.org/human-rights-vs-natural-rights. (last accessed 5 December 2017).
23. Ibid.
24. Ibid.
25. Ibid.
26. Ibid.
27. United States National Archives, "Declaration of Independence: A Transcription", America's Founding Documents. Available https://www.archives.gov/founding-docs/declaration-transcript (last accessed 5 December 2017).
28. Johannes A. van der Ven, "From Natural Rights to Human Rights: A Cultural War in the Modern Era", *Religion, State & Society* 41(2) (2013): 165.
29. Ibid.
30. Ibid, 164–5.
31. Mashood A. Baderin and Manisuli Ssenyonjo, "Development of International Human Rights Law before and after the UDHR", in *International Human Rights Law: Six Decades after the UDHR and Beyond*, Mashood A. Baderin and Manisuli Ssenyonjo (eds.) (Farnham: Ashgate, 2010), 5.
32. Ibid, 6. See e.g. the *Atlantic Charter of 1941* [online]. Available from: http://avalon.law.yale.edu/wwii/atlantic.asp.
33. University of Minnesota Human Rights Resource Center, "A Short History of Human Rights" in *Human Rights Here And Now: Celebrating the Universal Declaration of Human Rights*, Nancy Flowers (ed.). Available http://hrlibrary.umn.edu/edumat/hreduseries/hereandnow/Part-1/short-history.htm (last accessed 6 December 2017).
34. Baderin and Ssenyonjo, "Development of International Human Rights Law", 6, United Nations, *Charter of the United Nations*, 26 June 1945. Available http://www.un.org/en/charter-united-nations/ (last accessed 6 December 2017), Preamble, § 1.
35. Ibid, § 2.
36. University of Minnesota Human Rights Resource Center, "A Short History of Human Rights".
37. Ibid.
38. Susan Waltz, "Reclaiming and Rebuilding the History of the Universal Declaration of Human Rights", *Third World Quarterly* 23(3) (2002): 440.

39. Ibid, 441.
40. Ibid, 441.
41. Ibid, 441.
42. United Nations, *Charter*, art. 55, 26 June 1945.
43. Betton, "Human Rights, Globalism and Cultural Values", 1.
44. Ibid, 2.
45. Ibid, 2.
46. Ibid, 3.
47. Sashi Tharoor, "Are Human Rights Universal?", *World Policy Journal* (1999/2000): 3.
48. Ishay, "What Are Human Rights?", 359.
49. Waltz, "Reclaiming and Rebuilding", 442.
50. United Nations, "The Foundation of International Human Rights Law" (undated). Available http://www.un.org/en/sections/universal-declaration/foundation-international-human-rights-law/index.html (last accessed 6 December 2017).
51. United Nations, "The Foundation of International Human Rights Law".
52. See Orend, *Human Rights: Concept and Context*, 31.
53. International Justice Resource Center, "Overview of the Human Rights Framework" (undated). Available http://www.ijrcenter.org/ihr-reading-room/overview-of-the-human-rights-framework/#THE_INTERNATIONAL_HUMAN_RIGHTSFRAMEWORK (last accessed 6 December 2017).
54. United Nations, "The Foundation of International Human Rights Law".
55. International Justice Resource Center, "Overview of the Human Rights Framework".
56. Ibid.
57. Ibid.
58. Ibid.
59. Ibid.
60. University of Michigan, "Interdependence and Indivisibility of Economic and Political Rights" (undated). Available http://humanrightshistory.umich.edu/problems/indivisibility (last accessed 6 December 2017).
61. Orend, *Human Rights: Concept and Context*, 31.
62. Ishay, "What Are Human Rights?", 359.
63. Ibid.
64. Ibid.
65. Ibid.
66. Ibid.
67. Fausto Pocar, "Some Thoughts on the Universal Declaration of Human Rights and the 'Generations' of Human Rights" *Intercultural Human Rights Law Review*, 10(2015): 45.
68. Ibid.
69. Ibid, 46. *See*, "Introductory Note: Universal Declaration of Human Rights" UN Audio-visual Library of International Law. Available http://legal.un.org/avl/ha/udhr/udhr.html (last accessed 6 December 2017).
70. Pocar, "Some Thoughts on the Universal Declaration", 46.
71. Ibid, note 8.
72. Ibid, 47.
73. Dorothea Anthony, "Indivisibility of Human Rights: A Theoretical Critique" (2010) Research Thesis. Available https://www.uts.edu.au/sites/default/files/law-form-dorothea-anthony.pdf 1 (last accessed 6 December 2017).
74. Ibid.
75. Ibid, 5.
76. Anthony, "Indivisibility of Human Rights", 5, citing *Vienna Declaration and Programme of Action: Report of the World Conference on Human Rights*, Vienna, 14–25 June 1993, UN Doc A/CONF.157/23 (1993); 32 ILM 1661 (1993), I.5.
77. University of Michigan, "Interdependence and Indivisibility of Economic and Political Rights".

78. Heine Bielefeldt, "'Western' Versus 'Islamic' Human Rights Conceptions?: A Critique of Cultural Essentialism in the Discussion on Human Rights", *Political Theory* 28(1) (2000): 91.
79. Douglas Lee Donoho, "Relativism Versus Universalism in Human Rights: The Search for Meaningful Standards", *Stanford Journal of International Law* 27 (1990–91): 353.
80. Samuel P. Huntington, "The Clash of Civilisations?" *Foreign Affairs* 72(3) (1993): 24–5.
81. Ibid, 41.
82. Jack Donnelly, "Human Rights and Human Dignity", 303–16.
83. Ibid, 303.
84. Ibid, 315.
85. See Susan Waltz, "Universalizing Human Rights: The Role of Small States in the Construction of the Universal Declaration of Human Rights", *Human Rights Quarterly* 23(1) (2001), 44–72.
86. Ann Elizabeth Mayer, *Islam and Human Rights: Tradition and Politics* (Boulder, CO: Westview Press, 2012), 21.
87. Ibid, 22.
88. Ibid.
89. Ibid.
90. Ibid.
91. Ibid, 21.
92. Ibid, 13.
93. Pippa Norris and Ronald Inglehart, "Islamic Culture and Democracy: Testing the 'Clash of Civilizations' Thesis", *Comparative Sociology* 1(3–4) (2002), 235–64.
94. Xiaorong Li, "A Cultural Critique of Cultural Relativism", *American Journal of Economics and Sociology* 66(1) (2007): 151.
95. Abdullahi A. An-Na'im, "The Interdependence of Religion, Secularism, and Human Rights: Prospects for Islamic Societies", *Common Knowledge* 11(1) (2005): 59.
96. Henry J. Steiner, Philip Alston and Ryan Goodman, *International Human Rights in Context: Law, Politics, Morals*, 3rd edn (Oxford: Oxford University Press, 2012), 519.
97. Ibid, 540, quoting Louise Arbour, High Commissioner for Human Rights, on the Opening of the 61st Commission on Human Rights, Geneva, 14 March 2005.
98. See, for example, Michael Ignatieff, "Human Rights As Idolatry" in *Human Rights as Politics and Idolatry*, Amy Gutman (ed.) (Princeton: Princeton University Press, 2001), 58–60, 183.
99. Johannes Morsink, *The Universal Declaration of Human Rights: Origins, Drafting, and Intent* (Philadelphia: University of Pennsylvania Press, 1999), 25–6.
100. Ibid, 25.
101. Susan E. Waltz, "Universal Human Rights: The Contribution of Muslim States", *Human Rights Quarterly* 26 (November 2004): 815.
102. Ibid, 822.
103. Ibid, 820.
104. Ibid.
105. Ibid, 821.
106. Morsink, *The Universal Declaration*, 25.
107. Waltz, "Universal Human Rights", 823.

3. Islamic human rights instruments

This chapter looks at the efforts made by Muslims to engage with the international human rights discourse of the twentieth century. This engagement has sought to conceptualise human rights within an Islamic frame of reference and in doing so, a number of "Islamic" human rights instruments have been developed. This chapter will consider three of these documents, which broadly reflect the approaches and characteristics of the broader debate.

BACKGROUND

When the UDHR was adopted in 1948, most Muslim-majority countries were under colonial rule. Only five of the twenty-two current members of the Arab League existed then: Saudi Arabia, Syria, Iraq, Lebanon, and Egypt.[1] Beyond the Arab world, of the fifty-seven present member states of the Organisation of Islamic Cooperation (OIC), only the five states already mentioned, plus Turkey and Iran, were independent states at that time. These figures are important, as Tabet Koraytem argues, when thinking through the factors that are involved in Muslim acceptance or rejection of the UDHR. Certainly, this at least partly explains why its "universal" nature has been subject to debate among Muslims.[2] Only a small number of Muslim nations were independent or quasi-independent at the time when the UDHR was formally adopted.

At the same time, it is important to note that the UDHR was drafted with contributions from several Muslim-majority countries, or countries with a significant Muslim population like Lebanon. Charles Malik (d. 1987), a Lebanese diplomat, served as Chairman of the General Assembly's Social and Humanitarian Committee during the drafting of the UDHR.[3] Saudi Arabia and Pakistan were also notable contributors, the latter making an important contribution to the direction of certain articles and amendments. As Waltz explains, "in the debate on what would become Article 16 [regarding marriage], the Pakistan delegation resisted efforts by Saudi Arabia to change the provisions for marriageable age", since the unchanged text "more clearly conveyed the intent to prevent child marriages, and nonconsensual marriages".[4]

Article 18, on freedom of thought and religion, was also a particular point of debate. The issue of the right to change one's religion was controversial and was cited by Saudi Arabia (along with Article 16) as a reason why it ultimately abstained from voting for the UDHR. Article 18 now reads:

> Everyone has the right to freedom of thought, conscience and religion; this right includes freedom to change his religion or belief, and freedom, either alone or in community with others and in public or private, to manifest his religion or belief in teaching, practice, worship and observance.[5]

These efforts show that the Muslim-majority countries that were internationally recognised at the time, actively contributed to the drafting process of the UDHR. Syrian delegate Abdul Rahman al-Kayali (d. 1969), in particular, noted the collaborative nature of the drafting process:

> Civilisation [has] progressed slowly through centuries of oppression and tyranny, until finally the present declaration [has] been drawn up. It was not the work of a few representatives in the Assembly or in the Economic and Social Council; it was the achievement of generations of human beings who [have] worked towards that end. Now at last the peoples of the world [will] hear it proclaimed that their aim has been reached by the United Nations.[6]

On 10 December 1948, once the document was finalised, the following Muslim-majority countries voted in favour of the UDHR: Iran, Iraq, Lebanon, Pakistan, Syria, and Turkey. Despite the fact that Saudi Arabia was involved in the drafting group, it ultimately abstained.[7]

THE ARAB CHARTER ON HUMAN RIGHTS

Although a number of Muslim-majority nations and Arab nations became independent in the 1950s and 1960s, there was no rush to develop alternative human rights instruments. Most Muslim-majority states went on to become members of the UN and to adopt many of its human rights treaties, albeit at times with reservations.

Within the Arab region, attempts to develop specific human rights instruments appear to have begun with a 1979 seminar organised by the Secretariat of the Arab Union Jurists in Baghdad.[8] The seminar produced a draft document on human rights that was primarily focused on the Arab peoples, rather than Muslims in general. Following this, the Arab League proposed the drafting of an Arab charter for human rights. A draft was submitted and considered by a number of Arab League committees. However, no concrete outcome resulted, and the matter was set aside, since an Islamic Declaration of Human Rights and Duties was about to be adopted by the Organisation of Islamic Conference (OIC, now Organisation of Islamic Cooperation).[9]

Over the following years a variety of attempts were made to put together human rights instruments from the perspective of different Arab countries at a national level. The Tunisian League of Human Rights adopted, for example, the Tunisian Charter of Human Rights in 1985. Libya also developed what it called the Great Green Charter of Human Rights in 1988, and in 1990, Morocco similarly developed a human rights charter.[10]

The Arab Charter for Human Rights reappeared on the agenda in 1992, when the Arab League revised the initial draft of the Charter.[11] In 1993, it publicly supported the draft and suggested that the Council of the Arab League adopt it.[12] While the League formally adopted the Charter in 1994, no Arab state ever ratified it.[13] This is unsurprising, because, as An-Na'im points out, the Charter contained several rights prohibited in most Arab states, such as the right to strike.[14] Many authoritarian states were nervous about adopting an instrument like the Charter, because it could potentially expose their actions to scrutiny and give political legitimacy to persecuted minorities or people pursuing reforms or legal rights.

An-Na'im argues that "even if [the Arab Charter had been] widely ratified, it [would have been] unlikely to improve the protection of human rights in the region because of the serious weakness of its provisions", especially when compared to other human rights instruments.[15] Indeed, the Charter contains provisions which essentially allow states to circumvent difficult or challenging elements of the instrument by allowing them to enact laws that limit the operation of some articles. So even if a state had ratified the Charter, it could qualify its application of certain articles if necessary.

The Charter also did not have enough power to enforce its own standards in any significant way. In fact, the committee of human rights experts it established could only "examin[e] reports submitted to it by state parties to the Charter, and [report] on them to the Permanent Commission of Human Rights of the Arab League".[16]

If Arab governments were not particularly interested in human rights issues, why did the Arab League develop the Arab Charter at all? The most plausible explanation is that the international community was putting significant pressure on Arab states to recognise international human rights instruments. Indeed, as An-Na'im highlights, "the spokesperson of the Egyptian delegation ... described it as a regional shield against international pressures on Arab states in the field of human rights".[17] The Arab Charter can therefore be seen as a defensive response to international pressure to abide by international human rights treaties: that the Arab region could and would develop its own set of rights, and not be dictated to by the international community. The Charter was presented as a specifically "Arab" expression of human rights, for Arab peoples. Yet, it seems that in doing so the Charter significantly restricted the scope of particular rights.

The failure of the Charter to attract ratification led to efforts to revise it and eventually the Arab League adopted an updated version in 2004.[18] The revision of the Charter took place in the context of a "modernisation package" initiated by Arab League Secretary-General Amr Moussa,[19] and was a collaborative effort between the Arab League and the UN Office of the High Commissioner for Human Rights. The process brought together a number of human rights experts from different UN bodies, including nationals from several Arab countries, such as Saudi Arabia, Egypt, Algeria, and Qatar.[20] The 2004 Charter was a significant improvement over the previous version, though it still did not fully conform with international standards.[21] The Charter eventually entered into force in March 2008, and as of August 2016, seventeen states had signed the treaty, including Saudi Arabia, Egypt, Lebanon, Iraq, and Tunisia.[22] This represents over three-quarters of the Arab League's membership.

The Charter utilises much of the language of the international human rights discourse. It calls for a variety of economic, political, cultural, and social rights. It also contains important provisions about women, children, and migrants.[23] Despite this, the document has numerous shortcomings. For instance, Article 8 refers to the right to protection from physical or mental torture, or cruel, inhuman, and degrading treatment.[24] However, as Rishmawi points out, the article makes no reference to punishment, allowing corporal punishment and the death penalty (both of which have been described as cruel, inhumane, and degrading in other international human rights forums) to stand outside its provisions.[25] Other problems in the Charter include restricting the rights to peaceful assembly and association (Article 24), and to free primary education (Article 41(b)) only to citizens, As Rishmawi notes, this is inconsistent with the universal protections expressed in the ICCPR.[26] Many important children's rights, particularly civil and political rights, are also omitted.[27]

In summary, the 2004 Arab Charter represents a step in the right direction, but with significant shortcomings. It could be argued that it is perhaps a way of engaging with international human rights law, but with a whole range of restrictions.

THE UNIVERSAL ISLAMIC DECLARATION OF HUMAN RIGHTS

The Universal Islamic Declaration of Human Rights (UIDHR) was drafted by a private Muslim organisation called the Islamic Council of Europe.[28] It was adopted on 19 September 1981 at the International Islamic Conference in Paris at the headquarters of the United Nations Educational, Scientific and Cultural Organization (UNESCO).[29]

The UIDHR was an important attempt by a group of European Muslims to draft a human rights instrument similar to the UDHR, but using an "Islamic" framework. It takes into account the role of God in granting rights; the obligations of Muslim governments and organs of society; and the duties of people towards God and the state. Its foreword, written by Salem Azzam (d. 2008), Secretary-General of the Islamic Council of Europe, clearly emphasises its position on the origin of human rights:

> Islam gave to mankind an ideal code of human rights fourteen centuries ago. These rights aim at conferring honour and dignity on mankind and eliminating exploitation, oppression and injustice.
>
> Human rights in Islam are firmly rooted in the belief that God, and God alone, is the Law Giver and the Source of all human rights. Due to their Divine origin, no ruler, government, assembly or authority can curtail or violate in any way the human rights conferred by God, nor can they be surrendered.[30]

The foreword goes on to explain the aim of the document:

> [Since] human rights are being trampled upon with impunity in many countries of the world, including some Muslim countries … I sincerely hope that this *Declaration of Human Rights* will give a powerful impetus to the Muslim peoples to stand firm and defend resolutely and courageously the rights conferred on them by God.[31]

The UIDHR proposes that the concept of human rights is not a new one, but one that has been authentically part of Islamic tradition since the very birth of Islam. Rights stem from "belief that God, and God alone, is the Law Giver and the Source of all human rights".[32] Accordingly, they cannot be restricted by any government or head of state. The text of the UIDHR goes on to emphasise the importance of recognising the dignity of human beings, as well as eliminating exploitation, oppression, and injustice. It explicitly states that its purpose is the protection of human dignity—a protection required by both revelation and reason.[33] Importantly, however, the UIDHR also explicitly affirms that there are certain duties and obligations that have priority over rights.[34] The emphasis on religious duties over rights is a critical point shared by Islamic human rights schemes in general, and one that sets them apart from secular human rights schemes.[35]

Furthermore, it is clear that it is the Shari'a that ultimately governs the UIDHR's framework of rights. The rights articulated in the UIDHR can be restricted or even eliminated if "the Law", meaning the Shari'a,[36] requires. In other words, the Shari'a is the ultimate qualifier of the rights and freedoms affirmed by the UIDHR. Article 1, on the right to life, states: "Human life is sacred and inviolable and every effort shall be made to protect it. In particular no one shall be exposed to injury or death, *except under the authority of the Law*" [my emphasis].[37]

The constant reference to "the Law" in the Declaration creates many difficulties for its interpretation. Ebrahim Moosa describes the function of the Shari'a in the UIDHR as a "statutory limitation that could potentially trump several other clauses".[38] There are several cases where rights and freedoms are limited by a reference to the "Law". The central issue is, as Moosa rightly notes, that since the Shari'a is not codified in the sense that modern law is, this provision introduces "an element of arbitrariness".[39] Since there are many interpretations of what is or is not acceptable from a Shari'a perspective, qualifying particular rights in the name of the Shari'a is highly problematic. For instance, which school of law should dominate in the understanding of particular rights or establish permissible limitations? Furthermore, this clause also gives religious authorities great power over the definition and implementation of certain rights.[40] Thus, the repeated reference to the Shari'a is a major issue for the compatibility of the UIDHR with the modern concept of human rights.[41]

While the UIDHR is modelled on the UDHR, many of its provisions fall short of international human rights standards. Article 10, for example, which addresses the rights of minorities, states:

> a) The Qur'anic principle "There is no compulsion in religion" shall govern the religious rights of non-Muslim minorities;
> b) In a Muslim country religious minorities shall have the choice to be governed in respect of their civil and personal matters by Islamic Law, or by their own laws.[42]

Here, the reference to religious laws (whether Islamic or otherwise) in governing the civil and personal matters of non-Muslims calls into question the applicability of the first part.

The right to freedom of religion is expressed in Article 13, but is not absolute: it must be "in accordance with [one's] religious beliefs",[43] raising the question of whether converting from Islam is permitted. Meanwhile, Article 12 on freedom of speech contains another limitation by "the Law", qualifying the permissibility of speech acts that could be considered blasphemous.[44] Moving to gender issues, Article 19 affirms that "every spouse is entitled to such rights and privileges and carries such obligations *as are stipulated by the Law*" [my emphasis], and that "within the family, men and women are to share in their obligations *according to their sex, their natural endowments, talents and inclinations*" [my emphasis].[45] This fails to address the issue of the inequality between men and women that many see in Islamic tradition. The same problem occurs with Article 20, which covers the rights of married women and enshrines the different rights of divorce afforded to men and women in traditional Islamic law.[46] In sum, as Katerina Dalacoura notes, the UIDHR "glosses over the most thorny issues of Islam and human rights: apostasy, equality between Muslims and non-Muslims, and between men and women".[47]

THE CAIRO DECLARATION ON HUMAN RIGHTS IN ISLAM

The Cairo Declaration on Human Rights in Islam (CDHRI) was developed and adopted in Cairo in 1990 by the Organisation of Islamic Cooperation (OIC) at its nineteenth Conference of Foreign Ministers.[48] Like the UIDHR, the CDHRI is modelled on the UDHR, and also makes numerous references to the Qur'an, the Prophet's teachings and to Islamic legal tradition.[49]

The CDHRI, also like the UIDHR, regularly refers to the Shari'a. The CDHRI explicitly affirms that the Shari'a is the primary source of guidance for Muslims when interpreting its provisions. This is manifest throughout the document, especially in its two final articles, which state:

> Article 24. All the rights and freedoms stipulated in this declaration are subject to the Islamic Shari'a.
>
> Article 25. The Islamic Shari'a is the only source of reference for the explanation or clarification of any of the articles of this declaration.[50]

The insistence on the critical role of the Shari'a in its interpretation means that the CDHRI faces many of the limitations of the UIDHR. As described above and in Chapter 1, the Shari'a represents the totality of

Islamic moral and ethical guidance, and is not a codified body of law. When it is referred to in a legal document like this, it is often unclear what exactly is meant by it. Given the variety of rulings and opinions that exist within the Shari'a on many matters, it is not clear which interpretations or schools of thought should be given precedence. Ultimately, as Turan Kayaoğlu has pointed out, the CDHRI seems more about confirming state power, instead of empowering or protecting individuals, and this has a negative effect on the human rights it is supposed to protect: "In the absence of any international authority to decide on the [meaning of] Shari'ah, the Cairo Declaration effectively *diminishes* the universality of human rights by relegating them to the discretion of governments" [original emphasis].[51] The weight given to governmental discretion through the references to the Shari'a in the CDHRI is quite clear.

In addition, while there is support for particular human rights within the Shari'a as broadly understood, such support is usually more limited or conceptualised differently to modern international human rights standards. For instance, the right to freedom of expression in Islamic law is usually understood to be limited by a prohibition on blasphemy, for example, (which I will discuss in more detail in Chapter 9). The same issue arises in the CDHRI: while it affirms in Article 22 that "Everyone shall have the right to express his opinion freely", the second part of the clause, "in such manner as would not be contrary to the principles of the Shari'ah", curtails this right.[52]

There are also other problematic areas. Article 1 states that "all men [*sic*] are equal in terms of basic human dignity and basic obligations and responsibilities, without any discrimination on the basis of race, colour, language, belief, sex, religion, political affiliation, social status or other considerations".[53]

As Bielefeldt argues, "[t]his concept of equality ... remains vague because equality in dignity is not clearly connected to claims of equal *rights*" [original emphasis].[54] Similarly, in Article 6, the CDHRI states that "woman is equal to man in human dignity",[55] yet Bielefeldt points out that it "concludes with a statement that seems to support the traditional role division between husband and wife".[56] Meanwhile, Article 5 states that the right to marry and make a family should not be restricted by "race, colour, or nationality".[57] Again, Bielefeldt points out that "[the lack of any] rejection of restrictions based on religious difference [means] ... traditional shariah obstacles to interreligious marriages remain".[58] Finally, Article 10 appears to privilege Islam over other faiths by calling it "the religion of true unspoiled nature", and seems to ban proselytising among Muslims by stating that "it is prohibited to exercise any form of pressure on man [*sic*] ... in order to force him to change his religion to another religion or to atheism".[59] Reading between the lines, it appears that "his religion" here only refers to Islam. As Bielefeldt observes, protection of Islam is therefore given preference over the religious freedom of individuals and the equal treatment of different religions.[60]

CONCLUSION: THE UTILITY OF ISLAMIC HUMAN RIGHTS INSTRUMENTS

The question is, is there a need for Islamic human rights instruments? This issue centres on whether human rights should be understood as universally applicable to all human beings, or whether particular groups, like Muslims, should have their own conceptions of human rights. Or, to phrase the question another way, are there barriers that make the acceptance of international human rights standards problematic in an Islamic context, thus necessitating a specifically Islamic expression of human rights?

Some scholars argue that international human rights and Islamic notions of rights are conceptually different. For this reason, as Moosa argues, efforts should not be made to "conflate the two very different legal, ethical and moral traditions so that they instantly look compatible".[61] Moosa warns that even though it is possible to find "similarities" between the two regimes, this does not justify "the grafting of presumptions from one system to the other and in so doing packaging Muslim notions of rights as compatible to modern human rights practices".[62] In his view, the way to approach the issue is to examine "the extent to which modern Islamic thought would be open to a revisionist or reconstructionist approach in philosophy and ethical orientation".[63] For Moosa, examples of such thinking exist in the work of Fazlur Rahman (d. 1988) and Muhammad Iqbal (d. 1938).[64] Such an approach will result in a more authentic Islamic approach to human rights.

There is a view that some key figures who have worked to put forward Islamic human rights instruments have been associated with twentieth century Islamist organisations or movements. These movements historically emphasised a conflict between the West and Islam. For Islamists, Islamic tradition provides a far superior set of values and understanding of human beings, which takes into account the idea of God and the centrality of His sovereignty. Human rights are therefore not simply a matter of recognising human dignity. They are part of an overall God-centred framework, in which a Muslim is not simply an individual but a servant of God. Priority should be given to his or her duties to God and the community. This position stands in tension with the perspective propagated by the UDHR and other human rights treaties, where the focus is on the individual.

Despite this, some scholars argue that Islamic human rights schemes have a place in the defence of human rights, particularly in the Muslim context, and that we should be open to the idea that different cultures may produce different human rights schemes.[65] The attempts to draft various Islamic human rights documents are perhaps an indication that Muslims are engaging seriously with the human rights discourse. Many Muslims appear to be quite comfortable with the rights articulated in the UDHR, the ICCPR, and the ICESCR. However, other Muslims—and not only those who subscribe to an "Islamist" perspective—also feel that an indigenous conception of human rights is important to them, and that the UDHR promotes a particular Western conception of human rights for all cultures of the world. For these Muslims, human rights can or should only be understood within an Islamic framework.

It is true that Islamic human rights documents do not apply the same standards as international human rights instruments. This is largely because they constantly refer to the Shari'a, which is, by its very nature, fluid. The usefulness of Islamic human rights instruments is therefore limited if we are seeking to guarantee the kinds of rights as specified in international human rights instruments. However, they are useful in another respect. They do serve to normalise the discussion about human rights in Muslim-majority states and societies. As Abdullahi An-Na'im argues, the "protection of human rights anywhere in the world is a process, not an 'objective' that can be achieved once and for all".[66] Further, "human rights cannot be protected in an effective and sustainable manner without developing an internal popular human rights culture".[67] In many Muslim-majority states there is a lack of public space available for discussions on human rights. Thus, Islamic human rights instruments, even with all their limitations, provide a starting point by creating general awareness of the issues.

* * *

LOOKING AT AN ISSUE CLOSELY: THE OIC'S PERMANENT INDEPENDENT HUMAN RIGHTS COMMISSION

Turan Kayaoğlu, "The OIC's Permanent Independent Human Rights Commission: An Early Assessment" (2015) *The Danish Institute for Human Rights*, pp. 4–8. Extract*

This case, from a report by the Danish Institute for Human Rights, introduces the OIC's Independent Permanent Human Rights Commission (IPHRC) as another recent example of Muslim-majority states' efforts to interact with the international human rights discourse.[68]

> More recently, the OIC [Organisation of Islamic Cooperation] has become known for its promotion of the so-called defamation of religion agenda, challenging the right to freedom of expression. In 1999, OIC countries introduced the first of a series of resolutions asking governments to combat the defamation of religions. For the OIC, this was a much-needed step in the fight against rising Islamophobia, arguing that defamation of Islam often led to anti-Muslim discrimination. Western states, for their part, considered the resolutions contrary to free speech at best and universalising blasphemy laws at worst. These states argued that religious people have a right to protection from discrimination and defamation—but religions do not.
>
> In recent years, however, there are signs of the OIC moving towards a universal conception of human rights, strengthening its participation in the international human rights system. As part of a larger reform of the OIC, a Ten Year Programme of Action was launched in 2005, introducing a clear focus on universal human rights and the importance of mainstreaming them into all programmes and activities. The amended OIC Charter, adopted at the 11th Islamic Summit in Dakar in 2008, further strengthened this new focus on human rights. In his book, then Secretary General Ekmeleddin Ihsanoğlu writes that the summit "ushered in a new era for the Organisation and its members", and he continues:
>
> This new approach, in the objectives of the Charter, marked a great step forward in adapting to global human rights values and involves closer alignment of principle to the international instruments and the practices of other regional or intergovernmental organisations.

---

* Turan Kayaoğlu, "The OIC's Permanent Independent Human Rights Commission: An Early Assessment" (Copenhagen: The Danish Institute for Human Rights). Denmark's National Human Rights Institution. Wilders Plads 8K. DK-1403 Copenhagen K. Phone +45 3269 8888. www.humanrights.dk

In 2011, a human rights commission was established with the purpose to support member states in their implementation of international human rights obligations. And the same year, the OIC co-sponsored a UN resolution on religious discrimination, at least on the surface signalling a move away from the anti-defamation agenda.

Optimists see these initiatives as signs of the OIC's willingness to leave behind the Cairo Declaration, and instead promote a conception of rights that is more in line with international human rights. Skeptics see them as nothing but window-dressing. Some have pointed to the fact that the new human rights commission's mandate is severely restricted, and that it has little room for the commission to actually do something about the serious human rights violations of certain OIC member states.[69] Others note that despite having abandoned the term "defamation", the OIC still works actively for the introduction of blasphemy laws and other measures to criminalise criticism of Islam, to the detriment of the right to free speech.[70]

…

The establishment of the IPHRC signalled a newfound commitment to human rights issues within the OIC. The commission was charged with the promotion of human rights within OIC members as well as those of Muslim minorities. Having completed its fifth session in June 2014, the IPHRC's track record and trajectory are likely to disappoint optimists' hopes and justify skeptics' fears. So far, the IPHRC has failed to develop a single major initiative to promote and protect human rights in the Muslim world. Of greater concern is that the comments of the OIC and IPHRC leaders, as well as the debates and resolutions of the Commission itself, provide a bleak picture of the commission's commitment to international human rights. The universalist and progressive tendencies towards human rights that were present at the start of the commission have been replaced by parochial and reactionary attitudes.[71]

Changes in the leadership of both the OIC and IPHRC explain the IPHRC's misdirection. The departures of the OIC's Secretary General, Ekmeleddin İhsanoğlu, and the IPHRC's Chairwoman, Siti Ruhaini Duhayatin, have greatly diminished the progressive tone of the IPHRC. Increasingly, the IPHRC looks like a tool for OIC member states, as states have come to rely on the IPHRC both to deflect criticism from their human rights records and to promote their foreign policies. In the same sense, the IPHRC merely seems to engage in human rights in the international public sphere, rather than actually advance human rights in the OIC member states. The IPHRC is a relatively new human rights organisation—and some of its failings are due to its inexperience. However, the IPHRC's initial steps are likely to determine its future; initial institutional decisions, designs, and discourses will likely determine the IPHRC's path, inform its trajectory, and inform its long-term success.

NOTES

1. Tabet Koraytem, "Arab Islamic Developments on Human Rights", *Arab Law Quarterly* 16(3) (2001): 256.
2. Ibid.
3. Waltz describes Malik as a "stickler for procedure", who "recognised the importance of allowing all delegates to have their say on the draft Declaration". Susan Waltz, "Universalizing Human Rights", 58. Lebanon at the time was not a Muslim-majority country.
4. Waltz, "Universalizing Human Rights", 55.
5. United Nations, *Universal Declaration of Human Rights*, 10 December 1948, 217 A (III), art. 18. Available http://www.ohchr.org/EN/UDHR/Documents/UDHR_Translations/eng.pdf (last accessed 2 December 2017).
6. Waltz, "Reclaiming and Rebuilding", 446. Waltz gives al-Kayali's name somewhat differently.
7. The UDHR was adopted in a unanimous vote on 10 December 1948, but eight member states of the UN, mainly members of the Communist bloc, abstained: Saudi Arabia, South Africa, the USSR, Byelorussia, Ukraine, Poland, Czechoslovakia, and Yugoslavia. See Waltz, "Reclaiming and Rebuilding", 448.
8. Abdullahi A. An-Na'im, "Human Rights in the Arab World: A Regional Perspective", *Human Rights Quarterly* 23 (2001): 713.
9. Ibid.
10. Koraytem, "Arab Islamic Developments on Human Rights", 257.
11. An-Na'im, "Human Rights in the Arab World", 714.
12. Ibid.
13. Ibid.
14. Ibid.
15. Ibid.
16. Ibid, 715.
17. Ibid.
18. Mervat Rishmawi, "The Revised Arab Charter on Human Rights: A Step Forward?", *Human Rights Law Review* 5(2) (2005): 362.
19. Ibid.
20. Ibid, 363.
21. Ibid, 364.
22. The complete list of signatories is: Algeria (2006), Bahrain (2006), Egypt (signed 2004, not yet ratified), Iraq (2012), Jordan (2004), Kuwait (2006), Lebanon (2011), Libya (2006), Morocco (signed 2004, not yet ratified), Palestine (2007), Qatar (2009), Saudi Arabia (2009), Sudan (signed 2005, not yet ratified), Syria (2007), Tunisia (signed 2004, not yet ratified), the United Arab Emirates (2008), and Yemen (2008); International Centre for Not-For-Profit-Law, "Civic Freedom Monitor: League of Arab States", last updated 19 August 2016. Available http://www.icnl.org/research/monitor/las.html (last accessed 2 December 2017).
23. Rishmawi, "The Revised Arab Charter on Human Rights", 364.
24. League of Arab States, *Arab Charter on Human Rights*. 22 May 2004. Reprinted in 12 *International Human Rights Reports* 893 (2005). Entered into force 15 March 2008. Available http://hrlibrary.umn.edu/instree/loas2005.html (last accessed 16 December 2017).
25. Rishmawi, "The Revised Arab Charter on Human Rights", 367.
26. Ibid, 373.
27. Ibid, 370–71.
28. Koraytem, "Arab Islamic Developments on Human Rights", 257.
29. Ibid, 260.
30. Salem Azzam, "Universal Islamic Declaration of Human Rights: Adopted by the Islamic Council in Paris on 19 September 1981", *International Journal of Human Rights* 2(3) (1998): 102 (Foreword). The UIDHR is also available at the University of Minnesota Human Rights Library, *Universal Islamic Declaration of Human Rights*, adopted by the

Islamic Council of Europe on 19 September 1981/21 Dhul Qaidah 1401". Available http://hrlibrary.umn.edu/instree/islamic_declaration_HR.html (last accessed 2 December 2017).
31. Azzam, "Universal Islamic Declaration", 102 (Foreword).
32. Ibid.
33. Ibid, 103 (Preamble, § (d)).
34. Ibid, 103 (Preamble, § (f)).
35. See Ebrahim Moosa, "The Dilemma of Islamic Rights Schemes", *Journal of Law and Religion* 15(1/2) (2000–2001): 196.
36. The Explanatory Notes to the UIDHR explain that "the term 'Law' denotes the Shari'ah, i.e. the totality of ordinances derived from the Qur'an and the Sunnah and any other laws that are deduced from these two sources by methods considered valid in Islamic jurisprudence" (Azzam, "Universal Islamic Declaration of Human Rights", 108–9 (Explanatory Notes, § 1(b)).
37. Azzam, "Universal Islamic Declaration", 104, art. 1.
38. Moosa, "The Dilemma of Islamic Rights Schemes", 197.
39. Ibid.
40. Ibid.
41. See also Katerina Dalacoura, *Islam, Liberalism and Human Rights: Implications for International Relations*, rev. edn (London; New York: I.B. Tauris, 2003) 50–51.
42. Azzam, "Universal Islamic Declaration", 106, art. 10.
43. Ibid, 106, art. 13.
44. Ibid, 106, art. 12.
45. Ibid, 107–8, art. 19.
46. Ibid, 108, art. 20.
47. Dalacoura, *Islam, Liberalism and Human Rights*, 51.
48. Al-Ahsan, "Law, Religion and Human Dignity", 572.
49. Ibid, 573.
50. The CDHRI is accessible at the University of Minnesota Human Rights Library, Organisation of Islamic Conference, *Cairo Declaration on Human Rights in Islam*. 5 August 1990. UN GAOR, World Conf. on Hum. Rts., 4th Sess., Agenda Item 5. UN Doc A/CONF.157/PC/62/Add.18 (1993) [English translation]". Available http://hrlibrary.umn.edu/instree/cairodeclaration.html (last accessed 2 December 2017).
51. Turan Kayaoğlu, "It's Time to Revise the Cairo Declaration of Human Rights in Islam", Brookings Institute, 23 April 2012. Available http://www.brookings.edu/research/opinions/2012/04/23-cairo-kayaoglu (last accessed 2 December 2017).
52. Organisation of Islamic Cooperation, *Cairo Declaration*, art. 22.
53. Ibid, art. 1.
54. Heiner Bielefeldt, "'Western' Versus 'Islamic' Human Rights Conceptions?", 105.
55. Organisation of Islamic Cooperation, *Cairo Declaration*, art. 6.
56. Bielefeldt, "'Western' Versus 'Islamic' Human Rights Conceptions?", 105.
57. Organisation of Islamic Cooperation, *Cairo Declaration*, art. 5.
58. Bielefeldt, "'Western' Versus 'Islamic' Human Rights Conceptions?', 105.
59. Organisation of Islamic Cooperation, *Cairo Declaration*, art. 10.
60. Bielefeldt, "'Western' Versus 'Islamic' Human Rights Conceptions?', 105.
61. Moosa, "The Dilemma of Islamic Rights Schemes", 189.
62. Ibid.
63. Ibid, 187.
64. Ibid.
65. Ibid, 206–7.
66. An-Na'im, "Human Rights in the Arab World", 720.
67. Ibid.
68. Turan Kayaoğlu, "The OIC's Permanent Independent Human Rights Commission: An Early Assessment" (2015) *The Danish Institute of Human Rights*, 4–8. Available http://

www.humanrights.dk/sites/humanrights.dk/files/working_papers/2015%20matters_of_concern_kayaoglu_2015.pdf 4–8 (last accessed 2 December 2017).

69. *See* Marie Juul Petersen, "Islamic or Universal Human Rights? The OIC's Independent Permanent Human Rights Commission", Danish Institute for International Studies, 2012, and Turan Kayaoğlu, "A Rights Agenda for the Muslim World", Brookings Doha Center Publications, 2013.
70. Ann Elizabeth Mayer's working paper.
71. The OIC's decision to locate the IPHRC's headquarters in Saudi Arabia should give even the most neutral observer pause.

4. Human rights and the idea of "clash of civilisations"

INTRODUCTION

The supposed conflict between Islamic and Western conceptions of human rights appears to be based on essentialist, and often misguided, views of both "Islam" and the "West". One of the most famous examples of essentialist thinking is the essay "The Clash of Civilizations?" by political scientist Samuel Huntington in 1993.[1] Huntington's essay argued that differences between what he termed "civilisations" would become a fundamental source of conflict in the post-Cold War environment. Huntington described civilisations as "the highest cultural grouping of people and the broadest level of cultural identity that human beings have".[2] He identified eight major world civilisations, including "Western" and "Islamic", each of which shares common features, such as history, language, customs, institutions, values, and, most importantly, a distinct identity.

For Huntington, people within each civilisation hold very different views and beliefs from one another—beliefs that have evolved over many centuries and are thus culturally entrenched.[3] Differences between civilisations may include understandings of God, the status of the individual, the significance of institutions such as the family, or positions on freedom, authority, or equality.[4] Huntington describes the international debate over the nature of human rights as one example of such an irreconcilable difference.[5] He assumes that human rights are fundamentally Western, and thus non-universal. They have "little resonance" among non-Western "civilisations", including Islam.[6] Thus, Western promotion of human rights will not gain their acceptance but instead produces "a reaction against 'human rights imperialism'".[7]

Other theorists advance somewhat similar views, arguing particularly that human rights are not a universal idea. Jack Donnelly, for example, puts forward the view that, while non-Western traditions and cultures such as Islam may have ancient concepts of "human dignity", this is not necessarily equivalent to the idea of "human rights".[8] Rolf Hille, a

German theologian, suggests that an "open clash of cultures" is in fact "pre-programmed" by the very nature of Islamic law and tradition.[9]

This chapter will set out key elements of Huntington's theory, consider how it has impacted the debate on the universality of human rights, and discuss whether this has any ramifications for the discourse on Islam and human rights.

HUMAN RIGHTS FROM A WESTERN PERSPECTIVE

The debate about whether human rights stem from a particular civilisational perspective has a number of aspects to it. This relates to the debate on cultural relativism described in Chapter 2. Bielefeldt points out that cultural relativists on the left and those on the right (among whom he counts Huntington), "reject universal human rights".[10] Shaheen Sardar Ali also refers to the views of some Muslims who believe that human rights come from a "Western" perspective. These Muslims argue that human rights are secular and "independent of the authority of any specific religion".[11] The validity of the rights, therefore, comes from human acceptance and is not connected to religion or God[12] and therefore, perhaps not "Islamic".

Cultural relativists argue that human rights developed in Europe, emerging from the natural law discourse, and were shaped by the writings of Western thinkers.[13] Their works led to a new conceptualisation of the individual and his or her status within society. The emphasis on the human person as an individual became fundamentally important in the framework of Western society and in its conception of human rights in particular.

The emphasis on the individual and their inalienable rights provided later the framework for the development of universal human rights, which are based upon "individualistic values".[14] From this perspective, rights are primarily there to protect individuals. For Hille, this emphasis is evident in almost every article of the UDHR, which begins with the words: "Every human being has the right to ..." or "No person may ...".[15]

Thus, those who believe human rights are essentially Western argue that they are based on the fundamental status of the individual, and the idea of human rights unfolded alongside the development of the nation state in the West and its growing power. Rights emerged to curtail absolute state power and were framed in terms of protecting the individual vis-à-vis the state. In the Enlightenment period, the state's ability to use its coercive power against its people became a significant issue for many thinkers. These thinkers argued for restrictions to state power by promoting and strengthening the rights of the individual. Importantly, in this, there was no need to make reference to God as the authority for human rights.

However, as some thinkers have pointed out, it may be incorrect to frame Western conceptions of human rights in purely secular terms. For example, Riffat Hassan argues that although international human rights instruments may not refer to God, this does not mean "that God-centred or God-related concepts were excluded from them".[16] Within the Western context there are those who have argued for human rights based on scripture and religious traditions, just as there are those who have argued for a non-religious conception of human rights.

Indeed, many scholars have pointed out that there has not been a single uniform position on human rights within Western civilisation.[17] As Waltz observes, there are many prominent Western thinkers whose ideas in fact conflict with contemporary ideas about human rights.[18] For example, Aristotle (d. 322 BCE), considered one of the founders of Western philosophy, argued that the state should have priority over the individual.[19] The French philosopher Jean-Jacques Rousseau (d. 1778) likewise argued that "individual rights were subordinate to the general will".[20] The English moral philosopher Jeremy Bentham (d. 1832) famously described the idea of natural rights as "nonsense on stilts".[21] As Waltz aptly observes, "[i]t is one thing … to recognise the tradition of human rights within Western philosophy; [and] quite another to equate the two".[22]

HUMAN RIGHTS FROM AN ISLAMIC PERSPECTIVE

According to scholars who adhere to the "clash of civilisations" approach, whether Western or Muslim, Islamic civilisation has its own conception of human rights which is fundamentally different to how they are conceptualised in Western tradition. Despite the fact that Islamic civilisation encompasses a wide range of nations and cultures, this position sees it, in general, as having its own particular conception of human rights.

Divine Origin

A key point in this argument by Muslims is the idea that in Islamic law, human rights are divinely provided, or at least divinely inspired.[23] Since for Muslims Islamic law is based on divine guidance, human rights, which they believe are enshrined in Islamic law, are seen to be of divine origin. According to this view, human rights that are divinely ordained or sanctioned are superior to any other notions of human rights, particularly those based on human ideas or reason.[24] They are also believed to be conceptually different because they are framed as duties rather than as rights.

It is important to bear in mind that Islamic law is diverse and, in practice, allows for a great variety of interpretations that can either support or negate conceptions of human rights. It is critical to understand that Islamic law by and large is the result of human reasoning. It is not accurate to argue that Islamic law is divine guidance without any element of human input. The development of Islamic principles of jurisprudence was the work of Muslim scholars over centuries, their encounters with key Islamic texts, and their application in various socio-cultural contexts. Put another way, while Islamic law is closely connected to the teachings of the Qur'an and Sunna of the Prophet, the entire body of Islamic law should not be considered equivalent to God's commandments.

DUTIES VS RIGHTS

While some may argue that there is a greater emphasis on duty-based human rights in Islam in comparison to international conceptions of human rights, I argue that this difference is overemphasised.

The relationship between "rights" and "duties" is not a new debate. It has been the subject of philosophical and legal discussion since at least the time of Aristotle.[25] Many thinkers argue that there is, in fact, "an inextricable link between rights and duties".[26] For instance, recognising this relationship, Immanuel Kant argued that freedom provides the basis for "moral and legal responsibility".[27]

Since at least the twentieth century, scholars have therefore attempted to describe the legal nexus between human rights and duties.[28] According to Ali, there is a strong correlation between rights and duties in many rights traditions, including the Western tradition. She asks: "is there any difference in how a right … is enforced/enforceable if not by placing the corresponding duty on the object of the duty?"[29] Orend makes a similar point, quoting W.N. Hohfeld (d. 1918), a key American human rights theorist, who argued that there are four types of rights: "a claim, a liberty, a power, or an immunity".[30] In relation to the first type, namely, claims, he points out that "a claim-right imposes an obligation on other people and/or on social institutions. In the language of rights theorists, a claim-right imposes a correlative duty. The duty literally co-relates with the right. There is no claim right-holder without a correlative duty-bearer."[31]

Hohfeld argued that the notion of "duty" was an "invariable correlative" of the term "right" in the ordinary legal discourse of his time.[32] Or to put it another way, "the claim or enjoyment of a right ... [made] the imposition or performance of a duty imperative".[33]

Other contemporary scholars argue for the notion of individual duties based on an ontological argument. Since most human rights scholars today concur that human rights are inherent to human beings simply because they are human, could this same principle apply to the notion of duties? In other words, "does common humanity impose duties on human beings?"[34]

The first acknowledgment of individual duties in an international human rights instrument can be found in the American Declaration of the Rights and Duties of Man (1948). Ten articles of the Declaration refer explicitly to human duties.[35] The preamble also establishes the inherent connection between human rights and duties: "The fulfilment of duty by each individual is a prerequisite to the rights of all. Rights and duties are interrelated in every social and political activity of man. While rights exalt individual liberty, duties express the dignity of that liberty."[36]

Drafted during the same year, the UDHR also includes a reference to duties. Article 29 states: "Everyone has duties to the community in which alone the free and full development of his personality is possible."[37]

The African Charter on Human and Peoples' Rights too recognises the concept of human duties, as well as rights, but it is rather unique in the way it refers to this notion. The Charter actually contains a whole chapter on duties.[38] In terms of specific duties, Article 27 articulates an individual's duties towards his or her family, society, other communities and the international community:

> Article 27
>
> Every individual shall have duties towards his family and society, the State and other legally recognised communities and the international community.
>
> The rights and freedoms of each individual shall be exercised with due regard to the rights of others, collective security, morality and common interest.[39]

Article 28 also affirms an individual's duty not to discriminate and to "maintain relations aimed at promoting, safeguarding and reinforcing mutual respect and tolerance".[40] Article 29 further elaborates an individual's duties to preserve African cultural values and to contribute to African unity.[41]

Commentators note that this emphasis on duties in the African Charter stems from traditional thought which defined an individual's status in society in terms of their connection to the community.[42] Both rights (entitlements) and duties came from being a member of this group because each person fulfilled a role within it that was critical for the survival of the entire community.[43] Thus a saying evolved in many African societies: "you are a human being because of others, alone you are an animal".[44] This is the conception of duties that the African Charter attempts to articulate.[45]

Despite the elaboration of individual duties in these human rights instruments, Western scholars remain "divided on the relative significance of right versus duty".[46] Some argue that focusing on the terminology of a "right" or a "duty" is redundant because, "[w]hether we speak of rights or duties is at the end of the day merely a matter of perspective or style since nothing extra is conveyed by using instead of duty the language of right".[47] Baderin agrees because, for him, "expressing human rights either in the language of rights or that of duties is like presenting a coin from either of its two sides".[48] Moreover, "the need to claim rights arises only when the rights are denied or violated. Therefore even where the rights are expressed in the language of duties a claim can still be brought in [the] form of an action for restraint in case of a violation."[49] It seems therefore that the distinction between rights and duties is not as conceptually clear as is argued by some.

TERMINOLOGY OF RIGHTS

When we look more closely, we find that Islamic tradition is not unfamiliar with the terminology of rights. Discussions in fact stretch back to early Islam. The rights of human beings and their connection to God were prevalent in Islamic thought and practice. The Arabic term for right—*haqq*—is a frequently used word in the Qur'an, the traditions of the Prophet and in the discourse of Muslim theologians. *Haqq* can have a variety of meanings, depending on the context in which it is used, including right, claim, duty, or truth. In the Qur'an, *haqq* is mostly used to refer to truth, certainty, justice, or right. In Q. 51:19, for example, the term refers specifically to an entitlement (not a duty). In the hadith literature, the Prophet also uses the word *haqq* in a similar way. For example, when discussing inheritance, he said, "God has given everyone having a right (*haqq*) his right [in the inheritance], so there shall be no bequest for [a Qur'anic] heir."[50]

The idea of *haqq* developed by early Muslims related to both the notion of rights in relation to God and in relation to other human beings. Mohammed Arkoun (d. 2010), a distinguished Muslim scholar, notes that "Islamic thought has always included a discourse on the rights of God and the rights of man (*huquq Allah/huquq adam*), with the former having primacy and priority over the latter".[51] Islamic law also discusses the term in significant detail. As Moosa notes, however, in traditional Islamic thought "rights are framed within a religious-moral framework where the omission of a duty/right is subject to religious sanction and its commission results in the acquisition of virtue".[52]

INDIVIDUALISM

Another argument frequently made to distinguish between Islamic and Western conceptions of rights is that the Islamic approach emphasises the community over the individual. For example, Hille argues that in the Islamic view of rights "the collective, the *umma*, always takes precedence over the individual".[53] Based on this view, this emphasis on community clashes with Western ideas of rights that are framed around the individual. As a consequence, there would be a fundamental incompatibility between Islamic and Western notions of rights, or, as Hille would put it, a "pre-programmed" clash of civilisations.[54]

It is worth considering whether Islamic tradition does in fact minimise the importance of the individual and, consequently, individual rights. Even a cursory look at the Qur'an reveals that with respect to obligations, accountability, and the following of God's path, there is a clear emphasis on individual responsibility. For example, it is an individual's obligation to save themselves on the Day of Judgement.[55] Each individual is accountable for his or her own actions and no one may share in that responsibility. The Qur'an says: "Whoever accepts guidance does so for his own good; whoever strays does so at his own peril. No soul will bear another's burden." (Q. 17:15) Similarly, in many areas of Islamic law, such as contract law or property law, the individual is the central concern. Indeed, Joseph Schacht (d. 1969), a noted scholar of Islamic law, argues that in fact, "the formal structure [of] Islamic law is individualist" in nature.[56] He states:

> The solutions provided by Islamic law go decisively and consistently in favour of the rights of the individual, of the sanctity of contracts, and of private property, and they put severe limits to the action of the state in these matters. If Islam as a religion confronts man as an individual with his

> transcendent Maker, Islamic law protects man as an individual as much as possible from interference with his rights and interests by the state.[57]

Likewise, provisions for inheritance and the functioning of trusts are also "strictly individualistic".[58] Islam introduced a new system of inheritance whereby relatives who had previously been unlikely to receive any inheritance at all in seventh century Arabian society were given "fixed shares".[59] The way succession worked—"where every single heir succeeds directly to his individual share"—was "strictly individualist" in practice.[60]

The Mazalim tribunals are another example of Islamic law's recognition of the rights of individuals. Those tribunals were established during the Abbasid period specifically to hear the claims of individuals against state officials who, the individuals claimed, had violated their rights. In effect, those tribunals functioned "as a mechanism for redressing the rights of individuals against the power of the state".[61] Moreover, Islamic law also recognised the state's obligation to protect an individual's right to "life, religion, intellect, property, dignity and family", and this was widely debated by legal theorists from approximately the eleventh century CE.[62] Similarly, all schools of Islamic law agreed that the state could not simply confiscate (an individual's) private property.[63]

The argument that Islamic law is essentially about the protection of a community's rights over an individual's is therefore actually quite unfounded. In my view, the notion of the individual and the protection of individual rights with respect to the state is an essential part of Islamic tradition. Therefore, there is no real conflict between Islamic and Western conceptions of individual rights. As Schacht succinctly concludes: "Whatever may be the case of other features of traditional Islamic law, its fundamental concepts concerning the sanctity of contracts, the respect for private property, and the relationship of individual and state, are well in line with the trend of contemporary Western legal thought."[64]

RIGHTS IN PRACTICE

It is important to acknowledge that most Muslim-majority states today have poor human rights records. The surveys done by various UN bodies and other experts paint a bleak picture of human rights in these states. But this does not mean that Islamic tradition is necessarily the cause of this situation. Rather, there are a number of factors that may have contributed. It is possible to argue that many Muslim-majority states by and large do not actually follow Islamic precepts or values in their governance. Furthermore, an important study by Wade Cole challenges the link between religion and a country's human rights record. Cole finds that "religious composition is only weakly associated with human rights outcomes".[65] More importantly, "a country's cultural or religious affinity to the West does not insulate its citizens from gross violations of their rights", and "neither does cultural 'distance' from the West guarantee that [citizens'] rights will be abused".[66] The study challenges the assumption that human rights are essentially a characteristic of the West, finding that in many cases "countries with relatively close cultural ties to the West—such as Catholic, Orthodox, and Jewish [majority countries], for example—are often identified as the worst abusers of human rights".[67] Therefore, the argument that there is a significant incompatibility between Islam as a religious system and contemporary human rights based on the poor human rights record of many Muslim states is reductive and, in my view, ultimately incorrect.

QUESTIONING THE IDEA OF "CIVILISATIONS"

A key notion of Huntington's thesis that should be examined is "civilisation". Are there such things as overarching civilisations that share elements of culture, belief, and language, and do individuals really identify themselves with this? The notion of civilisation is actually an imagined entity. There are great limitations that come from thinking in such terms, which can negate the reality of cultural difference and other specificities within and between nations and cultures.

These points have been made by many scholars in response to Huntington's essay. Regarding the Muslim world more specifically, observers such as Pippa Norris and Ronald Inglehart have noted its great diversity as a result of different "historical traditions and colonial legacies, ethnic cleavages, levels of economic development, and the role and power of religious fundamentalists in different states".[68] As they argue, "it makes little sense to lump together people living in Jakarta, Riyadh, and Istanbul". Similarly, "[to suggest there is] a single culture of 'Western Christianity' is to over-simplify major cross-national differences".[69]

Mahmoud Kashefi argues that the events of the "Arab Spring" also appear to contradict Huntington's thesis that different civilisations hold to distinctly different value systems. In his view, the clashes "underline[d] the power of an emerging universal human culture … composed of basic human and citizenship rights".[70] It is notable that in the midst of the uprisings, Muslims and Christians stood together with those from distinctly different socio-economic levels and younger and older generations to demand the same things: "economic and employment opportunities, especially for educated youth; governmental accountability and opposition to corruption, as well as establishing the rules of law and respect [for] freedom, democracy, and human rights".[71] Moreover, the people were demonstrating against regimes consisting of individuals from the same cultural background, yet it was human rights, not religious or cultural identity, that was clearly at issue.[72]

Shadi Mokhtari agrees that human rights were at the forefront of the Arab Spring uprisings.[73] Indeed, it was the paradigm of human rights that was put forward as a basis for challenging Arab authoritarianism.[74] The protesters' desire for basic rights and freedoms that they saw as basic human entitlements was clearly demonstrated by Yemeni activist and Nobel Peace Prize winner Tawakkol Karman who stated in her acceptance speech:

> The people have decided to break free and walk in the footsteps of civilised free people of the world … Our youth revolution … is motivated by a just cause, and has just demands and legitimate objectives, which fully meet all divine laws, secular conventions and charters of international human rights. … the values and objectives of freedom, democracy, human rights, freedom of expression and press, peace, human coexistence, fight[ing] against corruption and organized crime, [a] war on terrorism, and resistance to violence, extremism and dictatorship, are values, ideals, demands and objectives of common human interest.[75]

Karman's perspective, and that of other Arab human rights activists, do not conform to Huntington's proposition that there is a confrontation between the "ideology of the West" and non-Western cultures.[76] In the view of these authors and activists, human rights now carry the status of "cultural universals",[77] and do not belong only to the West.

CONCLUSION

In sum, the idea that Western and Islamic conceptions of human rights are so different that they cannot be reconciled is not helpful for the promotion of human rights. Instead, we must work to find common ground between the two. The falsely framed confrontation between Western and non-Western conceptions of human rights does a disservice to the promotion of human rights in regions outside of the West. However, for the human rights discourse to find global acceptance, it must be acknowledged that there need to be ways of talking about human rights that are sensitive to different cultural contexts. The human rights discourse will be more easily accepted in non-Western contexts if it is articulated in a language and terminology that connects it to the cultural norms and values that are already present in a particular context.

While there are differences between traditional Islamic and modern international notions of rights, this does not mean they are insurmountable, nor that the two conceptions of rights are irreconcilable. Tensions between the two traditions particularly arise when commentators take essentialist views. Within each tradition there is a diversity of views and opinions and it is important to recognise this, especially when reflecting on Islamic tradition. Many modern Muslim scholars are drawing on the diversity of views within Islamic law to find points of intersection between Islam and international human rights standards. This scholarship is critically important and will be considered in the coming chapters on substantive human rights.

* * *

LOOKING AT AN ISSUE CLOSELY: DUTIES IN INTERNATIONAL HUMAN RIGHTS LAW

David Petrasek, "Taking Duties Seriously: Individual Duties in International Human Rights Law" (1999) *International Council on Human Rights Policy*. Available http://ichrp.org/files/reports/10/103_report_en.pdf, pp. 15–28. Extract*

One of the main arguments put forward in the debate about the compatibility of Islamic and international notions of human rights is the idea that Islamic notions of rights are really based on duties, rather than the notion of rights or entitlements. This case outlines some important references to duties (or responsibilities) in international human rights instruments, showing that the notion of duties is not foreign to the international human rights discourse.

Types of individual duties in international human rights standards

In international human rights standards, we find three kinds of duties on individuals:

---

* David Petrasek, "Taking Duties Seriously: Individual Duties in International Human Rights Law" (1999) *International Council on Human Rights Policy*. Available http://ichrp.org/files/reports/10/103_report_en.pdf (last accessed 1 March 2018). Republished by permission of the author.

duties on individuals vested with State authority to respect, promote and protect human rights;
duties on individuals to exercise their rights responsibly; and
more general duties individuals have towards others and their community.

The first two types of duty arise when individuals exercise their rights. The third type of duty arises independently of any particular human rights claim. All three types of duty are primarily legal, but in each there is an overlap with ethical obligations. ...

The duty on State authorities

To be enforceable, a right claimed by one person must imply a corresponding duty on someone else to take, or not to take, a certain course of action. Human rights guaranteed in international standards generally create duties on State authorities. A right to speak freely involves a duty on the authorities not to interfere with free speech and to devise and maintain laws and institutions to protect that right. A right to join trade unions implies a duty on the authorities and on employers not to punish people who do so, and so on. The mere proclamation of human rights is not enough: those in authority must act in a certain way to give effect to the right.

A distinction used to be drawn between human rights that create *negative* duties (prohibitions on acting in a certain manner) and human rights that create *positive* duties (requirements to act in a certain manner). It was argued that civil and political rights created negative duties—injunctions on the State not to torture, not to interfere with free speech, not to discriminate and so on. Economic, social and cultural rights, on the other hand, were said to create positive duties—for example, to establish schools to ensure the right of children to education, to build houses for the homeless and so on.

This distinction is rarely made nowadays, because it is widely agreed that most human rights, in whatever category they fall, require a variety of both positive and negative measures to be taken. For example, to prevent torture requires not only a prohibition in law, but also adequate training of police and prison personnel, and punishment of those who resort to torture. ...

There are many specific clauses in international human rights standards that place clear obligations on State authorities to take measures to ensure rights are respected. Indeed, for each human right one could identify a corresponding duty on individual State authorities, and in this way construct a fairly lengthy list of legal duties. ...

The duty on individuals to exercise their rights responsibly

International human rights standards also place duties on individuals to exercise their rights responsibly. They make clear that personal freedom is not absolute and that rights can be qualified. The right to freedom of expression does not allow a person to slander or libel someone else. The right to equality cannot be pursued to the point where it leads unfairly to someone else suffering inequality. The legitimate demands of minority groups for special protection of their rights must be balanced against the requirements of democratic government. Freedom of the press does not mean that journalists can publish legitimate military secrets or exhort their readers to violence. …

Duties towards others and the community

In the two previous categories, the individual duty arises in the exercise of rights: either a State authority is required to act (or not act) to give effect to the right, or the individual is required to act responsibly so as not to exceed the limits of the right. However, international human rights standards also place some general duties on individuals that exist independently of any particular human rights claim. These duties are often characterised in broad terms as "duties to the community", but they can be more specific. For example, a number of documents attach specific responsibilities to groups of individuals (for example, parents, doctors or law enforcement officials) who are in a position to exercise power over others. …

International human rights standards contain numerous references to the notion that individuals have certain general duties. The first and perhaps most important such reference is Article 29(1) of the Universal Declaration of Human Rights (UDHR), which says:

> *Everyone has duties to the community in which alone the free and full development of his personality is possible. …*

The two International Covenants [the ICCPR and the ICESCR] include in their preambles an identical reference to individual duties, which is based on Article 29(1) of the Universal Declaration:

> *The State Parties to the present Covenant …*
>
> *Realising that the individual,* ***having duties to other individuals and to the community to which he belongs****, is under a responsibility to strive for the promotion and observance of the rights recognised in the present Covenant,*
>
> *Agree upon the following articles …* [Emphasis added.] …

It is worth noting that the language of duties in the preambles of the Covenants makes clear that the individual has duties both to the "community" and to "other individuals", whereas Article 29(1) of the UDHR only mentioned the former. Though no full list of these duties is provided, it is clear from the language used in the preambles that at least one such duty on individuals is to promote and observe human rights.

NOTES

1. Samuel P. Huntington, "The Clash of Civilisations?", 22–49.
2. Ibid, 24.
3. Ibid, 25.
4. Ibid.
5. Ibid, 29, 40–41.
6. Ibid, 40.
7. Ibid, 41.
8. Donnelly, "Human Rights and Human Dignity", 306–7.
9. Rolf Hille, "Human Rights and Islam—Is the 'Clash of Civilizations' already pre-programmed?", *Evangelical Review of Theology* 30(4) (2006): 352–61.
10. Bielefeldt, "'Western' Versus 'Islamic' Human Rights Conceptions", 91.
11. Shaheen Sardar Ali, "The Conceptual Foundations of Human Rights: A Comparative Perspective", *European Public Law* 3(2) (1997): 270.
12. Ibid.
13. Ibid, 264.
14. Ibid, 270.
15. Hille, "Human Rights and Islam", 353.
16. Riffat Hassan, "On Human Rights and the Qur'anic Perspective", in *Human Rights in Religious Traditions*, Arlene Swidler (ed.) (New York: Pilgrim Press, 1982), 53.
17. Ali, "Conceptual Foundations", 265.
18. Waltz, "Reclaiming and Rebuilding," 437.
19. Ibid.
20. Ibid.
21. Ibid.
22. Ibid.
23. Ali, "Conceptual Foundations", 270.
24. Ibid.
25. Kwame Gyan, "The Duty (Responsibility) of the Individual in the African Charter on Human and Peoples' Rights as It Relates to International Human Rights", *University of Ghana Law Journal* 21 (2000–2002): 156.
26. Ibid.
27. Ibid, 158. See generally Mieczyslaw Maneli, *Juridical Positivism and Human Rights* (New York: Hippocrene Books, 1981), 257–260.
28. Gyan, "The Duty (Responsibility) of the Individual", 159.
29. Ali, "Conceptual Foundations", 273.
30. Orend, *Human Rights: Concept and Context*, 21.
31. Ibid.
32. Gyan, "The Duty (Responsibility) of the Individual", 159.
33. Ibid, 156.
34. Ibid, 160.
35. Ibid, 170.

36. *American Declaration of the Rights and Duties of Man.* Available https://www.cidh.oas.org/Basicos/English/Basic2.american%20Declaration.htm (last accessed 4 December 2017.
37. *Universal Declaration of Human Rights*, art. 29. Available http://www.un.org/en/universal-declaration-human-rights (last accessed 4 December 2017).
38. See *African Charter on Human and Peoples' Rights*, Chapter II. Available http://www.achpr.org/instruments/achpr/#a25 (last accessed 4 December 2017). The chapter consists of three articles: Articles 27–9.
39. *African Charter on Human and Peoples' Rights*, art. 27.
40. *African Charter on Human and Peoples' Rights*, art. 28.
41. *African Charter on Human and Peoples' Rights*, art. 29.
42. Gyan, "The Duty (Responsibility) of the Individual", 164.
43. Ibid, 165.
44. Ibid.
45. Ibid, 166.
46. Mohammad H. Kamali, "Fundamental Rights of the Individual: An Analysis of Haqq (Right) in Islamic Law", *American Journal of Social Sciences*, 10(3) (1993): 364. For details see Samuel J. Stoljar, *An Analysis of Rights* (London: Macmillan, 1984).
47. Ibid.
48. Mashood A. Baderin, "Human Rights and Islamic Law: The Myth of Discord", *European Human Rights Law Review* 2(2005): 174.
49. Ibid, 175.
50. Abu Dawud, *Sunan Abi Dawud*, Kitab al-wasaya, Bab ma ja'a fi al-wasiyya li-l-warith, No. 2870.
51. Mohammad Arkoun, *Rethinking Islam: Common Questions, Uncommon Answers* (Boulder, CO: Westview Press, 1994), 108.
52. Moosa, "The Dilemma of Islamic Rights Schemes", 193.
53. Hille, "Human Rights and Islam", 359. See also Jack Donnelly, "Cultural Relativism and Universal Human Rights", *Human Rights Quarterly* 6(4) (1984): 400–19.
54. Hille, "Human Rights and Islam", 352.
55. See, for example, Q. 2:48, 2:123, 80:34–7.
56. Joseph Schacht, "Islamic Law in Contemporary States", *American Journal of Comparative Law* 8(2) (1959): 138.
57. Ibid.
58. Ibid, 138–9.
59. Ibid, 138.
60. Ibid.
61. Baderin, "Human Rights and Islamic Law", 184.
62. Ibid, 182.
63. Schacht, "Islamic Law in Contemporary States", 140.
64. Ibid, 147.
65. Wade M. Cole, "Does Respect for Human Rights Vary across 'Civilizations'? A Statistical Reexamination", *International Journal of Comparative Sociology* 54(4) (2013): 374.
66. Ibid.
67. Ibid.
68. Norris and Inglehart, "Islamic Culture and Democracy", 239.
69. Ibid.
70. Mahmoud "Max" Kashefi, "The 'Arab Spring' and its Theoretical Significance: Samuel Huntington's 'The Clash of Civilizations' Revisited", *International Review of Modern Sociology* 39(1) (2013): 30–31.
71. Ibid, 36.
72. Ibid, 40.
73. Shadi Mokhtari, "Human Rights and Power amid Protest and Change in the Arab World", *Third World Quarterly* 36(6) (2015): 1207.
74. Ibid, 1208.

75. Nobel Foundation, "Tawakkol Karman—Nobel Lecture". Available https://www.nobelprize. org/nobel_prizes/peace/laureates/2011/karman-lecture_en.html (last accessed 4 December 2017).
76. Kashefi, "The 'Arab Spring' and its Theoretical Significance", 37–8.
77. Ibid, 38.

5. Islam and the state

INTRODUCTION

Around the world different states apply various models of government—from religion-based to liberal democratic systems—but is one model preferable when it comes to the promotion of human rights? Is a liberal democratic state the best model of governance for protecting human rights? What if a state is structured around a particular set of religious ideas—will human rights be hindered? More specifically, if a state governs by Islamic precepts, can human rights still be promoted?

Many studies affirm there is a link between political regime types and human rights. They suggest that democratic systems, on average, have better human rights records, compared to non-democratic regimes.[1] Democracies, on the whole, are more conducive to the promotion of human rights because they formally recognise the dignity and equality of the individual through processes that allow people to participate on an equal basis in the process of government. Democratic systems often seem to put more emphasis on policies that promote human rights. While there are different systems of democracy, the focus here is on liberal democratic systems. This can be found in countries such as the United States, a number of European countries, Australia, and Japan, for example.

Most liberal democracies emphasise the importance of human rights in their own countries, as well as around the world. As scholars have noted, a significant foreign policy objective of many Western states is the global spread of human rights.[2] The importance of human rights is also evident in domestic legislation and policy. Liberal democracies generally legislate a range of protections for minorities,[3] people who might otherwise be discriminated against. Yet as Jonathan Fox points out, liberal democracies are not always entirely secular: while some clearly separate religion and the state, others explicitly include religious laws in their legal framework and allow some religions to have privileges over others.[4] This chapter will therefore explore very briefly the relationship between religion, state, and human rights, consider whether Islamic models of governance can support human rights, and in doing so, examine the question of the compatibility of democracy with Islamic teachings and tradition.

HUMAN RIGHTS ISSUES IN MUSLIM-MAJORITY COUNTRIES

Several models of government have been employed by Muslim-majority states historically and today. Contemporary Muslim scholars have in general recognised the legitimacy of nation states, but there is no agreement about the best model of government.[5] Some countries, like Iran, are considered theocracies, where the head of state can be said to rule in the name of God. Others, such as Saudi Arabia, are monarchies, ruled by a king who comes to power through hereditary rule. There are even examples of "Islamic" democracies, although they differ in form and vary in their implementation of democratic ideals. Some examples include Pakistan and Malaysia. As Fox observes, about half of the world's Muslim population lives in democratic and semi-democratic states.[6] However, many Muslims continue to live under systems of governance that can be termed authoritarian or semi-authoritarian, even if they present themselves as democratic. In fact, a number of studies have argued that Muslim states are "disproportionately autocratic",[7] and in general have poor human rights records.[8]

Many members of the Organisation of Islamic Cooperation (OIC) currently recognise some form of Islam as the official religion of the state.[9] Many of these countries, which only weakly separate religion and the state, are also not very democratic. In fact, they are often far from participatory. In these societies, even if equality is promoted through law and policy, in reality, a variety of discriminatory practices exist.

For example, in Iran, many articles of legislation explicitly outlaw discrimination. Article 19 of the Iranian Constitution affirms equality for all, regardless of race or ethnic origin. The right of equality before the law is guaranteed by Article 3(14) and the religious freedom of recognised religious minorities is protected by Article 13.[10] For those religious minorities outside the three recognised religious traditions (Judaism, Christianity, and Zoroastrianism), their religious freedom is protected in a qualified manner by Article 14:

> The Government of the Islamic Republic of Iran and all Muslims are duty bound to treat non-Muslims in conformity with equitable norms and the principles of Islamic justice and equity and to respect their human rights. This

> principle applies to all who refrain from engaging in conspiracy or activity against Islam and the Islamic Republic of Iran.[11]

However, despite these provisions, a report by Human Rights Watch reveals that "the treatment of ethnic minorities has failed to meet the standard of equal treatment under the law for all Iranians regardless of their ethnic origin, set forth in the Iranian constitution and instruments of international law".[12] Moreover, reports suggest there is widespread discrimination against Baha'is, even though President Hassan Rouhani has promised to end religious discrimination.[13]

Similarly, there are numerous reports of discrimination against minorities and women in Pakistan. In 1979, a series of laws known as the Hudood Ordinances were promulgated by General Zia ul Haq, which dramatically changed Pakistan's system of criminal justice. The Zina Ordinance, amongst these provisions, which prohibits wilful sexual intercourse outside marriage,[14] is widely regarded to be discriminatory against women. It has resulted in the dramatic increase of the number of women in jail in Pakistan. Even committees appointed by the government have since demanded that it be repealed.[15]

RELIGIOUS EXCLUSIVITY AND HUMAN RIGHTS

If it is true that most Muslim states are failing to protect human rights, can we conclude that this is because of Islam? To answer this question, we should ask first: if a state identifies with a particular religion or exclusively promotes one religious tradition (that is, religious exclusivity), will it be more hostile to certain human rights? Or will the state potentially be reluctant to promote human rights in general? If the answer is yes, then we might conclude that the problem is not necessarily with Islam but with states that promote one religion exclusively.

Until relatively recently, most states around the world were closely connected to particular religious traditions, usually the religion of the majority. The state religion would influence matters of law, policy, and other aspects of day-to-day governance. The connection between state and religion is still evident in many parts of the world today. The link is widespread in Muslim-majority countries, although it also remains in some Western countries, particularly in parts of Europe. In the United Kingdom, for example, the Queen is the head of state and also the head of the Church of England. However, a link between religion and the state does not necessarily mean that the state propagates that religion in a way that curtails the rights of other religious traditions. In most democratic societies of the West, the notion of equality is highly valued and discrimination against minorities is formally prohibited.

Thus, a state may be associated with a particular religion for historical or cultural reasons, but how much this connection impacts the promotion of human rights is dependent on a number of factors. A study published by Fox in 2008 examined the impact of state religious exclusivity on a state's human rights record. "State religious exclusivity" was defined as "state support for some religions or one religion over others and state legislation of religious precepts as law".[16] The study found that "state religious exclusivity is associated with poorer human rights records".[17] This was the case for all states in the study, including democracies, but the link was weaker for "Western democracies".[18] Even when controlling for factors such as "regime", "economic development" or "religious tradition", state religious exclusivity was found to have a notable influence on human rights records, even within democratic states.[19] This is significant because previous studies have found that autocratic states have higher levels of state religious exclusivity,[20] and, in turn, "poorer human rights records".[21] However, Fox's study found that state religious exclusivity is a significant factor regardless of regime type.[22]

There are clearly different factors at play here. Within the data set, states with Islam as the state religion also had worse human rights records on average when compared to countries with a form of Christianity or a non-Abrahamic religion.[23] Fox also found that economic development positively impacts human rights, and that states with smaller populations also have better records.[24] It is not clear that we can conclude from this that having Islam as state religion is the cause of a country's poor rights record, any more than we can conclude that having a state religion causes it—only that the two are associated. In the case of most Muslim-majority countries, history, and in particular the legacy of colonial rule, must also be considered.

Fox's study should probably be read alongside Cole's examination (discussed in Chapter 4) of the link between religious composition and human rights records, in which Cole found only a weak association between the two.[25] Another study, published by Brian Calfano and Emile Sahliyeh in 2008, found that among member states of the OIC, "the presence of non-Islamic religious groups [within a state] increases the prospects of … democracy through the strengthening of political rights".[26] On the other hand, "intra-Islamic divisiveness … contributes significantly to a decrease in political rights and civil liberties".[27] Based on these results, they concluded that "to view Islam either as 'for' or 'against' democracy is too simplistic".[28] Rather, they suggest that "Islam, when it holds the status of a state's official religion, may provide ruling elites with the impetus to extend some rights, while taking others away, depending on the nature of the population they oversee".[29]

It seems evident that how deeply rooted the spirit of democracy is within a given society is a major factor that affects its human rights record. In states that are democratic in real terms, despite being linked to a particular religious tradition, the notion of equality and the protection of minorities are stronger. This leads us to the question of Islam's compatibility with democracy, which the remainder of this chapter will examine.

EVIDENCE FROM ISLAMIC TRADITION

In terms of Islamic models of governance, there is no one blueprint provided by the Qur'an or explicitly commanded by the Prophet Muhammad. Despite this, some Muslim thinkers do argue that Islam does envisage a specific model of governance. This belief is rooted in the idea that governance is such an important part of human life that it would be unthinkable for God to neglect to give specific instructions in this area. However, proponents of this view do not agree on what this model might be. This suggests that the views of such thinkers should be taken with a high degree of caution.

There are, however, certain teachings in both the Qur'an and the traditions of the Prophet that can be used to support particular systems of government. Khaled Abou El Fadl has examined this issue in detail and argues for the compatibility of Islam and democracy. As he explains, many verses of the Qur'an emphasise the pursuit of justice through "social cooperation and mutual assistance";[30] the importance of managing community affairs through consultative processes;[31] and "mercy and compassion in social interactions".[32] Some of the most illustrative Qur'anic verses are as follows:

> People, We created you all from a single male and a single female, and made you into races and tribes so that you should recognise one another. In God's eyes, the most honoured of you are the ones most mindful of Him: God is all knowing, all aware. (Q. 49:13)
>
> If your Lord had pleased, He would have made all people a single community, but they continue to have their differences. (Q. 11:118)
>
> It was only as a mercy that We sent you [Prophet] to all people. (Q. 21:107)

Many other teachings emphasise the need to be fair and just to all people; the importance of cooperation between peoples; and compassion when dealing with others (see Chapter 1).

Individual and state accountability is another theme that runs through Islamic discourses on governance. A ruler is not free to do whatever they want; rather, they are accountable to God and to their people. This idea is demonstrated most clearly in the inaugural speech of the first caliph, Abu Bakr (d. 13/634), who said:

> O people, I have been appointed over you, though I am not the best among you. If I do well, then help me; and if I act wrongly, then correct me. Truthfulness is synonymous with fulfilling the trust, and lying is equivalent to treachery. The weak among you is deemed strong by me, until I return to them that which is rightfully theirs, God willing. And the strong among you is deemed weak by me, until I take from them what is rightfully (someone else's), God willing.[33]

As Baderin argues, "by inviting the populace to help him when he did well and to correct him when he did wrong", Abu Bakr acknowledged the importance of community participation in good governance.[34] As Baderin puts it, "Islam considers governance a Trust (*Amanah*) primarily from God and subsequently from the populace to those in authority. Thus, those in authority are accountable to God in the hereafter and accountable to the populace here in this world."[35]

These Qur'anic texts, legal principles, and traditions of the Prophet contain many crucial ideas and values that can be used to develop a broader system of governance, government institutions, and policies through the prism of Islam. The fact that neither the Qur'an nor the Prophet provided a prescriptive model of governance means that there is flexibility inherent in Islamic tradition to devise approaches to governance that are sensitive to historical and societal change. As Abou El Fadl argues, "Islamic political thought contains both interpretive and practical possibilities that can be developed into a democratic system."[36] To achieve this will require the "will power, inspired vision and moral commitment" of Muslims; otherwise these "doctrinal potentialities may remain unrealized".[37] However, this potential means that Muslims can support the idea of democracy without fear that it compromises Islam.[38]

In fact, Abou El Fadl argues that "democracy … offers the greatest potential for promoting justice and protecting human dignity, without making God responsible for injustice or the degradation of human beings".[39] The Qur'an affirms that human beings are responsible (as God's representatives) for ensuring justice.[40] Abou El Fadl argues that "by assigning equal political rights to all adults, democracy expresses that special status of human beings in God's creation and enables them to discharge that responsibility",[41] and further, that a democratic system makes leaders accountable to their people, which limits the possibility that they "render themselves immune from judgment".[42] Governmental accountability is therefore "consistent with the imperative of justice in Islam".[43]

THE CALIPHATE

In Islamic political theory, specifically within Sunni tradition, the issue of governance centres on the notion of the caliphate. Abou El Fadl argues that it is possible to view the caliphate as based on a contract between the caliph (or ruler) and the people, rather than as a form of absolute rule.[44] On this understanding, the caliphate can in theory be seen as having a resemblance to representative government. According to Abou El Fadl, in Sunni political theory, key community members enter into an implied contract (*'aqd*) with the caliph who agrees to govern the people.[45] The importance of this contractual arrangement is played out most visibly when a caliph is given their *bay'a* (allegiance) in return for his commitment to enact the terms of the contract.[46] The stipulations of the contract, according to Muslim jurists, would usually include provisions ensuring the caliph's obligation to apply God's law; protect the Muslim state or territory, and rule justly. In return, the caliph has the promise of his people's obedience and support.[47] However, as Abou El Fadl notes, it is important not to read modern democratic concepts into this arrangement: "many of the concepts employed in [pre-modern Muslim] political discourses [only] suggest ... representative government but never fully endorse it".[48]

COMMUNITY CONSULTATION OR *SHURA*

Underpinning the notion of the caliphate (and Islamic governance more generally) is the importance of community consultation, referred to as *shura*. There are a number of key verses in the Qur'an which urge the Prophet Muhammad to consult with his people in different socio-political or ethical matters. For example, the Qur'an says:

> By an act of mercy from God, you [Prophet] were gentle in your dealings with them—had you been harsh, or hard-hearted, they would have dispersed and left you—so pardon them and ask forgiveness for them. Consult with

> them about matters, then, when you have decided on a course of action, put your trust in God: God loves those who put their trust in Him. (Q. 3:159)

It also refers to "[those who] respond to their Lord; keep up the prayer; conduct their affairs by mutual consultation; [and] give to others out of what We have provided for them" (Q. 42:38).

Islamic history reveals, however, that different forms of consultation have been used by Muslim states at different times. Consultative mechanisms have varied enormously in form and process, which suggests that no single model of consultation has been prescribed by God. The particular form of consultation depended not only on Islamic precepts, but also on the particular socio-political and cultural context of the time. Abou El Fadl argues that the concept of consultation as it appears in Islamic history should be understood as broadly signifying "resistance to autocracy, government by force, or oppression".[49]

The Prophetic period and that of the first four caliphs saw a relatively informal mode of consultation used. However, after the first two centuries or so, consultation became more formally institutionalised. Jurists developed the notion of "the people of consultation" (*ahl al-shura*), a group of community members who were, in theory, also given the authority to choose a ruler.[50] There were discussions among jurists about whether the results of this consultation were binding on the ruler or not. A minority of jurists argued that consultation was binding, whereas the majority held that the consultative process was "advisory and not compulsory".[51]

Because of the variety of forms that "consultation" has taken over time, there is nothing to prevent Muslims conceptualising it in a way that is most appropriate and relevant to their circumstances today. For example, the notion of consultation within a contemporary Islamic framework might resemble the consultative methods of liberal democratic societies. However, as Abou El Fadl argues, even if consultation is used as a means of participatory representation, it must be governed by other principles that "serve an overriding moral goal such as justice".[52] Consultation must be valued as a process in and of itself, not just because it produces particular results. This means that consultation should also allow for and tolerate dissenting views.[53]

THE ISSUE OF SOVEREIGNTY

The problem of sovereignty is a key objection to democracy for some Muslim thinkers. They argue that "sovereignty" belongs only to God and therefore people cannot be deemed "sovereign" beings. For instance, the Egyptian thinker Sayyid Qutb (d. 1966) argued that the only legitimate sovereignty is divine sovereignty: "There is no sovereignty (*hakimiyya*) but God's, no law (*shari'a*) except from God, and no power (*sultan*) of a person over another person, because all power belongs to God."[54]

Even in classical Islamic juristic tradition there are fervent debates about whether lawmaking is the task of the ruler or whether this usurps God's sovereignty. Many jurists held that lawmaking is for God only or, to put it another way, that God is the ultimate and only legitimate source of law. Does this then mean that Islam is not compatible with democracy as we understand it today? Is it possible to reconcile the idea of God as the ultimate lawmaker with the notion that people and their elected ruler can also have the authority to enact laws?

The belief in God's sovereignty is rooted in the Qur'an and in juristic discourses on governance and lawmaking, and strongly felt in contemporary Muslim consciousness. Thus, the idea that sovereignty can rest with the people, as liberal democratic systems propose, remains one of the most important challenges for reconciling Islam with democracy. Nevertheless, the debate should not be deemed a closed one.

Certainly, the Qur'an emphasises the sovereignty of God and His ultimate authority and status as the Creator of all. However, even within this conception of God's sovereignty, it is possible to attribute fundamental agency to human beings as well. Human beings were, according to the Qur'an, created on the earth to be a *khalifa* or viceregent (Q. 2:30), which necessarily requires them to have the ability to think, take action, and assume responsibility for their decisions. This responsibility and agency is a crucial expectation of God. The actions of human beings, whether within the workings of government or in day-to-day life, do not diminish the sovereignty of God; rather, it is an extension of it. As Abou El Fadl argues, "when human beings search for ways to approximate God's beauty and justice" they honour God's sovereignty.[55] This means that if human beings are required to recognise the sovereignty of God in Creation, they should also be willing to exercise the powers God has given them. As a consequence, they are required to manage their affairs, including government.

The objections to democracy that claim it places the execution of God's law into human hands usually rely on the assumption that the Shari'a is a "complete moral code".[56] While the notion of God's sovereignty can be conceptualised as all-encompassing, the fact remains that God has not prescribed laws for every possible situation. Clearly then, there is a need for human participation in law, lawmaking, and governance.

Many Muslims would argue that lawmaking by the people cannot change particular laws of God that Muslims believe must remain unchanged. The question arises, how do we distinguish between changeable and unchangeable laws? Islamic tradition with all its diversity has the ability to provide very different answers to this question. The unchangeable laws of God can be determined to be abstract principles that exist at a high level, for example, ensuring justice and fairness in society, the need to take care of the needy and disadvantaged, and the importance of protection of people's property. One could argue that such unchangeable laws are relatively few, and they could be applied in very different ways in different contexts and times. The vast majority of laws Muslims have developed over many centuries as part of their juristic literature would not fall into this unchangeable category. Those specific laws may be changed as society and its values and norms also change. The role of interpretation is critical here, and Muslim scholars and jurists are expected to use their God-given agency to deal with such questions.

It is clear, however, that for Muslims, the notion of God's sovereignty cannot simply be displaced by human sovereignty. As Abou El Fadl argues:

> A case for democracy presented from within Islam must accept the idea of God's sovereignty; it cannot substitute popular sovereignty for divine sovereignty but must instead show how popular sovereignty—with its idea that citizens have rights and a correlative responsibility to pursue justice with mercy—expresses God's authority, properly understood.[57]

There is therefore a crucial need to elaborate on the notion of a "dual sovereignty": one that places a degree of sovereignty in the people while, at the same time, recognising that fundamental sovereignty lies with God. *Ijtihad* (independent reasoning by Muslim scholars and jurists) can be used to develop an understanding that is authentic to Islamic tradition, while at the same time being sensitive and relevant to the contemporary context.

DEMOCRACY AS A "WESTERN" PRODUCT

Alongside the challenge of sovereignty, Muslim scholars point to other difficulties with democracy. One critical issue is the notion that democracy is a non-Muslim, Western construct that is not applicable in Muslim contexts. This position is rooted in the political Islamist discourse that emerged in response to colonialism and Western imperialism. The leaders of some anti-colonial Muslim movements resisted the importation of ideas from Western colonial powers, arguing instead for an indigenous form of government. In the post-colonial period this anti-imperialist position continues to hold some sway.

However, the origins of democracy should not distract us from asking the question: can democracy as a system of governance now be applied in a Muslim-majority context? In my view, democracy is not unlike other institutions that Muslims have adopted from non-Muslim societies: for example, economic systems or educational constructs. Without being too concerned about the origins of these institutions, Muslims have very comfortably adopted or developed similar versions to meet the needs of their own communities.

It could be argued that another reason for Muslim resistance to democracy where it exists is related to the status of leadership in contemporary Muslim societies. Many Muslim states are still, by and large, autocratic and dynastically based, which makes the idea of democracy quite uncomfortable. For these governments democracy places far too much emphasis on equality, participation, consultation, and accountability. However, democracy can easily be dismissed under the guise of anti-colonial or anti-imperial struggle, hiding the reality that it is often a strategy employed by semi-authoritarian or authoritarian rulers to maintain the status quo. The rejection of democracy often uses the language and symbols of religion to further its legitimacy, but in reality, there is probably little in Islam that can be used to wholly reject democracy.

CONCLUSION

Can an Islamic system of governance therefore accommodate democratic principles? Given that there is no specific blueprint for governance provided by Islamic tradition, I believe it is possible to develop an Islamic model that is based on democratic values. Forms of Islamic democracy are possible if the question of sovereignty can be resolved. As Fred Dallmayr argues, "there is no compelling reason to deny the possibility of the emergence of democracies with chiefly 'Islamic characteristics'", such as we have seen in Turkey and Indonesia, for example.[58] Likewise, Calfano and Sahliyeh argue that there is no reason not to believe that "a certain type of democracy may flourish in states where Islam is the official religion", although it may not look like a Western democracy.[59]

It seems to me that an Islamic government could adopt some aspects of contemporary liberal democratic systems. For example, a balance of power can be maintained to ensure that no single institution of government becomes authoritarian. The executive, the judiciary, and the legislature must all remain in balance, and mechanisms can be developed to ensure this.

An Islamic democratic system of governance must also be mindful of the need to treat all people fairly and justly, in line with Qur'anic commandments. It would also need to ensure that there are mechanisms in place to hear the voice of the people through, for example, free and fair elections. The right to be consulted and the right to participate in the workings of government are not just a democratic ideal but an Islamic one too. An Islamic democracy would also need to ensure freedom of religion. Protection of religion is one of the fundamental aims of Islamic law and clearly explicated in the Qur'an. A Muslim-majority state should be able to recognise its religious majority while still protecting its minorities and their rights. In other words, a Muslim-majority state can be based on the notion of equal rights for all citizens, regardless of their religious beliefs. The state may not be obliged to give all religious traditions the same "status" as Islam, but it should make sure that non-Muslims are not discriminated against.

There is no one model of government prescribed by Islamic tradition, nor specific commandments that insist on a particular type of governance. Although there are historical examples of Islamic governance, they are interpretative models, not fixed forms. Muslim jurists have always debated the topic of governance and have never come to an agreement on the matter. In the contemporary context, a variety of governance models can potentially be supported by Islamic tradition, ranging from those supported by certain political Islamist groups, such as "Islamic state" models, to liberal democratic models. What is clear is that it is wrong to suggest that Islam only offers one possible model of government or that democracy contradicts the principles of Islam. Democratic values can be applied within an Islamic polity, while at the same time recognising God's sovereignty and authority. In summary, the key characteristics of democracy do not conflict with the fundamentals of Islam.

Muslims therefore must not be fixated on a particular form of government. Governance is essentially about ensuring justice and fairness, fair treatment, and preventing chaos, division, hatred, enmity, and injustice. Any model that can achieve this—whether liberal democratic or otherwise—should be a legitimate form of Islamic government.

* * *

LOOKING AT AN ISSUE CLOSELY: THE VIEWS OF MALIK BENNABI AND RACHID GHANNOUCHI ON DEMOCRACY

Azzam Tamimi, "Islam and Democracy from Tahtawi to Ghannouchi", *Theory, Culture & Society* 24(2) (2007), pp. 53–5. Extract*

This case discusses the views of Malik Bennabi and Rachid Ghannouchi on democracy. Both thinkers have made important contributions to the debate on the compatibility of Islam and democracy.

One very influential figure from within the Islamic circle itself has been Malik Bennabi (1905–73). Credited with having laid the foundations of the contemporary Islamic democratic school of thought, Bennabi, an Algerian thinker of French culture, believed that the coming of Europe had enabled the Muslims to escape from their decadence … (Bennabi, 1991).

From the early 1950s until his death, Bennabi wrote and lectured on what he described as the grand issues: civilisation, culture, concepts, orientalism and democracy. In a lecture entitled "Democracy in Islam" delivered in French at the Maghreb Students Club in 1960 he attempted to answer the question "Is there democracy in Islam?" He pointed out that defining the concepts of "Islam" and "democracy" in a conventional manner would lead to the conclusion that, with respect to time and location, the connection between the two is non-existent. He suggested that deconstructing the concepts in isolation from their historical connotations and redefining democracy in its broadest terms, without linguistic derivatives and free from any ideological implications, would lead to a different conclusion:

> Democracy ought to be looked at from three angles: democracy as a sentiment toward the self, democracy as a sentiment toward the other, and democracy as the combination of the socio-political conditions necessary for the formation and development of such sentiments in the individual.

That is why he strongly believed that democracy should be considered an educational enterprise for the whole community, administered through the implementation of a comprehensive curriculum that encompasses

---

* Azzam Tamimi, "Islam and Democracy from Tahtawi to Ghannouchi", *Theory, Culture & Society* 24(2), (2007), pp. 39–58.

psychological, ethical, social and political aspects. Bennabi believed that an Islamic model of democracy is attainable, one that would, in his opinion, be a superior model of democracy. Whereas in other models the main objective is to endow man with political rights enjoyed by the "citizen" in Western countries, or social securities enjoyed by the "comrade" in Eastern countries, Islam endows man with a value that surpasses every political or social value. …

[Bennabi's disciple Rachid] Ghannouchi conceives of democracy as a political system that derives legitimacy from the public. In a democracy, he explains, the people elect, audit and, when necessary, replace the ruler by means of mechanisms that may vary from one democratic regime to another. However, all such democratic models share in common the mechanism of free election. Democracy, he says, establishes the principle of the alternation of power through the ballot box, guarantees a number of basic liberties for the public, such as the freedom of expression and the freedom of forming political parties, and protects the independence of the judiciary. Democracy is a mechanism that guarantees the sovereignty of the people over the ruling regime and that instantiates a number of important values that shield the public against injustice and despotism (Tamimi, 2001).

Building on Bennabi's theory, Ghannouchi's main aim has been to emphasise the need for democracy, prove its compatibility with Islam and analyse the obstacles hindering its success in the Arab region. The challenge for contemporary Islamic thinkers is to develop an Islamic theory of governance based on democratic procedure. An Islamic model of democracy, which is a marriage between the Islamic value system and code of ethics on the one hand and democratic procedures on the other, will, in Ghannouchi's opinion, not only solve the problem of despotism rampant in Muslim lands but also fulfill the many broken promises of liberal democracy.

The Muslims, according to him should have no problem with the mechanisms devised by Western democracy; these, he maintains are good but not without room for improvement. According to him, the real problem with liberal democracy lies not in these mechanisms but in the fuel that feeds them: the materialist philosophy that eventually transformed these mechanisms, through the role played by finance and the media, into ploys, ultimately producing choices that represent not the people but influential financial and political centers.

The Islamic contribution, according to Ghannouchi, would be primarily in the form of a code of ethics, a transcendent morality that seems to have no place in today's democratic practice. It is deficiency in such transcendental morality, he warns, that ultimately turns democracy into "rule of the people by the rich and powerful for the interest of the rich and the powerful" (see Tamimi, 2001). He cites the example of elections in the United States, where money, the media and lobbies play the most crucial role in deciding not only who wins the election but also who runs for office. What Islam provides is not only a set of values for self-discipline and for the refinement of human conduct, but also a set of restrictions to combat monopoly and a set of safeguards to protect public opinion.

He is optimistic that, by assimilating the Western democratic system, Islam can, for the benefit of humanity, preserve the positive aspects of democracy. This, he suggests, can be achieved by transforming the Islamic principle of *shura*, which implies involving the *Ummah* in government, from a mere admonition, or a set of general principles, to a proper governing institution. This, he envisages, should be similar to what the Western "mind" did with Muslim discoveries in geometry and algebra, developing them "so marvelously into visible technologies; a feature of the Western genius and scientific revolution" (Tamimi, 2001).

NOTES

1. Bruce Bueno de Mesquita, George W. Downs, Alistair Smith, and Feryal Marie Cherif, "Thinking Inside the Box: A Closer Look at Democracy and Human Rights", *International Studies Quarterly* 49(3) (2005): 439–57.
2. Jonathan Fox, "State Religious Exclusivity and Human Rights", *Political Studies* 54 (2008): 934–5.
3. Ibid, 935.
4. Ibid, 934–5.
5. See, for example, National Imams Consultative Forum, "An Australian Muslim Perspective on Some Key Contemporary Concerns" (2015), para. 29. Available arts.unimelb.edu.au/__data/assets/pdf_file/0005/2159807/NICF-Statements.pdf (last accessed 20 December 2017).
6. Fox, "State Religious Exclusivity", 932.
7. M.S. Fisch, "Islam and Authoritarianism", *World Politics* 55(1) (2002): 4–37 and M.I. Midlarsky, "Democracy and Islam: Implications for Civilizational Conflict and the Democratic Peace", *International Studies Quarterly* 42(3) (1998): 458–511.
8. Fox, "State Religious Exclusivity", 928.
9. Brian Robert Calfano and Emile Sahliyeh, "Determining Democracy in the Organization of the Islamic Conference", *Social Science Quarterly* 89(3) (2008): 753. The organisation changed its name to the Organisation of Islamic Cooperation in 2011.
10. Human Rights Watch, "The Legal Framework" in *Iran: Religious and Ethnic Minorities: Discrimination in Law and Practice*, September 1997 9(7(E)). Available https://www.hrw.org/legacy/reports/1997/iran/Iran-04.htm#P143_18379 (last accessed 6 December 2017).
11. Human Rights Watch, "[Iran] The Legal Framework".
12. Human Rights Watch, "Summary and Recommendations" in *Iran: Religious and Ethnic Minorities: Discrimination in Law and Practice*, September 1997 9(7(E)). Available https://www.hrw.org/reports/1997/iran/Iran-01.htm (last accessed 6 December 2017).

13. Bah'ai International Community, "Situation of Bah'ais in Iran: Current Situation" (2016). Available https://www.bic.org/focus-areas/situation-iranian-bahais/current-situation#wqtEuzeyWPvSWdf7.97 (last accessed 6 December 2017).
14. *The Offence of Zina (Enforcement of Hudood) Ordinance, 1979*. Ordinance No. VII of 1979. 9 February 1979. Available http://www.pakistani.org/pakistan/legislation/zia_po_1979/ord7_1979.html (last accessed 6 December 2017).
15. Martin Lau, "Human Rights, Natural Justice and Pakistan's Shariat Courts" in *Religion, Human Rights and International Law: A Critical Examination of Islamic State Practices*, Javaid Rehman and Susan C. Breau (eds.) (Leiden: Martinus Nijhoff Publishers, 2007), 359.
16. Fox, "State Religious Exclusivity", 928.
17. Ibid, 944.
18. Ibid. In Fox's view, the weak connection between state religion and human rights records in Western democracies is likely because of the stronger human rights practices in these states and the relatively low level of variation between Western democracies on the human rights variable, 940.
19. Ibid.
20. See Jonathan Fox, "World Separation of Religion and State into the 21st Century", *Comparative Political Studies* 39(5) (2006): 537–69.
21. Fox, "State Religious Exclusivity", 944–5.
22. Ibid, 944.
23. Ibid.
24. Ibid.
25. Cole, "Does Respect for Human Rights Vary".
26. Calfano and Sahliyeh, "Determining Democracy", 763.
27. Ibid.
28. Ibid.
29. Ibid.
30. Khaled Abou El Fadl, *Islam and the Challenge of Democracy* (Princeton: Princeton University Press, 2004), 5, referring to Q. 49:13 and 11:119.
31. Ibid, 5.
32. Ibid, referring to Q. 6:12, 6:54, 21:107, 27:77, 29:51 and 45:20.
33. Ibn Kathir, *Al-Bidayah wa al-Nihayah* (6/305, 306).
34. Mashood A. Baderin, "The Role of Islam in Human Rights and Development in Muslim States", in *Religion, Human Rights and International Law: A Critical Examination of Islamic State Practices*, Javaid Rehman and Susan C. Breau (eds.) (Leiden: Martinus Nijhoff Publishers, 2007), 334.
35. Baderin, "The Role of Islam in Human Rights", 333.
36. Abou El Fadl, *Islam and the Challenge of Democracy*, 5.
37. Ibid.
38. Ibid, 5–6.
39. Ibid, 6.
40. Ibid.
41. Ibid.
42. Ibid.
43. Ibid, 3.
44. Ibid, 11.
45. Ibid.
46. Ibid.
47. Ibid.
48. Ibid, 12.
49. Ibid, 17.
50. Ibid.
51. Ibid.
52. Ibid, 18.

53. Ibid.
54. Sayyid Qutb, *Ma'alim fi al-Tariq* (Beirut: Dar al-Shuruq, 1979), 24–5.
55. Abou El Fadl, *Islam and the Challenge of Democracy*, 9.
56. Ibid.
57. Ibid, 30.
58. Fred Dallmayr, "Whither democracy? Religion, Politics and Islam", *Philosophy and Social Criticism* 37(4) (2011): 445.
59. Calfano and Sahliyeh, "Determining Democracy", 763.

6. Religion, the state and human rights

INTRODUCTION

Freedom is an element of many human rights, including one of the most fundamental: freedom of religion. The right to freedom of religion concerns the extent to which individuals, and groups, are free to choose a religion and to practise it. For states, this means that individuals within their territory must not be coerced into adopting a particular faith, set of beliefs, or theological position, and one religious group should not be favoured in relation to others. This position relies on the assumption that there is no place for the state to interfere in the domain of religious belief, and that religious groups should have maximum freedom to practise their beliefs. However, the idea that the state should stay outside the domain of religion does not mean that the state must be anti-religious. Instead, it should remain neutral towards all religious groups and their practices. This means that it must deal with all religious groups fairly and equally, without giving one group an advantage over others.

This chapter considers the question: is there an ideal model for managing the relationship between religion and the state? For human rights scholars, how a state responds to the idea of religion and to the communities within its jurisdiction can have a bearing on how human rights are promoted and protected.

MODELS OF RELIGION–STATE SEPARATION

There are many models for managing the relationship between religion and the state, and many approaches that a state can adopt concerning religious communities. Indeed, there may not be one perfect model that can be followed. Although state neutrality is a widely accepted principle, there are many approaches that a state can adopt towards religion.[1] Some models involve a closer relationship between the state and certain religions, although they do not necessarily discriminate against the rest. Others are very anti-religious and even hostile towards religious expression in the public sphere. The impact of these different models on freedom of religion may vary from state to state, depending on other contextual factors.

Terms like "secularism", "*laïcité*", or "neutrality" arise in the discourse on states and the policies or practices they use to manage religion, particularly in the public sphere. Each term broadly refers to an institutional separation between the state and religion. The *Oxford Dictionary of English* defines secularism as "the principle of separation of the state from religious institutions".[2] Neutrality is a broader term, defined as "not supporting or helping either side in a conflict, disagreement, etc."[3] It is often used interchangeably with the word "impartiality". The French term *laïcité* is often translated as secularism, but has particular features, which will be discussed below.

MODELS OF SECULARISM

Secularism is usually understood as something more subtle than the strict separation of religion and state. It can be thought of as a particular understanding of the relationship between religion and the state, which emphasises the importance of state neutrality vis-à-vis religion so that individual and collective freedoms are protected. Secularism is a feature of many liberal democratic states, where the principle is translated into law. According to this principle, the state should clearly recognise freedom of religion for all and should not get involved in matters of religion. For Rafael Palomino, there are usually two rationales presented for it: first, because the state considers it to be the best way to protect freedom of religion, and second, because it is seen as a means to avoid strife and division.[4] There are many different legal arrangements that are possible, and the state is usually required to "strike a balance between freedom and equality", a balance which can be difficult to achieve.[5]

European Models

Even within liberal democracies, many of which are in Europe, it is difficult to find many fully religiously neutral states. Some democratic states, for instance Denmark, Norway, and Malta, promote Christianity as the official religion of the state. These states allow certain advantages for Christian groups by providing tax concessions or by helping to facilitate their work in other ways. In Germany, while churches have "no official say in German politics", the state collects taxes from Christians and distributes them to the churches.[6] Churches are legally recognised as "corporations by public law" and their representatives often have significant authority; they sit, for example, on the boards of broadcasting corporations, participate in meetings of state education departments, and decide on religious curricula.[7]

These states allow for some public presence of religion, but this does not necessarily mean the state discriminates against other religious groups. Having said that, of course, the very fact that the state provides certain advantages to particular religious groups could be conceived of as discrimination. As Palomino observes, even when a state is attempting to be impartial, there can be "unintended consequences such as certain advantages and special regulations for major religions", while minority religions are denied "access to certain legal benefits such as public funding, tax exemptions, or the ability to provide religious or spiritual counselling in hospitals and prisons".[8] Favouring the state's dominant religion can be seen as the propagation of an unfair advantage for the majority. Often the state has laws in place that enshrine certain privileges for the majority group, and it is difficult for minority groups to argue for similar privileges.

Even in cases like this, however, the state can still actively try to minimise the negative ramifications for minority religions. This seems to work in some democratic societies. One example is the United Kingdom, where the state recognises the Church of England as the official church of the state, but this does not necessarily mean state discrimination against other Christian groups or other religions, such as Islam, Judaism, Hinduism, or Buddhism.

France

Another model of secularism is evident in France. For a range of historical reasons, the French model of secularism rejects the idea that religion should have any public role in French society. In this model, which is based on the principle of *laïcité*, religion may only play a role in the private sphere.

Laïcité, as a constitutional principle, emerged out of a particular historical context, involving long conflict between the Catholic Church and French republican institutions.[9] As Dominique Decherf notes, "since the end of the religious wars of the sixteenth and seventeenth centuries, [France has] known only one large majoritarian religion. Either one was within the Catholic Church, or one was a freethinker outside of it."[10] *Laïcité* is thus a product of the former dominance of the Catholic Church and the rebellion of French society against that dominance. In 1905, therefore, when France legally enacted the separation of church and state, the term was and still is understood by the French as "freedom *from* the moral authority of a single dominant religion", here Catholicism, rather than freedom to practise a particular religion.[11] *Laïcité* is defined in the current French constitution as assuring "the equality of all citizens before the law, without distinction to their origin, race, or religion. It *respects* all religious beliefs [my emphasis]."[12]

In France, it is seen as crucial that religion should not influence state policy, laws, or institutions, and that religious symbolism is separated from the public sphere. The debate around the issue of Muslim women wearing the *hijab* (the hair covering observed by many Muslim women) is reflective of this particular character of French secularism. The hijab is seen by its opponents as something that "invades the sacred space of the *Republic*".[13] Michel Machado argues that "in French schools, the [hijab] is seen as a constant call for rebellion against non-Muslim order".[14] It is feared as a precedent that may escalate to "secluding girls from courses and activities, if not from school altogether".[15] According to Machado, French authorities, and indeed the average person on the street, believe that every person living in France and sending their children to school must accept French culture.[16] This clashes with the view that children have rights as believers and should not be coerced where their religious freedom is concerned.[17]

Former Soviet Union

While French secularism may be perceived as hostile towards public displays of religion, though tolerant of religious expression in the private sphere, there are also models of secularism where intolerance is the norm. The most notable examples of this extreme secularism are the Communist regimes of the former Soviet Union and China. The Soviet Union was the most extreme in its rejection of religion, considering it a form of corruption. Again, this approach to secularism can be traced to historical events. The Russian Orthodox Church, during the time of the Tsars, "had occupied a privileged position as the state religion of the [Russian] Empire".[18] It was estimated that seventy per cent of the population were adherents of the church.[19] During the Russian Revolution of 1917, which began Communist rule in Russia, Lenin and the Bolsheviks, who were militantly atheist in ideology, acted quickly to impose control on any independent aspects of society that might oppose the revolution, including religion.[20] Indeed, many religious groups were hostile to the Bolsheviks. One of the first acts of the government was to legislate the separation of the church from the state and educational institutions.[21] This was not an attempt to guarantee freedom of worship but to crush the previous power of the Orthodox Church in particular. Thus, the 1936 Russian constitution guaranteed "freedom of religious confession", but only atheists were permitted to propagate their beliefs.[22] The power of the Orthodox Church in society, as well as that of other religious groups, was eventually successfully destroyed.[23] In the aftermath of Stalin's death in 1953, the government continued to make it a duty for "members of the Communist party, teachers, doctors, scientists and others in positions [of] authority" to propagate atheism.[24] They were taught that religion was "institutionally obsolete", although it could be a private "force in the lives of many citizens".[25] Nevertheless, "asocial, treacherous religion" was explicitly contrasted "against human collective accomplishments, which were the only deserving objects of faith".[26] While the Russian experience is of historical interest now, it still shows how an extreme form of secularism can function.

China

In China, religion has historically been seen as something that politically and socially poses a threat to stability. Unlike in the former Soviet Union, however, the state's suspicion of and interference in religion is not only recent policy. It is a long-established pattern, strengthened by countless emperors and their bureaucrats who enforced a "comprehensive religious management system".[27] Historian Daniel Bays notes that "there has hardly been a Chinese political regime from the Tang dynasty (618–907) to the present that has not required a form of registration or licensing of religious groups or has not assumed the right to monitor and intervene in religious affairs".[28] Chinese scholar Zhuo Xinping classifies the religion–state relationship in pre-modern China as "state-lead, church-follow".[29] Changgang Guo and Fengmei Zhang describe it as a "master–slave relationship" in which "the state [was] always dominant", and religion "never acquire[d] a freedom detached from the secular regime in the Western sense".[30]

Except for a brief hiatus in the first half of the twentieth century, when the absence of a strong state made it impossible to effectively regulate religion, modern China has more or less followed this pattern.[31] After 1950, Bays describes the dominant theme as one of "state and Communist Party control, interference, and repression".[32] When the People's Republic of China was founded in 1949, the Chinese Communist Party claimed to be an "atheist" party with Marxism as its "guiding principle".[33] Like the Bolsheviks in Russia, the Party sought to gain control over any social organisation that could conceivably oppose it, including religious organisations.[34] Into the late 1950s, the Communist

Party increasingly emphasised the ideological opposition between Marxism and religion.[35] Repression of religion was justified in the name of "stability".[36] Recently, however, the Communist Party appears to have become more tolerant of religion, responding to a rapid and unexpected growth in religious activity.[37] Some measure of religious freedom is now allowed, "as long as religious organisations do not endanger political and social stability".[38] Mickey Spiegel describes the approach taken since 1982 as one of "control and containment",[39] which means allowing "limited yet meaningful religious participation" in the wide range of religious groups that have sprouted in the decades since the Cultural Revolution.[40] It should be noted, however, that "profound tensions" continue, and the state remains interventionist in the management of religious organisations.[41]

Singapore

Singapore is another interesting example of the application of secularism. Singapore is composed of a number of different ethnic groups, often overlapping with religious traditions. Managing tensions resulting from ethno-racial identity is a key concern of the government, rather than regulating religious practice in itself. In its attempt to create an overarching secular national identity, one that trumps loyalty to particular cultural and religious allegiances,[42] it has implemented policies that, according to political scientist David Brown, are designed "to attenuate and sanitise the cultural values of each component ethnic community in Singapore so as to make them compatible with each other and with the ideological preference of the governing elite".[43] In a *White Paper on Shared Values* presented in Parliament in 1991, the government's strategy was made explicit: "to identify a few key values which are common to all the major groups in Singapore, and which draw on the essence of each of these heritages".[44] According to Kerstin Steiner, these shared values were then to be "interpreted and conveyed according to the various cultural and religious traditions".[45] For example, the *White Paper* refers to these values being expressed "in Malay and Muslim terms" for Malays, "in terms of Bible stories and Christian traditions" for Christians, and for "many Chinese by reference to Confucian, Buddhist or Taoist teachings". In due time, the expectation was that "all communities [would] gradually develop more common, distinctively Singaporean characteristics".[46] This kind of secularism appears to allow different religious and ethnic groups in the country some degree of flexibility to interpret the state's model of secularism.

ARE HUMAN RIGHTS SECULAR?

A number of scholars argue that secularism is probably the only way that human rights can be adequately promoted and protected, given the religious diversity of societies in most countries around the world. It is worth remembering that human rights themselves have not always been secular, however. As discussed in Chapter 2, many scholars claim that human rights emerged in the West primarily as a response to modern conditions; specifically, to protect individuals from the power of the state. However, this denies the historical connection of rights to religion; in particular, to Christian ideas. As political scientist Michael Freeman points out, human rights "emerged in the West … as a *religious* response to a set of problems that was both religious and political at a time when religion and politics were inseparable [original emphasis]".[47] Only gradually thereafter did human rights become secularised.[48]

The influential Enlightenment thinker John Locke, whose ideas have been mentioned in Chapter 2, argues in the first of his *Two Treatises of Government* that the natural freedom of human beings is bounded by the law of nature, the source of which is God.[49] Natural law was a way of expressing the idea that there are "certain moral truths that applied to all people, regardless of … where they lived or the agreements they had made".[50] According to Locke, God is the source of natural law,[51] although knowledge of it is obtainable by reason alone.[52] As natural law applies to everyone, all human beings are naturally equal, "unless God had set one above another 'by any manifest declaration of [H]is will'".[53]

Put simply, Locke framed the notion of natural rights within a religious, Christian framework.[54] He refers to the purpose of God's creation of humankind, the obligations that human beings have to one another, and to God. It was only during the following century that Locke's conception of natural rights was "weakened and secularised", when "disputes about religious truth led some to believe that God's will was beyond our [human] understanding, and that morality must therefore be secular".[55]

According to Freeman, the example of Locke shows that "theocentric, duty-based moralities have the potential to develop robust conceptions of human rights".[56] It was only subsequently that references to religion or religiously based ideas as a means to justify particular political or philosophical theories became problematic for some. Eventually, even morality was conceived by many as a secular idea. The idea that religion could provide acceptable answers to practical or philosophical problems came to be seen as problematic during the Enlightenment, which emphasised the importance of human reason and scientific achievement. Later, in the West, Christianity (or more specifically, the church) eventually came to be perceived as a collaborator in state oppression, corruption, and exploitation. The ensuing backlash of anti-religious scholarship challenged the role of religion vis-à-vis the state. In 1789, the French Revolution destroyed whatever little connection was left between religion and the notion of the rights of human beings.[57]

This account reveals that human rights may not need to be distanced from religion. The human rights discourse that emerged in the West has a historical connection with religious ideas. That a subsequent disconnection of rights from a religious framework took place does not necessarily mean this is a preferable approach. The idea of a natural law stemming from God, alongside religious conceptions of morality and of obligations to God and to each other, can be used by religious traditions to support notions of contemporary human rights from their own perspectives.

At the end of the Second World War, with the establishment of the UN and drafting of the UDHR, it became important that human rights be engaged with through a secular prism. For the UN to function in a global setting, encompassing numerous religions and potentially conflicting belief systems, it was necessary to take a neutral position. As discussed in Chapter 2, to achieve such neutrality the UN adopted secular language in its framework and justification of human rights. Moreover, some of the major global powers at the time, such as the Soviet Union, were anti-religious. This meant that using any kind of religious justification for human rights would be met with serious opposition. A pragmatic approach was therefore the most feasible option in adopting a human rights discourse that could be acceptable to all. The UDHR is a prime example of this compromise, being based on "the dignity and worth of the human person", rather than any religious doctrine.[58] If the UN had grounded the universal rights of the UDHR in religious language or symbolism, it would not have been able to achieve the level of international support that was necessary for it to be finally adopted by the General Assembly in 1948.

As discussed in Chapter 2, even though the rights of the UDHR were framed in neutral or secular terms, contributors to the drafting process came from many different religious traditions. State representatives who contributed to the draft came from backgrounds as varied as Christianity, Islam, Judaism, Hinduism, and non-religious or atheistic backgrounds. Many of these individuals would likely have taken the view that even if religious language was not explicitly used to justify particular rights, this does not mean they are incompatible with scripture and tradition and must be rejected. Indeed, it is possible to find many connections and areas of compatibility between the two.

SECULARISM, ISLAM, AND HARMONISATION

There are many human rights advocates who believe that the value of human rights is that they are universal and thus take precedence over local and/or religious values.[59] This position is problematic for many people who are religious, and in particular for many Muslims who care about their religion but are also keen to support human rights norms. For them, a strictly secular approach would not work. For these Muslims, the discourse would feel more comfortable with Islamic norms, values and language.

Many Muslims see secularism as a Western ideology, which only serves to dilute the role of religion. This view largely stems from particular Muslim encounters with secularism during the twentieth century. The most notable were in Turkey under the leadership of Kemal Atatürk (d. 1938) and in Iraq and Syria with their Baathist regimes. Many argue that human rights violations under these secular regimes went hand in hand with attempts to destroy the status of Islam completely. In Turkey, for example, Atatürk militantly pushed religion away from the state, confining it solely to the private sphere. The Islamist movements of the twentieth century also played a significant role in painting secularism as anti-religious, arguing that it was a Western way of destroying the role of religion in Muslim societies. These legacies still colour the perception of secularism that Muslims have today. For this reason, proponents of human rights in Muslim societies need to pay particular attention to the sensitivities associated with the term "secularism" for many Muslims.

Resistance to the human rights discourse, based on the idea that it is a Western concept or part of a new colonial project, is very widespread among Muslims. Certainly, in some cases, if Muslims tried to promote human rights in their local contexts without using religious language they would be viewed very sceptically, and indeed seen as promoting a foreign, non-indigenous, or neocolonial project. It is therefore important to work for harmonisation between human rights and Islamic principles and values.

Opposition between human rights and Islamic values should therefore be avoided to make progress in the implementation of human rights in Muslim contexts. Muslim societies need human rights to be contextualised and they must be allowed to use a religious framework to achieve this. Indeed, Freeman argues that "human rights activism must be grounded in local culture" for it to be effective.[60] Taking into account the religious or cultural sensibilities of particular nations or communities is thus the only way to advance the implementation of human rights.

CONCLUSION

While secularism is highly regarded and promoted by many states as the ideal environment for the protection of human rights, recent scholarship, particularly emerging out of the challenges that countries like France are facing in managing their religious communities, suggests that some peoples' rights are being protected at the expense of others. The debate on secularism also reveals a number of other issues. Are human rights really secular? Do they need to be divorced from all religious overtones to be safeguarded or promoted? And why should human rights be used as a benchmark to evaluate the appropriateness of long-standing religious or cultural practices? These questions are particularly important for Muslims, many of whom need human rights to have some level of Islamic legitimacy in order for them to be embraced.

* * *

LOOKING AT AN ISSUE CLOSELY: ABDULLAHI AN-NA'IM'S PERSPECTIVE ON SECULARISM

Abdullahi An-Na'im, "The Interdependence of Religion, Secularism, and Human Rights", *Common Knowledge* 11(1) (2005), pp. 62–4. Extract*

In this case Abdullahi An-Na'im, discusses the strengths and limitations of secularism as a model of governance for protecting human rights, especially freedom of religion.

Secularism in Islamic societies will not succeed if based on preconceived Western notions of the concept and thus understood locally as an imposition. In particular, I believe (and as I have written before) that "it is grossly misleading to speak of complete separation or total union of

* Abdullahi An-Na'im, "The Interdependence of Religion, Secularism, and Human Rights: Prospects for Islamic Societies", *Common Knowledge*, 11(1) (2005) pp. 56–80.

any religion and the state. Any state, as well as its constituent organs and institutions, are conceived and operated by people whose religious or philosophical beliefs will necessarily be reflected in their thinking and behaviour".[61] Entire separation of religion and state is not possible, nor in my view desirable, because religion is not separable from politics. How can citizens be prevented from acting politically according to their most basic beliefs? Even were such a requirement established, how could it be enforced in a way consistent with the integrity and legitimacy of the political process?

There is, theoretically, a continuum of "secularisms" from the extreme of fusion to that of absolute separation between religion and state. The question is therefore which forms are more consistent with the rationale of secularism adopted here. Drawing on the premise that secularism is dynamic and deeply contextual, a recent study of the relationship between religion and state in Britain, Germany, the Netherlands, the United States, and Australia has concluded that the minimum requirement for a positive relationship is neutrality: "that people are neither advantaged or [*sic*] disadvantaged by their adherence to their secular or faith-based tradition".[62] The state should neither favour nor disfavour one particular religious tradition over another.[63] The problem with this minimum requirement, however clearly it is necessary, is that no public policy is ever completely neutral: citizens are always believers (in something). The question, then, is how people can exercise free democratic choice in accordance with their own beliefs (religious or otherwise) while the neutrality of the state is maintained. Again, my conclusions are that (a) the possibility exists only if belief systems are internally transformed and that (b) belief systems will be transformed only where the interdependence of religion, secularism, and human rights is well established.

But belief systems—religions—are not the only paradigm that requires transformation in this dynamic. Secularism suffers from a basic limitation or, rather, a need for limitation: it must confine its normative content to a minimum if it is to achieve its purpose—safeguarding political pluralism in heterogeneous societies. In other words, secularism is able to unite diverse communities of belief and practice into one political community precisely and only because the moral claims it makes are minimal. All secularisms, it is true, prescribe a civic ethos on the basis of some specific understanding of the individual's relation to the community. But my point here is that the content of most varieties of secularism is so narrow that it cannot serve as an interreligious and cross-cultural foundation for human rights as a universal norm. From a pragmatic or political viewpoint, this limitation is serious because religious believers will fail to be inspired by the doctrine of human rights if founded solely on secular grounds. It may be necessary, indeed, to seek a religious justification for the principle of secularism itself. I am not saying that a serious engagement of religion is essential for either human rights or secularism to be legitimised (everywhere and always) but rather that that engagement is necessary to obtain the consent of most religious believers. And religious adherents constitute the clear majority of all human beings.

A related concern is that secularism is unable to address the objections or reservations that religious believers may have about particular standards of human rights or specific principles of secular governance. For instance, since discrimination against women is often justified on religious grounds (in many societies throughout the world), these systematic and gross violations of human rights cannot be eliminated without addressing their allegedly religious rationale. To do so, however, risks violating freedom of religion, a fundamental human right as well. A purely secular discourse can be respectful of religion in general, but its rebuttal of one religion's justifications for discrimination against women is unlikely to convince that religion's adherents. In other words, the minimal normative content that makes secularism conducive to inter-religious coexistence diminishes its capacity to support human rights as a universal principle without reference to some other moral source. Likewise secularism by definition fails to address the need of religious believers to express the moral implications of their faith in the public domain. Secularism alone, then, is a necessary but insufficient condition for realising the political stability that forms part of its own rationale. But secularism can be enhanced by insisting on a contextual understanding of the rationale and functioning of secular government in each location.

NOTES

1. Rafael Palomino, "Legal Dimensions of Secularism: Challenges and Problems", *Contemporary Readings in Law and Social Justice* 4(2) (2012): 209.
2. "Secularism" in *Oxford Dictionary of English*, 3rd edn, A. Stevenson (ed.) (Oxford: Oxford University Press, 2010).
3. "Neutrality" in *Oxford Dictionary of English*, 3rd edn, A. Stevenson (ed.) (Oxford: Oxford University Press, 2010).
4. Palomino, "Legal Dimensions of Secularism", 214.
5. Ibid, 213.
6. Abdul Hadi Hoffmann, "Muslims in Germany: The Struggle for Integration" in *Islam and the Questions of Minorities*, Tamara Sonn (ed.) (Atlanta: Scholars Press, 1996), 51.
7. Ibid.
8. Palomino, "Legal Dimensions of Secularism", 213–14.

9. Robert Zaretsky, "How French Secularism Became Fundamentalist", *Foreign Policy*, 7 April 2016. Available http://foreignpolicy.com/2016/04/07/the-battle-for-the-french-secular-soul-laicite-charlie-hebdo/ (last accessed 6 December 2017).
10. Dominique Decherf, "French Views of Religious Freedom", *The Brookings Institution*, 1 July 2001. Available http://www.brookings.edu/research/articles/2001/07/france-decherf (last accessed 6 December 2017).
11. Ibid.
12. Robert Zaretsky, "How French Secularism".
13. Michel Machado, "Muslims in France: Jacobinism Confronts Islamism" in *Islam and the Question of Minorities*, 67.
14. Ibid.
15. Ibid.
16. Ibid.
17. Ibid.
18. Felix Corley, *Religion in the Soviet Union: An Archival Reader* (Basingstoke, UK: Palgrave Macmillan, 1996), 13.
19. Ibid.
20. Ibid, 13.
21. Sonja Luehrmann, *Secularism Soviet Style: Teaching Atheism and Religion in a Volga Republic* (Bloomington, IN: Indiana University Press, 2011), 1.
22. Ibid.
23. Ibid.
24. Ibid,1–2.
25. Ibid, 2.
26. Ibid.
27. Changgang Guo and Fengmei Zhang, "Religion and Social Stability: China's Religious Policies in the Age of Reform", *Third World Quarterly*, 36(11) (2015): 2184–5.
28. Daniel H. Bays, "A Tradition of State Dominance" in *God and Caesar in China: Policy Implications of Church–State Tensions*, Jason Kindopp and Carol Lee Hamrin (eds.), (Washington DC: Brookings Institution Press, 2004).
29. Guo and Zhang, "Religion and Social Stability", 2185.
30. Ibid.
31. See Bays, "A Tradition of State Dominance", 31.
32. Ibid, 34.
33. Guo and Zhang, "Religion and Social Stability", 2187.
34. See Jason Kindopp, "Fragmented Yet Defiant: Protestant Resilience under Chinese Communist Party Rule" in *God and Caesar*, 123.
35. Guo and Zhang, "Religion and Social Stability", 2187.
36. Ibid, 2184.
37. Ibid, 2188–9. See also Jason Kindopp, "Policy Dilemmas in China's Church–State Relations: An Introduction", in *God and Caesar*, 1–2.
38. Guo and Zhang, "Religion and Social Stability", 2189.
39. Mickey Spiegel, "Control and Containment in the Reform Era" in *God and Caesar*, 40.
40. Kindopp, "Policy Dilemmas", 3.
41. Ibid, 2.
42. Kerstin Steiner, "Religion and Politics in Singapore—Matters of National Identity and Security? A Case Study of the Muslim Minority in a Secular State", *Osaka University Law Review* 58 (2011): 112.
43. David Brown, "Democratization and the Renegotiation of Ethnicity" in *Towards Illiberal Democracy in Pacific Asia*, Daniel A. Bell et al. (eds.), (New York: St. Martin's Press, 1995), 156.
44. Steiner, "Religion and Politics in Singapore", 112.
45. Ibid.
46. Ibid.

47. Michael Freeman, "The Problem of Secularism in Human Rights Theory", *Human Rights Quarterly* 26 (2004): 386.
48. Ibid.
49. Ibid, 387.
50. Alex Tuckness, "Locke's Political Philosophy" in *The Stanford Encyclopedia of Philosophy* (Spring 2016 Edition), Edward N. Zalta (ed.). Available http://plato.stanford.edu/entries/locke-political/ (last accessed 6 December 2017).
51. See Freeman, "The Problem of Secularism", 387.
52. Alex Tuckness, "Locke's Political Philosophy".
53. Freeman, "The Problem of Secularism", 387, citing John Locke, *Two Treatises of Government* (1970), 287.
54. Ibid, 387–8.
55. Ibid, 389.
56. Ibid, 388.
57. Ibid, 390.
58. Ibid, 391.
59. Ibid, 376.
60. Ibid, 377.
61. An-Na'im, "Sharia and Positive Legislation: Is an Islamic State Possible or Viable?" in *Yearbook of Islamic and Middle Eastern Law 1998/1999*, vol. 5, Eugene Cotran (ed.) (The Hague: Kluwer, 2000), 40. See also Harold J. Berman, *Faith and Order: The Reconciliation of Law and Religion* (Atlanta, GA: Scholars, 1993), 1–20, 35–52.
62. Stephen V. Monsma and J. Christopher Soper, *The Challenge of Pluralism: Church and State in Five Democracies* (Lanham, MD: Rowman and Littlefield, 1997), 209.
63. Monsma and Soper, *Challenge of Pluralism*, 209.

7. Islam, human rights and women

INTRODUCTION

Perhaps one of the most controversial issues in the discourse on Islam and human rights is the "status" of women in Islam. There is a strong public perception that Islam as a religion discriminates against women and that Muslim women are often segregated, oppressed, and denied many of the rights and freedoms that Muslim men take for granted. There have been many high profile cases of women being subject to horrendous crimes in Muslim-majority countries, such as honour killings, or being made to bear the responsibility for sexual abuse or rape, when in reality they were the victims of such abuse.

The first part of this chapter therefore examines briefly the "status" of women in Islam, going back to Islam's primary sources to explore whether these foundational texts and early practices are inherently discriminatory against women. It examines the role of cultural practices and norms in the development of Islamic tradition and explains why the Qur'an instituted a number of revolutionary reforms for women, yet left other cultural practices in place. New scholarship is also presented to show how contemporary Muslim scholars are reinterpreting what appear to be discriminatory elements within Islamic tradition, embracing the egalitarian spirit behind Qur'anic texts on women, and finding compatibilities between international human rights and Islamic law. The second part of this chapter sets out the international human rights mechanisms that promote and protect the rights of women around the world today. It reflects on the conceptual framework for these rights, as well as the mechanisms that supervise and enforce them. Given that many of the concerns about the rights of Muslim women are grounded in the practices of Muslim-majority states, the last part of the chapter focuses on Muslim states' engagement with the Convention on the Elimination of all Forms of Discrimination against Women. Finally it provides the views of a number of Muslim scholars today who argue for the reform of Islamic law in relation to women and find a degree of compatibility between international human rights law and Islamic norms.

WOMEN IN ARABIA BEFORE ISLAM

In virtually all societies in the pre-modern period, discrimination against women was probably common. Forms of discrimination varied from society to society, but in general, men were regarded as superior to women. The view that women were inferior to men was a prevalent socio-cultural norm in most societies around the world at that time. Even in pre-modern Western cultures, "women of all classes, regardless of their status, were subordinate to the authority of men and were considered property in the eyes of the law".[1]

In the West Arabian culture where Islam emerged, discriminatory attitudes and practices towards women were also prevalent. While these practices and attitudes varied from tribe to tribe, some of the most common are mentioned in the Qur'an. For example, female children were seen as a liability and a source of shame, and female infanticide—the deliberate killing of female babies—was practised by certain tribes.[2] The trading of women through marriage agreements is another practice mentioned in the Qur'an,[3] as well as the custom of polygyny, where a man could rightfully marry numerous wives but a woman could only take one husband.[4] In the area of inheritance, women were also denied equal rights prior to Islam in that culture.

When Islam emerged in the early seventh century CE it had to engage with the cultural context of this time, including the views that were held about women. This context formed the starting point from which the Qur'an took a position on such matters. The Qur'an responded to the cultural context and introduced a series of reforms that challenged many elements of the status of women at that time. However, these teachings did not fully abolish the discriminatory practices and ideas that were already in existence in that society.

QUR'ANIC REFORMS OF PRE-ISLAMIC GENDER DISCRIMINATION

The Qur'an offers clear advice concerning gender discrimination, particularly in the Arabian context. Its broad position was to reject existing discriminatory practices and to look towards a fairer treatment of women in general. Indeed, some observers argue that Islam is among the the first religions "in the world to honour women and … stipulat[e] that women should be treated as independent human beings".[5] The Qur'an specifically prohibited female infanticide,[6] and a number of hadith record that the Prophet focused on changing attitudes towards female babies by encouraging feelings of "love, affection and mercy" for female children.[7] The Qur'an also insisted on women having the right to own property and to inherit.[8] Although its inheritance provisions did not demand equal shares for women in most cases, it mandated a basic minimum share,[9] something that women had not been guaranteed before in that culture. The Qur'an restricted polygyny to a maximum of four wives, putting an end to the practice of unlimited wives that was "common practice in that society".[10] Although it could have prohibited the practice entirely, as Abdullah Yusuf Ali explains, polygyny continued to be allowed in a restricted form, "to prevent injustice to orphans, widows, and war captives … In the battle of Uhud, many men died and the Muslim community was left with many orphans, widows, and captives of war".[11] The Qur'an allowed marriage to them so they could be protected from exploitation, as unmarried women and orphans were vulnerable in that society. Polygyny meant that women's rights and property were safeguarded within the bounds of marriage.[12] Indeed, polygyny was only permitted in situations where a husband could guarantee justice and equal treatment to multiple wives.[13] The Prophet reportedly said, "[h]e who has two wives and does not demonstrate justice, fairness, and equality amongst them will come on the Day of Resurrection with one of his sides hanging down [paralysed]".[14]

The Qur'an also gave women agency in relation to their marriage contracts.[15] Women were given the right to contract marriage without a guardian (*wali*).[16] Fundamental to this was the idea of the role of the husband and wife as principal transacting parties. A woman could no longer be married without her consent.[17] Women also became the recipients of their dowries, whether it was a sum of money or property. The Qur'an also prohibited the practice of forcing a wife to make a will in her husband's favour that gave her dowry or any other gifts she had received back to him.[18] The Prophet's insistence on a particular form of marriage contract meant that the rights and obligations of all parties were clear, and the community could hold them to account. The pre-Islamic *zihar*, a particularly humiliating form of divorce where a husband compared his wife to his mother's back, was also abolished.[19] The Qur'an also allowed wives to initiate divorce proceedings.[20]

A broader outcome that stemmed from the Qur'anic and Prophetic regulation in this area of family law was, thus, the achievement of relative equality within the family unit. As Abdullahi An-Na'im observes, while "this level of achievement may not appear impressive by some modern standards, but it has meant very significant improvements in women's rights when viewed in historical perspective".[21]

Another critical area of reform propagated by the Qur'an and the Prophet centred on increasing the visibility of women in society. Under the leadership of the Prophet women began to play a more significant role in public life. There is at least one reference in the Qur'an to women who felt free to address and even argue with the Prophet on various matters.[22] In these examples, women's views were listened to and responded to with respect. Women who demonstrated particular skills and therefore potential value to the community were recognised and respected by the Prophet and his immediate successors, regardless of their gender. It is also evident that women played a significant role on the battlefield, both during and after the time of the Prophet. Nehaluddin Ahmad gives several examples of female Muslim warriors who fought in battles alongside the Prophet and during the time of the first four caliphs.[23] The views of the Prophet's wife Umm Salama (d. 59/679) prevailed over those of many men during the crisis of Hudaybiyya.[24] Finally, the Prophet's wife A'isha (d. 58/677–8) famously led an army against the fourth caliph Ali (d. 40/661), in what is known as the Battle of the Camel.

These Qur'anic and Prophetic reforms were revolutionary in the Arabian context at the time and introduced a radically new way of thinking about women, male–female relations, and family law. Many pre-Islamic practices concerning women were revised and reformed, if not wholly rejected. The reforms in this area were substantial, although they would not perhaps be deemed radical today. They challenged the status quo and called into question the unequal and discriminatory gender norms that were prevalent at that time.

DETERIORATION OF WOMEN'S RIGHTS IN THE POST-PROPHETIC PERIOD

However, pre-Islamic cultural and social values towards women still persisted to varying degrees and not all of the reforms or instructions concerning women were adopted fully in practice. While the legal positions propagated by the Qur'an in the areas of marriage and divorce were enacted, cultural attitudes towards women remained discriminatory in many Muslim societies. As Fazlur Rahman argues, "although woman's inferior status has been written into Islamic law, it is by and large the result of prevailing social conditions rather than of the moral teaching of the Quran".[25] To put it another way, social attitudes did not change in line with the emphasis on the reforms advocated in the Qur'an and the traditions of the Prophet.

An example of this was the continued dominance of men in positions of power, most obviously in the political, legal, and theological arenas. Indeed, some scholars argue that soon after the Prophet's death, "Muslim women were removed from public and political life."[26] Since the male-dominated norms did not allow the participation of women fully in the public sphere, over time, interpreting the Qur'an and debating Islamic law also became almost the exclusive responsibility of men.[27] Male scholars and judges, according to some, were free to "define critical ideas and analyse fundamental concepts in terms that reflected not only a purely male perspective but also the perspectives of the male political authorities".[28]

The marginalisation of women was at times justified by drawing on certain hadith. A key example is the reported statement of the Prophet, "Those who entrust their affairs to a woman will never know prosperity."[29] A number of scholars have analysed the context of this hadith and argued that it began to be narrated almost twenty-five years after the death of the Prophet.[30] Their analysis suggests that this hadith may have emerged immediately after the battle between A'isha, the Prophet's wife, and Ali, who was then the caliph. Given that A'isha's forces were defeated, this saying attributed to the Prophet began to be narrated in this context, and later on became what Muslims consider to be an authentic hadith.

One element of the exclusion of women from public life was the enforcement of norms of dress. Ziba Mir-Hosseini describes the notion of *hijab* (the hair-covering worn by many Muslim women), as it is found in the literature of *fiqh* (jurisprudence), as signifying a woman's "confinement". She notes that this idea is based on two juristic conceptions: first, that a woman's body is *'awra*, or "a source of shame, that must be covered both during prayers (before God) and in public (before men)", and second, that a woman's public presence is described as *fitna* (temptation) and a "threat to the social order".[31] It was therefore concluded that "a woman's body should be covered at all times—and the best way to ensure this [was] confinement or seclusion".[32] These ideas reflected the socio-cultural conditions and "practice of the time", and were particularly a response to "developments during Abbasid rule, for example … the presence in public of slave girls, who [were] forbidden to cover in order to distinguish them from free women".[33]

These cultural norms continued to marginalise women, preventing them from playing significant roles in community and political life. As seen above, political and legal arguments were made to justify the position that women could not hold public positions of power. Discriminatory interpretations of certain Islamic texts also curtailed freedom and equality for women in other aspects of society. For example, despite the fact that a woman's right not to be married without her consent was addressed by the Qur'an and hadith, the cultural norms and custom of the time when Islamic law was being developed, in the early centuries of Islam, maintained that a woman in some circumstances could be "given away" in marriage by a close male relative without her consent. Similarly, the Qur'anic commandment that permitted wives to initiate divorce was ultimately curtailed by interpreting women's freedom to initiate divorce restrictively, while husbands' rights of divorce were not.

In Q. 2:282, the mention of two women in place of one man as witnesses in a commercial transaction was eventually used as a precedent to determine the value of all women's testimony.[34] The verse reads, in part "And call to witness from among your men two witnesses; but if there are not two men, then one man and two women from among those whom you choose to be witnesses."

However, Q. 2:282 appears to be highly contextual. The women in this case were most likely expected to give testimony in a case related to a commercial transaction, which, in seventh century Medina, was typically the domain of men. This socio-cultural reality meant that, in this case, the woman in question was given half the legal status of a man because she was deemed to have less knowledge about this area of commercial life. The verse most probably was not meant to imply that women in all cases must be regarded as lesser witnesses. The example was highly specific: given that women, in general, did not play a very significant role in commercial matters in that society, the Qur'an asked Muslims to have at least one male and two female witnesses in this area. There was no suggestion that women are fundamentally unable to undertake this duty, nor that women are intellectually inferior to men. Rather, the Qur'an aimed to ensure justice and fairness and to avoid disputes in the area of commerce. As Nehaluddin Ahmad suggests, if the Qur'an was "laying down a norm that in matters of testimony two women would be treated as being equal to one man", then "wherever the question of witnessing arises, [it] would have treated the women in this way in a consistent matter".[35] Moreover, as Ahmad notes, "[t]here are seven other verses about recording evidence in the Qur'an, yet none of them [specifies] the requirement of two female witnesses".[36] Yet instead of recognising its particular socio-cultural context, the application of this verse has often been extended by many jurists and used to argue that women must always be regarded as half the value of men when giving testimony.[37] The way this Qur'anic text was used by jurists is an example of how prevalent social attitudes towards women came to dictate the way certain Qur'anic texts were interpreted.

The issue of polygyny is another example of socio-cultural influences on the interpretation of a particular Qur'anic verse. Classical Islamic law allows a man to have up to four wives at the same time. However, as Niaz Shah argues, the wording of Q. 4:3 suggests that the principle behind the verse is justice. Polygyny was only permitted to do justice to orphans and close relatives of war captives;[38] it was not a broad right given to Muslim men.

In general, while in the Prophet's time the tendency was to grant a high degree of freedom to both men and women within marriage, this freedom was gradually curtailed in relation to women. This is an example of the significant tension between the legal and social spheres. Islamic law recognises that women have agency and grants them legal capacity as capable decision-makers. However this legal status has not always translated itself into social practice. Indeed, as An-Na'im observes, "although Muslim women's legal personality is complete in theory, [in reality] their access to opportunities" to exercise that capacity is restricted.[39] This is because the segregation of men and women in many Muslim societies means that women are often confined to the home, or expected to wear a full-body veil outside the home. This has "tend[ed] to diminish the practical value of Muslim women's theoretical entitlement[s]".[40] In other words, women have very little room to freely move between the private and public spheres. Women may have gained formal legal capacity, but in practice they may not be free to make independent decisions in many cases.[41]

Having examined some of the textual and historical background to traditional Islamic legal positions on women, in the second part of this chapter I will briefly explore how the rights of women are dealt with in international human rights law.

THE RIGHTS OF WOMEN IN INTERNATIONAL HUMAN RIGHTS TREATIES

Human rights instruments that affirm the status of women and protect their human rights have evolved considerably since 1945. Many of the first human rights documents that were developed did not have a significant impact on the situation of women around the world. This initial lack of impact was an impetus for women's rights advocates to develop more effective instruments with a broader global reach. As with many human rights treaties, those protecting women's rights evolved over time. Natalie Hevener suggests that women's rights have progressed through three conceptual stages: "protective, corrective, and non-discriminatory".[42] Protective rights evolved to reflect a view of women as "a group [who] should not or cannot engage in specified activities", implying that women were "subordinate, weak and disadvantaged".[43] Corrective rights also envisioned women as "a separate group … need[ing] special treatment", but aimed to "improve the specific treatment" of women, without any explicit "comparison to the treatment of men in the [same] area".[44] Finally, non-discriminatory rights affirm that "men and women [are] entitled to equal treatment".[45] They "treat women in the same manner as men",[46] regardless of biological differences.

The human rights of women are enshrined in a variety of international human rights instruments that affirm gender equality and protect against discrimination. For instance, the UDHR emphasises the fundamental principles of equality and non-discrimination with respect to all of the rights mentioned in it.[47] Article 2 states "Everyone is entitled to all the rights and freedoms set forth in this Declaration, without distinction of any kind, such as race, colour, sex, language, religion, political or other opinion, national or social origin, property, birth or other status."[48]

The International Covenant on Civil and Political Rights

The International Covenant on Civil and Political Rights (ICCPR) elaborates the civil and political rights contained in the UDHR. After affirming that its rights should be enjoyed equally by both men and women, it sets out a number of articles that have particular significance for women. For instance, Article 23 affirms that women, as well as men, have the right to give their free and full consent to marriage, although only upon reaching marriageable age.[49] Governments must also ensure that rights and responsibilities during marriage and at its dissolution are based on equality for men and women.[50] In General Comment 19, the Human Rights Committee elaborated that equal rights and responsibilities encompass "all matters arising from … [the] relationship, such as choice of residence, running of the household, education of the children and administration of assets",[51] as well as any arrangements made in the context of "legal separation" or divorce.[52] This means that any discrimination with respect to "divorce, child custody, maintenance or alimony, visiting rights or the loss or recovery of parental authority" must be rectified by the state.[53] Concerns in this area are evident in the discussions that the Human Rights Committee has conducted with a number of Muslim-majority states. For instance, in the context of its examination of the third periodic report of Kuwait (2016), the Human Rights Committee expressed dissatisfaction at the government's "lack of progress" addressing certain "discriminatory provisions" in its legislation that concern "polygamy, the minimum age of marriage, the ability of women to conclude a marriage contract, divorce, parental authority … and the ability of Kuwaiti women to pass on their nationality to their children and foreign spouses on an equal footing with Kuwaiti men."[54] Similarly, when examining the second periodic report of Tajikistan (2013), the Committee noted with concern "the resurgence of patriarchal attitudes and stereotypes" about women in the context of the family.[55]

The ICCPR also provides that all citizens, regardless of sex, be given the same opportunities in the conduct of public affairs.[56] This includes the right to vote, be elected and have access to public service.[57] In relation to the second periodic report of Tajikistan, the Human Rights Committee also noted that women in Tajikistan were "underrepresented in the public sector, particularly in decision-making positions".[58] It urged the government to take "special measures" to rectify the situation.[59]

Finally, the ICCPR also explicitly protects pregnant women from the death penalty.[60]

The International Covenant on Economic, Social and Cultural Rights

The Covenant on Economic, Social and Cultural Rights affirms, in Article 3, that all of its rights are to be enjoyed equally by men and women. In General Comment 16 (2005), the Committee on Economic, Social and Cultural rights explains that this provision places particular obligations on state parties, including (among other obligations) "to refrain from discriminatory actions that directly or indirectly result in the denial of the equal right of men and women to their enjoyment of economic, social and cultural rights";[61] to set aside any laws, policies or other measures that contradict Article 3;[62] and to actively work toward "the elimination of prejudices, customary and all other practices that perpetuate the notion of inferiority or superiority of either of the sexes, and stereotyped roles for men and women".[63] In this regard the Committee has affirmed that the "stereotyped image of women as only mothers and wives" is contrary to the Covenant.[64] In relation to the second to fourth periodic reports of Mauritius (2010) (which is not a Muslim-majority country), the Committee raised this concern with the state party, noting "the persistence of stereotypes regarding the division of responsibilities between women and men in the family, the community and in public life, where men are still considered the main source of income for the family and women are expected to be primarily responsible for household chores".[65] The state was therefore encouraged to promote "the equal sharing of responsibilities in the family, community and public life".[66]

The Covenant also offers a number of special protections for women. These include the right to accept or reject employment; the right to work in "just and favourable conditions" and to receive "equal remuneration for work of equal value"; and equal opportunity for promotion.[67] While reviewing the second periodic report of Lebanon (2016), the Committee expressed concern in this regard about the few women participating in Lebanon's labour force,[68] and encouraged it to implement special measures to investigate the "root causes of women's low participation".[69]

Other provisions address the issues of marriage and consent, as well as family assistance,[70] which includes, according to the Committee, ensuring that the marriageable age is the same for girls and boys; that both sexes have "an equal right to choose if, whom and when to marry"; and that women, alongside men, have the same access to marital assets and inheritance if their spouse dies.[71] In many cases states are encouraged to examine their personal status laws for discriminatory provisions and even to consider constitutional reform, if necessary.[72]

Parenting and childrearing are also recognised as requiring special protection, and the ICESCR affirms the importance of leave with pay or adequate social security benefits as a way of assisting working mothers.[73] All of these provisions involve state expenditure, a fact that Article 2(1) seems to recognise. It requires governments to take an active role in making these provisions "progressively" realisable.[74]

The Convention on the Elimination of All Forms of Discrimination against Women

The Convention on the Elimination of All Forms of Discrimination against Women (CEDAW) is the "most comprehensive and important" instrument for protecting women's rights.[75] The convention sets out a wide range of provisions which aim to eliminate all forms of discrimination against women. It emphasises equality between men and women and calls for a range of state actions to achieve this. The convention emphasises the fact that women's rights should be protected in both the public and private spheres of life.[76]

CEDAW has four parts: Part 1 deals with the historical and cultural exclusion of women; Part 2 endorses women's participation in public life, especially in the political field; Part 3 covers the socio-economic rights of women, including in areas such as education and employment; and Part 4 deals with the law and its institutions.[77] States are called on to repeal all discriminatory laws and practices and to promote the equality of women.

These provisions have significant implications for states. As Ali observes, "not only must they abolish all existing discriminatory legislation and practices", they must also address more subtle forms of discrimination, such as "stereotyped concepts of male and female roles in society". CEDAW's rights-based framework thus "represent[s] a significant difference from previous legislation that was usually welfarist and 'protective' in tone".[78]

While all of CEDAW's provisions concern the rights and status of women, a number of articles are particularly relevant to our discussion. Firstly, Article 15 affirms that women and men are equal before the law and have the same legal capacity.[79] This means that a woman should have freedom to apply for "financial credit", hold property or manage a business in her own right.[80] A woman's testimony must also be given equal "respect" and "weight" to that of a man's in court,[81] because to do otherwise is to "diminish her standing as an independent, responsible and valued member of her community".[82]

Article 16 prohibitions discrimination with respect to women's status in marriage and in the context of family relations. This article has quite broad application. In General Recommendation 21, the Committee affirmed that women should have equal standing "in the family and society" because activities in this context are "invaluable for the survival of society".[83] Therefore, to regard domestic roles as "inferior" is to violate the "principles of justice and equality" in the Convention.[84] The Committee has expressed concern about this issue in relation to a number of state party reports, including the eighth periodic report of Bangladesh (2016), where the government was chastised for the "limited efforts made by the State party to eliminate such stereotypes which constitute serious barriers to women's equal enjoyment with men of their human rights and their equal participation in all spheres of their life".[85] Similarly, the Committee expressed concern about "the persistence of deeply entrenched traditional stereotypes regarding the roles and responsibilities of women and men in the family and in society, which overemphasize the role of women as caregivers" in Qatar.[86] The Committee rejected the argument that customary or religious law may prescribe different rights or responsibilities for men and women during marriage; for instance, that the husband may be granted the role of "head of household and primary decision maker".[87] The Committee stressed that this contravenes the principle of equal status in the Convention.[88] Likewise, the practice of polygyny goes against "a woman's right to equality with men", not to mention the "emotional and financial consequences" that this practice can have for women.[89] Article 16 also preserves a woman's right to freely choose a marital partner and prohibits forced marriages or marriages entered into for "payment or preferment … [or] financial security".[90] It prohibits the arrangement of marriage for women or girls without their consent by other members of the family, as well as different legal marital ages for boys and girls.[91] Equality also means that women should have equal rights when it comes to "guardianship, wardship, trusteeship and adoption"[92] and in the allocation of marital property upon divorce;[93] and be treated without discrimination in the distribution of inheritance.[94] In this regard, while reviewing the eighth periodic report of Bangladesh (2016), the Committee expressed concern that no legislation had been enacted to ensure the equal division of property in the event of divorce or "recognizing, defining, or setting out rules for control over marital property during marriage".[95]

Article 7 affirms that women should not be discriminated against when it comes to public or political life. This refers to taking up political roles, as well as "the exercise of legislative, judicial, executive and administrative powers", "public administration" and participation in "political parties, trade unions, professional or industry associations, women's organizations, community-based organizations and other organizations concerned with public and political life".[96] Traditionally, these roles have been dominated by men, while women have been confined to the private realm[97] or prevented from active participation due to cultural or religious norms or "men's failure to share the tasks associated with the organization of the household and with the care and raising of children".[98] In relation to the initial report of Qatar (2014), the Committee lamented the non-participation of women on the Shura Council, as well as their "low representation … in ministerial positions and in other decision-making positions in the Government, including in the foreign service, as well as in the judiciary and the legal profession".[99]

Criticisms of CEDAW

Those who see international human rights instruments as "Western" ideals typically consider CEDAW to be an instrument that promotes a specific and limited framework of gender equality.[100] One of the most prominent criticisms of CEDAW is that it does not recognise the significant diversity that exists in cultures and societies across the world. CEDAW is seen by some as imposing one particular model of equality. Accordingly, if the different socio-cultural conditions of women around the world are not taken into account, then only some women will benefit from the convention's approach. In other words, CEDAW is considered by some to be an ideological document that only advances a Western model of equality, and is thus unlikely to make a significant difference to the lives of many women around the world because it does not speak to their experience.

Indeed, as Warren observes, "[t]he role of international law and its applicability in non-Western cultures is a matter of controversy".[101] In Muslim contexts, some scholars argue that "the best way to address women's [rights] is not to dictate … a list of universal standards to meet, but rather to encourage liberalised interpretations of texts and laws by Islamic scholars themselves".[102] In An-Na'im's view, "international standards are meaningless to Muslim women unless they are reflected in the concrete realities of the Muslim environment".[103] As he observes, many cultural and religious traditions, including Islam, can be suspicious toward attempts to impose what is perceived as outside standards.[104] For such standards to be accepted, they need to be framed as not foreign but "compatible with the fundamental values of Islam".[105] International standards of human rights, including the rights of women, must therefore be provided with "Islamic legitimacy".[106] Furthermore, in the legal systems of Muslim-majority states, "policy arguments are insufficient bases for challenging [existing] rules".[107]

An-Na'im points out that international standards must interact with the Shari'a; but this does not necessarily mean relying on its historical formulations.[108] The provisions of the Qur'an and Sunna on women's rights can be revisited and interpreted differently,[109] because "the Qur'an is a living text and can be reinterpreted to meet contemporary needs of … Muslim societies".[110]

Another criticism of CEDAW and of the international framework for the protection of women's rights is that it creates a "normative conflict between equality and non-discrimination … on the one hand, and [the] right to freedom of religion and belief … on the other".[111] In cultures where religious traditions and customary practices create gender hierarchies, the right to freedom of religion actually legitimises these inequalities. As Ali observes, "it follows … that if the freedom to manifest or practice one's religion [leads] to discrimination against women, such discrimination could be [justified] on the basis of [this] right".[112] Thus, despite its objective to empower women through human rights, CEDAW is "said to have failed in providing a clear methodology to resolve these conflicting rights".[113] This means that "at the level of domestic law, complications [can] arise" in the interaction "between state law, customary norms and religious injunctions".[114] Ali observes that this often results in the application of the most patriarchal versions of these norms or laws.[115]

Muslim-majority States and their Engagement with CEDAW

Despite the concerns of some Muslim scholars about the universal applicability of CEDAW, its legitimacy and application in Muslim-majority societies, most Muslim-majority states are state parties to the convention. Of the fifty-seven members of the Organisation of Islamic Cooperation, all but Iran, Sudan, and Somalia have signed and ratified CEDAW.[116] However, many of these states have entered reservations against key articles, often citing the Shari'a for justification.[117] These reservations make up the greatest proportion of substantive reservations against CEDAW.[118] The large body of reservations has led some women's rights groups to claim that these states "never meant to implement CEDAW[,] hence the numerous reservations they have institutionalised to block any possible useful implementation".[119] Indeed, some reservations go to the heart of fundamental rights,[120] such as nationality, legal capacity, and equality in the family.

One example of a state that has cited adherence to Islam as a justification for entering a reservation to CEDAW is Malaysia, which states the following general comment before listing a number of articles that it will not be bound by: "The Government of Malaysia declares that Malaysia's accession is subject to the understanding that the provisions of the Convention do not conflict with the provisions of the Islamic Shari'a law and the Federal Constitution of Malaysia."[121]

Likewise, before listing two specific provisions it is not bound by, Saudi Arabia states that it is "not under obligation to observe" any terms of CEDAW that contradict "the norms of Islamic law".[122]

Kuwait declares that it is not bound by Article 16(f) on adoption, "inasmuch as it conflicts with the provisions of the Islamic Shariah, Islam being the official religion of the State".[123] Elsewhere, it has elaborated more fully on how the Islamic Shariah impacts the rights of women:

> Polygamy, marriage contracts, divorce and other matters are governed by the Islamic sharia. The approach adopted by the State of Kuwait in establishing the rules and frames of reference for equality, non-discrimination and enhancement of human dignity is based on the provisions of the Islamic sharia and principles enshrined in the Kuwaiti Constitution. Women in Islam enjoy rights consistent with their manifold duties in society.[124]

Moreover, "The Kuwaiti courts also recognize women as persons with full legal capacity and women are not prevented from delivering testimony in ordinary (non-sharia) courts. However, different rules are applicable to women's testimony before personal status (sharia) courts, in which a man's testimony is equivalent to the testimony of two women."[125] Kuwait also cites the Islamic Sharia as the reason behind this rule.[126]

Egypt has also entered a reservation against Article 16 in its entirety:

> Reservation [is made] to the text of article 16 concerning the equality of men and women in all matters relating to marriage and family relations during the marriage and upon its dissolution, without prejudice to the Islamic Sharia's provisions whereby women are accorded rights equivalent to those of their spouses so as to ensure a just balance between them. This is out of respect for the sacrosanct nature of the firm religious beliefs which govern marital relations in Egypt and which may not be called in[to] question and in view of the fact that one of the most important bases of these relations is an equivalency of rights and duties so as to ensure complementary [*sic*] which guarantees true equality between the spouses.[127]

Other states "have not expressly cited Islam as reason for reserving their position, but … [this] may well be inferred from the text of what appears a general reservation".[128] Both Pakistan and Tunisia, for instance, qualify their adherence to CEDAW by saying that they adhere to it as long as it does not conflict with the provisions of their constitutions,[129] which affirm the place of Islam as the state religion.

While Pakistan has entered a general reservation against CEDAW, it has taken concrete steps to address the status of women in its territory. The government has created a Permanent Commission on the Status of Women; declared honour killings murder; increased the political participation of women; and formulated a National Policy for Women.[130] It has also appointed women to the Council of Islamic Ideology, the body that "advises the legislature on whether or not a law is repugnant to Islam"[131] and makes recommendations on how to balance the requirements of state and Islamic law.[132] While only one woman is required to sit on the council at any time, Pakistan has appointed three.[133] Many of CEDAW's provisions have also been incorporated into Pakistan's constitution, "such as the definition of discrimination, 'equality before the law', 'equal protection of the law' and principles of affirmative action".[134] Pakistan has also passed legislation improving legal protection for women who may be subject to harmful traditional and customary practices.[135]

Moreover, the Federal Shariat Court has ruled in favour of the rights of women in a number of important cases. In one case concerning the principle of gender equality, the Court considered whether women were permitted to be appointed judges. After reviewing the textual evidence and juristic positions on the matter, it concluded that "there was no explicit injunction in the Qur'an or *Sunna* against the appointment of women to the judiciary, so it is not prohibited in Islam".[136]

In a subsequent case the Court reviewed a provision of the Citizenship Act 1951 that "denied citizenship to a foreign husband of a Pakistani woman".[137] The Court affirmed that men and women were created equal and as a result, found that "section 10 of the Citizenship Act is discriminatory, negates gender equality and is in violation of Articles 2-A and 25 of the Constitution of Islamic Republic of Pakistan and also against international commitments of Pakistan and most importantly is repugnant to Holy Qur'an and *Sunnah*".[138] The government was ordered by the Court to amend the provision.[139]

However, despite these measures, human rights groups stress that Pakistan still has a long way to go in terms of the realisation of women's human rights. A 2014 report by a Pakistani human rights organisation, the Aurat (Women) Foundation, found that in the country on a daily basis, "six women were murdered, six were kidnapped, four were raped and three committed suicide".[140] In fact, in 2011 a poll of experts by the Thomson Reuters Foundation rated Pakistan as the third most dangerous country for women in the world.[141] Dowry-related violence and acid attacks are still common, as is family violence.[142] Women's unequal status remains enshrined in several pieces of legislation, despite a number of constitutional guarantees of equality.[143] Moreover, the Committee on the Elimination of All forms of Discrimination against Women has noted "the persistence of patriarchal attitudes and deep-rooted stereotypes concerning women's roles and responsibilities that discriminate against women and perpetuate their subordination within the family and society".[144] According to Mahmuda Islam, in inheritance a substantial difference exists between the Qur'an's injunctions and actual practice: "Women rarely inherit their share, but even if they do, the [practical] ownership lies with the male members of the family, such as [a] husband or brother".[145] The 1984 Law of Evidence "reduces the testimony of women to half in financial matters", and "puts responsibility for [an illegitimate] child's maintenance upon the mother".[146] The controversial Hudood Ordinances omit marital rape as a crime,[147] and both women and children can be accused of the crime of *zina* (unlawful sexual relations).[148]

Human rights organisations attribute the ongoing failure to improve the status of women, and to promote and protect their human rights, to societal attitudes towards women. Zara Jamal argues that "a certain mentality is deeply ingrained in strictly patriarchal societies like Pakistan. ... Women must struggle daily for basic rights, recognition, and respect. They must live in a culture that defines them by the male figures in their lives".[149] Moreover, the implementation of laws and policies designed to improve the position of women remain largely "in the hands of male government functionaries and the police", which continues to exacerbate the problem.[150]

Despite its reservation, Tunisia has also made important progress towards guaranteeing the rights of women and improving their status in

Tunisian society. In relation to its periodic report (fifth and sixth, considered on 7 October 2010), the state was commended for its advancement toward "gender equality in education";[151] for encouraging the involvement of women in the public sphere, which resulted in a greater number of women candidates for the 2009 elections, and "the increase of women's representation in the parliament";[152] for amending various pieces of legislation that discriminated against women;[153] and for introducing measures to reconstruct societal attitudes towards women.[154]

Nevertheless, the Committee emphasised that measures were still needed to address "patriarchal attitudes", "deep-rooted stereotypes" and "adverse cultural norms, practices and traditions",[155] as well as further discriminatory legislation.[156]

From the very beginning the monitoring committee of CEDAW has expressed concern about the number and scope of state reservations to CEDAW and how they impact implementation of CEDAW's rights.[157] On a number of occasions it has urged state parties to reconsider their reservations or to consider narrowing them, particularly with regard to Articles 2 and 16, which are considered to be "core provisions" of CEDAW and "central to [its] objects and purpose".[158] These are two articles that feature commonly in the reservations of Muslim-majority states. However, Marsha Freeman believes that while these reservations show that the states "currently do not accept all aspects of [CEDAW's] non-discrimination norms", it affirms that "they do not wish to remove themselves entirely from the conversation".[159] The reservations therefore provide a useful starting point for dialogue.[160] Through high level engagement at an intellectual level, it may be possible for reservations to be removed if a state party is satisfied that the rights do not infringe "religious law",[161] or in this case the Shari'a. The reservations may therefore provide a useful opening for such conversations to occur.

TOWARDS MORE EMPHASIS ON EQUALITY

Despite the difficulties many Muslim societies seem to face today in coming to terms with gender equality as elaborated in international human rights instruments, a strong argument can be made in favour of this equality. This is largely based on what the Qur'an has to say on gender-related issues, the reforms it introduced in seventh century Arabia, and the Prophet's own teachings and practices in this area. Based on these sources, a number of Muslim scholars are arguing that there is no particular difficulty in harmonising international human rights norms and Islamic norms in the area of women's rights.

The Qur'an insists that both men and women were created equal by God and are equally accountable. For example, both men and women have similar obligations to God and are subject to similar punishments for going against His commandments.[162] Shah calls attention to the Qur'an's view that men and women are equally responsible for their actions: "Every soul is held in pledge for its deeds" (Q. 74:38). The word "soul" emphasises this gender neutrality.[163] From a Qur'anic point of view, whether a person is God-fearing and righteous is the key question. It says, "Anyone, male or female, who does good deeds and is a believer, will enter Paradise and will not be wronged by as much as the dip in a date stone" (Q. 4:124). It is religious belief and practice (not gender) that distinguishes people one from another. There is virtually nothing in the Qur'an to suggest that in the eyes of God, men, as a category of people, are better than women. Rather, righteousness, or what the Qur'an terms *taqwa*, is the most important value proclaimed by the Qur'an: "In God's eyes, the most honoured of you are the most righteous ones (*atqa*)" (Q. 49:13). Regardless of gender, *taqwa* is valued by God.

The Qur'an also affirms the equal value of men and women's lives. The Qur'an prohibits the killing of any person (Q. 17:33), and this crime is punishable regardless of the gender of the perpetrator or the victim. This is a theme that is evident in other verses of the Qur'an—the insistence on gender equality in the area of justice. A key verse on this matter states "You who believe, be steadfast in your devotion to God and bear witness impartially: do not let hatred of others lead you away from justice, but adhere to justice, for that is closer to righteousness (*taqwa*). Be righteous: God is well aware of all that you do" (Q. 5:8).

This verse addresses all who believe, not just men. The theme of equality is further exemplified in the story of the creation of humanity, where Adam and Eve are said to have been created from a single soul to complement one another.[164] In its account of the Fall from the Garden of Eden, there is no suggestion in the Qur'an that either Adam or Eve were guiltier of transgression. Both disobeyed God and both sought and received forgiveness from Him.[165] Both men and women are essential in the creation story and in creation in general. There is no suggestion in the Qur'an that one is inferior to the other.

Ali argues that "the basic teachings of the *Quran* focus[ed] on efforts to improve the condition of, and strengthen[,] the weaker segments of society … [including] orphans, slaves, the poor [and] women".[166] For these reforms to "take root [in] a tribal, patriarchal society, an outright break with the past would not have served any useful purpose".[167] Instead, she notes, they "la[id] the foundations of an egalitarian society based on the principles of social justice".[168] The extent of the changes instituted by Islam and the reason why women were not given the same rights as men in every sphere are, as Ali observes, "perhaps difficult to appreciate today" in our context, where gender equality is assumed. But fourteen hundred years ago such changes would have been radical, and it is imperative to recognise that the Qur'an and the Prophet's teachings on women emerged in that context.

In sum, a survey of the Qur'an and the practice of the Prophet suggests that there is no strong basis for the notion of inequality between men and women in Islam. The Qur'an and the Prophet challenged many common discriminatory practices and attitudes towards women that existed in seventh century Arabia and put into place a range of rules and regulations to alleviate the oppression of women in many realms. But these reforms were not properly put into practice due to cultural resistance and perhaps misinterpretation on the part of some jurists who wished to ensure the continuation of the cultural status quo. Discrimination thus remained, was cemented in Islamic tradition, and is still practised in many contemporary Muslim societies today. In the contemporary period, these discriminatory messages are the focus of Muslim human rights advocates, who argue that the egalitarian message of the Qur'an should be revived.

EXAMPLES OF CONTEMPORARY MUSLIM SCHOLARSHIP

While Islam is often perceived as a religion that oppresses or subjugates women under the authority of men, a number of contemporary Muslim scholars are challenging such views by revisiting discriminatory positions or interpretations of key Qur'anic verses. Of particular importance are the voices of a number of prominent female (as well as male) scholars, whose works challenge the view that the Qur'an is inherently discriminatory against women. Their writings seek to reinterpret what they describe as the traditional patriarchal interpretations that have dominated the understanding of some Qur'anic texts. In the following section I will give a brief overview of the work of a number of these scholars and examine briefly the methodology they propose, where relevant, to promote the egalitarian message of the Qur'an.

Amina Wadud

Amina Wadud (b. 1952), an American convert to Islam who has written extensively on Islam and women's rights, argues that "the method

Muslims traditionally have employed to read the Qur'an is … 'atomistic'".[169] By this, Wadud means that most Qur'anic exegetes read the text "begin[ning] with the first verse of the first chapter and proceed[ed] to the second verse", and so on.[170] As Asma Barlas puts it, "[l]ittle or no effort [was] made to recognise themes [or] to discuss the relationship of the Qur'an to itself thematically".[171] Wadud asserts that reading the Qur'an in such a fragmented and decontextualised way has failed to recognise "its internal coherence, or *nazm*, … [and] the broad principles that underlie its teachings".[172] Wadud therefore argues that the Qur'an should be read "as a textual whole, while … contextualising its teachings".[173] According to Barlas, "Wadud's … reading of the Qur'an" thus aims to "understand … its ethos and spirit and not merely its letter".[174]

The methodology Wadud proposes in her most important work, *Qur'an and Woman*, is to consider three aspects of the text. Firstly, the context in which it was revealed; secondly, its linguistic composition; and thirdly, the text as a whole, or as Wadud puts it, its "world-view".[175] In this regard Wadud argues that the Qur'an must be understood as a text that "responded to particular circumstances in Arabia at the time of the revelation".[176]

Wadud thus "explains the Qur'an's teachings in terms of the social and historical contexts Islam sought to reform and also in terms of the linguistic … structures of the text itself".[177] On the question of the Qur'an's view of women, Wadud argues that "there is no essential difference in the value attributed to women and men",[178] although there were "functional distinctions in the context of seventh century Arabia".[179] The Qur'an therefore took a differing approach to different prevailing cultural practices: it immediately prohibited deplorable practices such as "infanticide … [and] denial of inheritance to women"; modified others such as "polygamy, unconstrained divorce, [and] conjugal violence"; and "remained neutral" in relation to still others, especially forms of "social … [and] marital patriarchy".[180] According to Wadud, interpreters are in error when they use "contextually specific functions" (that is, social roles) to support the idea that men are inherently superior.[181]

Asma Barlas

Asma Barlas (b. 1950), a Pakistani-American academic, argues that the Qur'an does not advocate traditional patriarchy because it does not represent God as Father or male. In fact, it emphatically forbids representing God as Father.[182] Moreover, she argues, "the Qur'an … [does not] teach that men are ontologically superior to women or are entitled to rule over them or even to be heads of the household".[183] Rather, it describes women and men as each other's mutual "guides" (*awliya'*) and establishes love and mercy as the foundation of marriage.[184] The only way in which the Qur'an distinguishes between human beings is on the basis of their God-consciousness (*taqwa*), which can be attained without discrimination by both men and women.[185] This is the basis upon which she argues that the Qur'an opposes patriarchy and supports equality.[186]

Like Wadud, Barlas argues that the Qur'an must be read in a holistic way. She refers to the Qur'an's warning not to "read God's Message piecemeal and selectively",[187] referring to both 15:90 (where the Qur'an chastises those who "divide it into parts") and 6:91 (where the Qur'an reproaches the people of Israel for making the scripture given to Moses "into separate sheets, showing some but hiding many").[188] Barlas also states that the Qur'an must be read for its "best meanings".[189] Certainly, Muslims can read the Qur'an in multiple ways, but not all readings may be equally good or acceptable. The Qur'an does not define what it means by "best" but leaves it to Muslims to decide, urging them to use their own intelligence or reasoning (*aql*) to decipher God's signs for themselves.[190] For Barlas, this allows Muslims to exercise their own capacity and choices in constructing religious knowledge.[191]

Kecia Ali

Kecia Ali (b. 1972) is another American scholar of Islam whose focus is Islamic jurisprudence and women. Ali argues that traditionally, scholars have overlooked the diversity that exists in the scholarly interpretation of texts. There are significant differences and contradictory positions within the realm of Islamic jurisprudence and Qur'anic exegesis. It is therefore too simplistic to speak of one "Islamic law". Ali thus argues that it is important to recognise that "Islamic legal rules are to a significant extent the product of human and therefore fallible interpretive processes, and thus are susceptible to reform."[192] This is particularly the case where the religio-legal rules that govern marriage and divorce are concerned.[193] Indeed, "Muslim jurisprudence was an open rather than a closed system" in which "jurists expounded, explained, debated, and justified their stances on legal matters both mundane and lofty, social and ritual".[194] Minority views remained part of a canon of legal thought and are "available for later thinkers to draw on".[195] Today, scholars can use these to "derive fresh solutions to legal problems based on independent recourse to foundational texts (*ijtihad*)".[196]

Riffat Hassan

Riffat Hassan (b. 1943), a Pakistani-American scholar, also points out the ongoing impact of the removal of women from public life. As men were tasked with the job of interpreting the Qur'an and hadith, they took on responsibility for defining the "ontological, theological, sociological, and eschatological status of Muslim women".[197] This, in turn, provided the foundation for the "misogynistic and androcentric tendencies" that are evident in Islamic tradition today.[198] For Hassan, the way to challenge this foundation is to develop a "feminist theology" that will not only free Muslim women but have liberating benefits for men themselves as it challenges those "unjust structures and laws that make a peer relationship between men and women impossible".[199]

Fazlur Rahman

Fazlur Rahman (d. 1988), another Pakistani-American scholar, argues that the Qur'an must be understood as "the divine response, through the Prophet's mind, to the moral-social situation of the Prophet's Arabia".[200] As such, all Qur'anic verses were "revealed … in a specific time in history and within certain circumstances, … [as] expressions relative to those circumstances".[201] Rahman outlined two movements in interpreting the Qur'an. First, Muslims must "understand the import … of a given [Qur'anic] statement by studying the historical situation or problem to which it was the answer".[202] Having extracted a general principle from this answer, Muslims must then consider how it is "to be embodied in the present concrete sociohistorical context".[203] As he wrote: "To the extent that we achieve … this double movement successfully, the Qur'an's imperatives will become alive and effective once again."[204]

Abdullahi An-Na'im

Abdullahi An-Na'im (b. 1946), a Sudanese-American academic who has written extensively on Islam and human rights, suggests that the best way to achieve change is through "alternative Islamisation through the reformation of Shari'a".[205] Rather than "abandon[ing Islam] to the fundamentalists", An-Na'im argues that Islam can be mobilised to help "motivate women" and counter the idea that women's rights are "alien Western notions".[206] The best way to achieve this, according to An-Na'im, is "to show that the rights of women are Islamic".[207]

Khaled Abou El Fadl

Khaled Abou El Fadl (b. 1963), currently a professor of law in the United States, makes a distinction between what he terms Islamic law and "Muslim law".[208] Islamic law developed from the "normative teachings of the Prophet Muhammad and his disciples",[209] yet at the same time, Muslims incorporated legal or cultural practices from the regions and peoples surrounding Arabia, including Jewish law and practices from "Persia, Mesopotamia, Egypt and other Roman provinces".[210] Many of these were not consistent with Islamic law or even contrary to it; nevertheless, they became part of the rules that were applied in Muslim societies.[211] Abou El Fadl notes the impact that such prevailing cultural norms and practices had on attitudes towards women. For example, while women were quite active in public life during the Prophet's time (as scholars, poets or narrators of hadith) they were eventually marginalised by discriminatory attitudes from men (such as those that were evident in pre-Islamic, Greek, and Roman cultures).[212] In fact, "most of the misogynistic traditions and interpretations of Islamic law that [later] arose" may have come from men's refusal to accept women's presence in the public sphere.[213]

WOMEN'S RIGHTS—CHALLENGES AND POSSIBLE MEANS OF RECONCILIATION

Perhaps the greatest tension between Islamic law and international human rights law with respect to the rights of women is the fact that Islamic law recognises that men and women are equal ontologically, but "does not advocate absolute equality of roles between them, especially in the family relationship".[214] The distinction of roles that this creates in the family sphere has been a subject of concern to the Human Rights Committee, as it is contrary to its efforts to challenge "traditional, cultural, and religious attitudes" that are "used to justify violations of women's right to equality".[215] The same tension is also evident in Muslim states' engagement with CEDAW, and lies behind many states' specific reservations to Articles 2 and 16 of the convention, which concern marriage and family matters.[216]

This is a potentially irreconcilable issue for Islamic law and international human rights law. Muslim governments, communities, and individuals are often reluctant to challenge prevailing family and social structures because these institutions are considered cornerstones of Muslim societies. As Norris and Inglehart's research shows, the main cultural fault line between Muslim societies and the West appears to be on gender issues.[217] Thus, any changes will need to be supported with clear evidence from Islamic tradition so that Muslims are convinced of its legitimacy.

Despite this, within the realm of marriage and family matters there are several areas where it appears possible to achieve greater compatibility between international human rights norms and Muslim practices. In the following section I will outline some of the main areas of challenge, as well as the strategies that scholars have put forward to mitigate the difficulties.

Marriage (Polygyny and Consent)

Based on Q. 4:3, the legal systems of many Muslim-majority states permit Muslim men to marry up to four wives at the same time. However, this freedom does not extend to Muslim women (or even to non-Muslim men). Article 23(4) of the ICCPR and Article 16(1) of CEDAW both affirm the principle of equality in marriage. The Human Rights Committee has affirmed that polygyny is incompatible with equality in terms of the right to marry under the ICCPR. It is "inadmissible discrimination against women", and "should be definitely abolished wherever it continues to exist".[218] The monitoring committee of CEDAW has also affirmed that "polygamous marriages contravene a woman's right to equality with men and can have such serious emotional and financial consequences for her and her dependents that such marriages ought to be discouraged and prohibited".[219] Thus there exists a tension between what is permitted for men in marriage under Islamic law and international human rights standards that affirm equality for men and women.

According to Amina Wadud, there are particular reasons why the Qur'an allowed polygyny. Firstly, she notes that Qur'an 4:3 is about the treatment of orphans rather than the institution of marriage. In the context in which the verse was revealed, "Some male guardians, responsible for managing the wealth of orphaned female children, were unable to refrain from unjust management of that wealth (4:2). One solution suggested to prevent mismanagement was marriage to the female orphans."[220] This ensured that "the economic responsibility of maintaining the wife would counterbalance the access to the wealth of the orphaned female through the responsibility of management".[221] In essence, according to Wadud, this verse is about justice.[222] However, the Qur'an also set a clear limit as to how many wives a man could take,[223] something that was contrary to societal norms at that time.

As discussed earlier, this Qur'anic command can be understood as a contextual solution for ensuring that certain vulnerable members of society were taken care of in the early Muslim community.[224] Since the practice was only permitted, and not prescribed, there is an argument that it can be phased out of state practice, enabling the tensions between international human rights law and Islamic law in this regard to be resolved.[225] Moreover, many of the other arguments commonly cited in favour of polygyny are no longer compelling today. For instance, it has been argued that men with more financial capability should take care of additional wives. Yet today, many women are financially independent and do not need the financial support of a man.[226] Another argument for polygyny comes from the possibility that a women may be barren and unable to bear children.[227] However, there are many other options today for couples having difficulty conceiving, not to mention caring for orphaned children around the world.[228]

Moreover, while Islamic law allows polygyny, both classical and contemporary scholars emphasise that for it to be permissible, co-wives must be treated "justly". Some contemporary scholars, such as Baderin, see this stipulation as a way of controlling the practice, since "being able to do justice between co-wives is seldom given any consideration by men".[229] Furthermore, Baderin points out that in Muslim-majority societies, "the permissibility of polygamy is often abused in a way that actually works against the family institution itself".[230] Because of this, based on the principle of *maslaha* (public welfare), polygyny could therefore be restricted; again, easing the tension with international human rights law.

Divorce

Islamic law considers marriage to be a contractual relationship between two parties, and similar to other contracts, it can be dissolved through specified procedures.[231] In terms of Islamic law, the most common type of divorce arises from the right given to the husband to initiate divorce through *talaq*.[232] This allows him to dissolve the marriage unilaterally without having to give reasons. A right to divorce is also given to the wife: she may either dissolve the marriage judicially, where, usually, she must establish fault on limited grounds,[233] or through a process known as "discharge at the wife's request" (*khul'*), whereby she must usually return her dower to her husband.[234] However, even if a wife initiates the dissolution of her marriage through *khul'*, the husband may still withhold his consent, thus preventing the divorce.[235]

Because the process of dissolution is much easier for men in comparison to women,[236] this aspect of Islamic law has been identified as greatly incompatible with provisions such as Article 16(1)(c) of CEDAW, which grants women equal rights with men "during marriage and at its dissolution".[237] General Comment 28 of the Human Rights Committee also affirms this interpretation, confirming that the "grounds for divorce and annulment should be the same for men and women".[238]

Importantly, a number of Muslim-majority states have already taken steps to address this issue, bearing in mind their international human rights obligations, by either legislating that husbands may not divorce their wives through *talaq* or ensuring that women are compensated if they are unilaterally divorced without a valid reason.[239] In Malaysia, a married couple is required to come before a court before divorcing, which then either allocates an "arbiter" or takes on this role itself. According to Amina Wadud, this arrangement "creates greater parity between the rights and responsibilities of both [parties to the marriage]".[240]

Wadud also argues that a husband's unilateral power to initiate divorce was a common cultural practice at the time when the Qur'an was revealed. Therefore, "There is no indication that the unilateral right to repudiation needs be continued, or if continued, that it need be only for the husband. Although the Qur'an stipulates conditions for equitable separation or reconciliation, it does not make a rule that men *should* have uncontrolled power of repudiation."[241] Indeed, there is nothing in the Qur'an to suggest that women could not have that same power.[242]

Bharath Venkatraman suggests that given that there are a number of different positions on women and divorce under Islamic law, the most favourable position can be preferred. For example, if the "Maliki school's framework for granting judicially decreed divorces to women" was adopted, this would comply with CEDAW.[243] The Maliki school traditionally allows a woman to divorce on broader grounds than other schools, including a husband's cruelty, refusal or inability to maintain his wife, desertion, or serious disease or ailment that would make continuance of the marriage harmful to the wife.[244] Baderin also suggests that state "judicial control" over divorce could also be beneficial,[245] justified either through the doctrines of public welfare (*maslaha*) or encouraging good and preventing evil (*hisba*).[246] Limiting divorce to dissolution by judicial order (*faskh*) could help to remove some of the "procedural advantage" husbands have in this area, while also offering a strategy that is already permissible under Islamic law.[247]

Inheritance

Islamic law specifies that in most circumstances a male beneficiary should receive double the amount of inheritance to that of a female beneficiary.[248] This is based on Q. 4:11, which states: "Concerning your children, God commands you that a son should have the equivalent share of two daughters." Muslim scholars often point out that Islam probably was the first religious tradition to grant women a fixed share of inheritance and argue that this formula for distributing inheritance is equitable because, under Islamic law, women have less financial responsibility than men.[249] However, Baderin notes that this prescription is "inconsistent with the principle of equality for women".[250]

According to Wadud, a strict application of the "two-to-one" formula in determining inheritance is an "oversimplification" of the Qur'an's teachings in this regard. Qur'an 4:11–12 actually sets out several methods for distributing inheritance, and some of these give a greater proportion of inheritance to female inheritors.[251] For Wadud, the principle underlying the various divisions of inheritance in the Qur'an is equity, which "must take the actual *naf'a* (benefit) of the bereft into consideration".[252] Indeed, she argues, the Qur'an does not aim to set out every possible set of circumstances for distributing inheritance, but gives illustrative "scenarios" that may help families consider what is equitable. In any case, families are also permitted to bequeath "one third" of their inheritance as they wish and without restriction, "without decreasing the divisions of the remaining wealth".[253]

According to Venkatraman, differences in the amount of inheritance granted to men and women can be revisited and perhaps reformulated to recognise the contemporary reality that women are often financially independent from men or breadwinners in their own right.[254] Moreover, there are mechanisms within Islamic law that can be used to establish greater equity for women. The doctrine of *hiba* (gift) allows the gifting of any part of the estate to a particular person.[255] Therefore, one argument is that a testator could take the initiative to ensure equal shares of inheritance for their male and female heirs, despite the problems associated with such an idea in Islamic law.

However, from a state perspective it may be legally or judicially difficult to compel such changes to traditional inheritance laws. In 1959, Iraq attempted to legislate equal shares of inheritance for men and women in all circumstances; however, the legislation was eventually repealed because it lacked popular support.[256] Since the rules for inheritance are explicitly stated in the Qur'an, many Muslims feel that they are challenging the direct word of God by bequeathing their inheritance differently. Thus, for now, the tensions between Islamic law and international human rights law are likely to remain.

Veiling

On the issue of veiling, the Human Rights Committee regards the requirement (or the expectation) that women wear particular clothing in public—such as the veil—as a potential violation of several articles of the ICCPR, including Article 26 on non-discrimination.[257]

Asma Barlas notes that the practice of veiling stems from two sets of verses of the Qur'an: Qur'an 33:59–60 and Qur'an 24:30–31.[258] These verses have been used today to legitimise various forms of veiling—"from the *hijab* (a head veil that leaves the face uncovered) to the *burqa* (a head-to-toe shroud that hides even the feet; some models even mandate wearing gloves so as to hide the hands)"—on the basis of the argument that women's bodies are alluring to Muslim men and need to be hidden.[259] Importantly for Barlas, neither of these Qur'anic texts addresses all women in general.[260]

Fatima Mernissi goes on to explain that when these verses were revealed in the context of seventh century Arabia, women were commonly subjected to harassment when out and about in public, including the "humiliating practice of *ta'arrud*", which essentially meant "taking up a position along a woman's path to urge her to fornicate".[261] When the Prophet made enquiries as to why women were being approached in this way he was told by the perpetrators "[w]e only practice *ta'arrud* with women we believe to be slaves".[262] Therefore, Qur'an 33:59 was revealed to encourage Prophet Muhammad's wives to distinguish themselves from other women by wearing their *jilbab* [cloak] in a certain way. This "was not a question of a new item of clothing, but of a new way of wearing a usual one, distinguishing themselves by an action".[263] By encouraging these women to wear the *jilbab* in that way, the Qur'an was ensuring that they were distinguished from women who were slaves and "presumed … to be nonbelievers and thus fair game". Therefore, "only in a slave-owning … society … does the *jilbab* signify sexual nonavailability".[264] The *jilbab* was encouraged so that believing women were easily recognisable and protected in a society that had an entirely different social structure from today.[265]

Baderin also identifies a possible means of reconciling Islamic law and international human rights law on this issue, based on the differences of opinion within Islamic law on the issue of the extent to which women must cover themselves to protect their human dignity. He believes while some schools of Islamic law require women to cover themselves entirely in public or in the presence of strangers, other schools permit "exposure of the face, the hands up to the wrists and the feet up to the ankles".[266] Instead of states requiring women to dress in a particular way, they can allow women the freedom to voluntarily choose between the two positions that are offered by Islamic jurisprudence, thus upholding their freedom to choose and "striking a balance" between the two legal regimes.[267]

CONCLUSION

The overall picture that emerges from the Qur'an and the practice of the Prophet is a desire to free women from discriminatory pre-Islamic practices and to improve their status vis-à-vis men. The Qur'an specifically prohibited detrimental cultural practices, such as female infanticide; introduced a number of rights that were considered revolutionary for that historical period; and gave women agency and legal capacity, something many women probably did not have before in Arabia. Despite these initiatives, prevailing cultural attitudes remained influential, and it was not long before women lost many of these rights in all but theory. In light of the strong emphasis on women's rights in international human rights instruments and the situation of women on the ground in many parts of the Muslim world, a number of scholars are returning to the egalitarian spirit of the Qur'an's teachings about women and thinking about how this spirit can be applied in our contemporary context. The work of these scholars is revealing compatibilities between Islamic law and international human rights law and showing that there is an Islamic basis for non-discriminatory norms. Demonstrating the Islamic legitimacy of women's rights is an important step towards making improvements in the actual lives of Muslim women around the world. Despite the bleak picture in many parts of the Muslim world at the moment, there is hope that things will begin to change.

* * *

LOOKING AT AN ISSUE CLOSELY: MALAYSIA'S RESERVATIONS TO CEDAW

Marsha A. Freeman, "Reservations to CEDAW: An Analysis for UNICEF" (2009) *United Nations Children's Fund* [UNICEF]. Available https://www.unicef.org/gender/files/Reservations_to_CEDAW-an_Analysis_for_UNICEF.pdf, pp. 16–8. Extract*

Malaysia's reservations to CEDAW provide an example of one Muslim-majority state's interaction with the UN treaty body system and its attempts to grapple with what it understands to be the requirements of the Shari'a and international standards concerning the status and rights of women.

Malaysia

Malaysia's reservations present an unusual set of issues. The first is the scope of the reservations, as the State party's actions have been somewhat confusing. Upon accession in 1995 the State entered a general reservation referring to both *Sharia* law and the Federal Constitution:

> The Government of Malaysia declares that Malaysia's accession is subject to the understanding that the provisions of the Convention do not conflict with the provisions of the Islamic *Sharia*' law and the Federal Constitution of Malaysia. With regards thereto, further, the Government of Malaysia does not consider itself bound by the provisions of articles 2 (f), 5 (a), 7 (b), 9 and 16 of the aforesaid Convention.

Article 2(f) requires States parties to, "without delay, … take all appropriate measures, including legislation, to modify or abolish existing laws, regulations, customs and practices which constitute discrimination against women". This echoes the language of Article 5(a), requiring States parties to modify the social and cultural patterns of conduct of men and women, with a view to achieving the elimination of prejudices and customary and all other practices which are based on the idea of the inferiority or the superiority of either of the sexes or on stereotyped roles for men and women.

The reservations to these two provisions clearly indicate refusal or inability to address the traditions, customs, and stereotyping that underlie discrimination against women. In 1998, however, the State withdrew its reservation to Article 2(f). As to Article 5(a), the State "modified" the reservation, indicating that Article 5(a) was "subject to the division of inherited property" under *Sharia*, thereby apparently agreeing to address custom, tradition, and stereotyping, but leaving in place discriminatory inheritance law.

CEDAW Article 7(b) provides for women, on a basis of equality, "to participate in the formulation of government policy and the implementation thereof and to hold public office and perform all public functions at all levels of government". In 1998 the State "modified" this reservation to provide that Article 7(b) "shall not affect appointment to certain public offices like the Mufti, *Syariah* Court Judges, and the Imam which is in accordance with the provisions of the Islamic *Shariah* law", apparently limiting the reservation to apply only to appointment to religious courts.

Upon accession Malaysia also reserved Article 9 (nationality). Reservations to the entire article are rare, as they not only deny equality with respect to women's transmission of nationality to children (9(2)), but they also result in failure to guarantee women's ability to retain their nationality upon marriage to a foreigner (9(1)). This right has been enshrined in international law since the Convention on the Nationality of Married Women was adopted in 1958,[268] and Malaysia acceded to it in 1959. In 1998 it withdrew the reservation to Article 9(1).

Malaysia also reexamined its reservation to Article 16 (equality in marriage and divorce). Reserving the entire article was a devastating dismissal of any concern for equality in the family, and the state quickly reevaluated. In 1998 the reservations to some parts of Article 16 were withdrawn: 16(b) relating to free choice of spouse and consent to marriage; 16(d) relating to equal rights and responsibilities with respect to children; 16(e) relating to family planning; 16(h) on equal rights to ownership, disposition, and management of property. Apparently the concept of equality with respect to property rights does not, in the eyes of the State party, extend to inheritance, as the remaining reservation to Article 5 quite clearly indicates that equal inheritance rights are not supported.

The procedural issues surrounding the Malaysian government's entry of reservations, attempted modification, and withdrawal of some, are the subject of some concern among legal scholars. As a practical matter, however, "… the consensus seems to have been reached to consider Malaysia's reservations are those remaining after the partial withdrawal".[269]

The second overarching reservation issue relates to Malaysia's religious and ethnic makeup and the way in which its multiple legal systems apply to the different groups. While Islam is the majority religion, and Malaysia is a member of the Organization of the Islamic Conference, that majority is not overwhelming (60% in 2002). The population includes significant numbers of Christians, Hindus, Buddhists, Confucians, and animists, whose freedom to follow their religion is constitutionally protected. Marriage and divorce of Muslims [are] governed by *Sharia*. For non-Muslims, the Law Reform (Marriage and Divorce) Act of 1976 applies to personal status. All other matters are determined by federal law applied uniformly to all population groups.

The State party report alludes to customary as well as Islamic and statutory law and states that "the concept of women's equality in Malaysia is based on the culture and traditional beliefs of its various ethnic groups with the influence of religious values".[270] However, neither the reservations, the State report, nor the constructive dialogue with the Committee addresses the status of customary and non-Muslim religious laws, or the status of women under any of them. The NGO Shadow Report submitted by the National Council for Women's Organisations[271] states that in East Malaysia (Borneo) native custom and the customary legal system apply where at least one of the parties is a native. This issue remains a mystery. Given the considerable impact of customary practices on women's lives, study and clarification of this situation is warranted.

An additional source of confusion and sex discrimination is the variation of Islamic law from state to state (13 states and the Federal Territories). Several states have enacted very conservative versions of Islamic personal status laws. The role of Malay custom in the various state-level understandings of *Sharia* also is unclear. Since the government's obligations under CEDAW include implementation at local levels, the impact of both conservative Islamic law and the interplay of custom and religious practice at the more local levels should be examined.

NOTES

1. Susan A. Lentz, "Revisiting the Rule of Thumb: An Overview of the History of Wife Abuse", *Women & Criminal Justice* 10(2) (1999): 10–11.
2. Christie S. Warren, "Lifting the Veil: Women and Islamic Law", *Cardozo Journal of Law & Gender* 15 (2008–2009): 42. See Karen Armstrong, *Muhammad: A Biography of the Prophet* (San Francisco: Harper, 1992), 60.
3. See Shaheen Sardar Ali, *Conceptualising Islamic Law: CEDAW and Women's Human Rights in Plural Legal Settings: A Comparative Analysis of Application of CEDAW in Bangladesh, India and Pakistan* (New Delhi: UNIFEM—South Asia Regional Office, 2006), 26.
4. Q. 4:3, 4:129.
5. Warren, "Lifting the Veil", 42.
6. See Q. 6:151; 17:31; 81:8–9.

7. Ali, *Conceptualising Islamic Law*, 27.
8. Q. 4:7; 4:11.
9. Ali, *Conceptualising Islamic Law*, 29.
10. Niaz A. Shah, "Women's Human Rights in the Koran: An Interpretive Approach", *Human Rights Quarterly* 28 (2006): 890.
11. Shah, "Women's Human Rights", 890, citing Abdullah Yusuf Ali, *The Meaning of the Holy Qur'an*, 5th edn., 1993, 184, n. 508.
12. Shah, "Women's Human Rights", 890.
13. Q. 4:3, 4:129.
14. Warren, "Lifting the Veil", 40, citing Kathleen A. Portuin Miller, "The Other Side of the Coin: A Look at Islamic Law as Compared to Anglo-American Law—Do Muslim Women Really Have Fewer Rights than American Women?", *New York International Law Review* 16 (2003): 85.
15. Ali, *Conceptualising Islamic Law*, 21.
16. Ibid.
17. Warren, "Lifting the Veil", 39.
18. Ali, *Conceptualising Islamic Law*, 30, referring to Q. 4:20.
19. Q. 58:2–4.
20. See Q. 2:228–31, 4:128.
21. Abdullahi An-Na'im, "The Rights of Women and International Law in the Muslim Context", *Whittier Law Review* 9 (1987–1988): 495.
22. Q. 58:1.
23. Nehaluddin Ahmad, "Modern Debate on the Socio-Political Rights of Muslim Women", *Asia-Pacific Journal on Human Rights and the Law* 1 (2012): 55.
24. Ibid, 56.
25. Ali, *Conceptualising Islamic Law*, 25, citing Fazlur Rahman, "Status of Women in the *Quran*" in *Women and Revolution in Iran*, G. Nashat (ed.) (Boulder, CO: Westview Press, 1983).
26. Warren, "Lifting the Veil", 45. See Azizah al-Hibri, "Islam, Law, and Custom: Redefining Muslim Women's Rights", *American University Journal of International Law and Policy* 12 (1997): 5–8.
27. Warren, "Lifting the Veil", 45; see also Ali, *Conceptualising Islamic Law*, 12–13.
28. Warren, "Lifting the Veil", 46. See al-Hibri, "Islam, Law, and Custom", 7.
29. Ali, *Conceptualising Islamic Law*, 22.
30. See, for instance, Ali, *Conceptualising Islamic Law*, 22.
31. Ziba Mir-Hosseini, "The Politics and Hermeneutics of Hijab in Iran: From Confinement to Choice", *Muslim World Journal of Human Rights* 4(1) (2007): 3.
32. Ibid.
33. Ibid.
34. This verse has since been used as the basis of legislation in a number of Muslim-majority jurisdictions, including Pakistan.
35. Nehaluddin Ahmad, "Comment: Women's Testimony in Islamic Law and Misconceptions. A Critical Analysis", *Religion and Human Rights* 6 (2011): 18.
36. Ibid.
37. Ali, *Conceptualising Islamic Law*, 45–6.
38. Shah, "Women's Human Rights", 890.
39. An-Na'im, "The Rights of Women", 495.
40. Ibid, 495–6.
41. Ibid, 496.
42. Ali, *Conceptualising Islamic Law*, 16, citing Natalie Kaufman Hevener, *International Law and the Status of Women* (Boulder, CO: Westview Press, 1983), 4.
43. Ali, *Conceptualising Islamic Law*, 16.
44. Ibid, citing Hevener, *International Law and the Status of Women*, 4.
45. Ibid, 16–17.
46. Ibid, 17, citing Hevener, *International Law and the Status of Women*, 4.

47. See Articles 1 and 2 of the UDHR.
48. United Nations General Assembly, *Universal Declaration of Human Rights*, 10 December 1948, 217 A (III). Available http://www.refworld.org/docid/3ae6b3712c.html (last accessed 6 December 2017).
49. United Nations General Assembly, *International Covenant on Civil and Political Rights* (*ICCPR*), 16 December 1966, United Nations, Treaty Series, vol. 999, p. 171. Available http://www.refworld.org/docid/3ae6b3aa0.html (last accessed 6 December 2017), Article 23(2).
50. *ICCPR* Article 23(4).
51. Human Rights Committee, "General Comment No. 19: Article 23 (The Family)". 27 July 1990. Available http://tbinternet.ohchr.org/_layouts/treatybodyexternal/TBSearch.aspx?Lang=en&TreatyID=8&DocTypeID=11, [8] (last accessed 6 December 2017).
52. Ibid.
53. Ibid, [9].
54. Human Rights Committee, "Concluding Observations on the Third Periodic Report of Kuwait". 11 August 2016. UN Doc CCPR/C/KWT/CO/3, [14].
55. Human Rights Committee, "Concluding Observations on the Second Periodic Report of Tajikistan". 22 August 2013. UN Doc CCPR/C/TJK/CO/2, [6].
56. *ICCPR* Article 25.
57. Ibid.
58. Human Rights Committee, "Concluding Observations on the Second Periodic Report of Tajikistan", [6].
59. Ibid.
60. *ICCPR* Article 6(5).
61. Committee on Economic, Social and Cultural Rights (Comm ESCR), "General Comment No. 16 (2005) The Equal Right of Men and Women to the Enjoyment of all Economic, Social and Cultural Rights (art. 3 of the International Covenant on Economic, Social and Cultural Rights)". 11 August 2005. UN Doc E/C.12/2005/4, [18].
62. Ibid.
63. Ibid, [19].
64. Comm ESCR, "Concluding Observations on the Second Periodic Report of Lebanon". 24 October 2016. UN Doc E/C.12/LBN/CO/2, [27].
65. Comm ESCR, "Concluding Observations of the Committee on Economic, Social and Cultural Rights: Mauritius". 8 June 2010. UN Doc E/C.12/MUS/CO/4, [15].
66. Ibid.
67. United Nations General Assembly, *International Covenant on Economic, Social and Cultural Rights* (*ICESCR*), 16 December 1966, United Nations, Treaty Series, vol. 993, p. 3. Available http://www.refworld.org/docid/3ae6b36c0.html, Articles 6 and 7 (last accessed 6 December 2017).
68. Comm ESCR, "Concluding Observations on the Second Periodic Report of Lebanon", [27].
69. Ibid, [28].
70. *ICESCR* Article 10(1).
71. Comm ESCR, "General Comment No. 16 (2005) The Equal Right of Men and Women", [27].
72. See, for instance, the review of the second to fourth periodic reports of Mauritius (2010) where the state party was requested to consider "ongoing constitutional reform and [that] all personal laws relating to adoption, marriage, divorce, burial or devolution of property on death are governed by the principle of non-discrimination". Comm ESCR, "Concluding observations of the Committee on Economic, Social and Cultural Rights: Mauritius", [14].
73. *ICESCR* Article 10(2).
74. *ICESCR* Article 2(1).
75. An-Na'im, "The Rights of Women", 508.
76. An-Na'im, "The Rights of Women", 508.
77. See Ali, *Conceptualising Islamic Law*, 72–3.
78. Ibid, 73.

79. United Nations General Assembly, *Convention on the Elimination of All Forms of Discrimination against Women (CEDAW)*, 18 December 1979, United Nations, Treaty Series, vol. 1249, p. 13, Article 15 (a) and (b). Available http://www.refworld.org/docid/3ae6b3970.html (last accessed 11 January 2018).
80. Committee on the Elimination of All forms of Discrimination against Women (Comm EDAW), "General Recommendation No. 21: Equality in Marriage and Family Relations" (1994). UN Doc A/49/38. Available http://www.un.org/womenwatch/daw/cedaw/recommendations/recomm.htm#recom12, [7] (last accessed 8 December 2017).
81. Ibid, [8].
82. Ibid.
83. Ibid, [12].
84. Ibid.
85. Comm EDAW, "Concluding Observations on the Eighth Periodic Report of Bangladesh". 18 November 2016. UN Doc CEDAW/C/BGD/CO/8, [16].
86. Comm EDAW, "Concluding Observations on the Initial Report of Qatar". 10 March 2014. UN Doc CEDAW/C/QAT/CO/1, [21].
87. Comm EDAW, "General Recommendation No. 21", [17].
88. Ibid.
89. Ibid, [14].
90. Ibid, [16].
91. Ibid, [38].
92. Ibid, [20].
93. Ibid, [28].
94. Ibid, [35].
95. Comm EDAW, "Concluding Observations on the Eighth Periodic Report of Bangladesh", [42].
96. Comm EDAW, "General Recommendation No. 23: Political and Public Life" (1997). UN Doc A/52/38. Available http://www.un.org/womenwatch/daw/cedaw/recommendations/recomm.htm#recom12, [5] (last accessed 8 December 2017).
97. Ibid, [8].
98. Ibid, [10].
99. Comm EDAW, "Concluding observations on the initial report of Qatar", [27].
100. See Bharath Anandi Venkatraman, "Islamic States and the United Nations Convention on the Elimination of All Forms of Discrimination against Women: Are the *Sharia* and the Convention Compatible?", *American University Law Review* 44 (1994–1995): 2004.
101. Warren, "Lifting the Veil", 59.
102. Ibid, 61. See also Leila P. Sayeh and Adriaen M. Morse, Jr, "Islam and the Treatment of Women: An Incomplete Understanding of Gradualism", *Texas International Law Journal* 30 (1995): 331–2.
103. An-Na'im, "Rights of Women", 515.
104. Ibid.
105. Ibid.
106. Ibid.
107. Ibid, 497.
108. Ibid, 514.
109. Ibid, 497.
110. Shah, "Women's Human Rights", 881.
111. Ali, *Conceptualising Islamic Law*, 3.
112. Ibid, 88.
113. Ibid.
114. Ibid, 3.
115. Ibid.
116. Özlem Altıok, "Muslim Family Laws and CEDAW: A Factsheet" (2015). Available https://www.socwomen.org/wp-content/uploads/Muslim-Family-Laws.pdf, 3 (last accessed 8 December 2017).

117. Marsha A. Freeman, "Reservations to CEDAW: An Analysis for UNICEF" (2009). Available http://www.unicef.org/gender/files/Reservations_to_CEDAW-an_Analysis_for_UNICEF.pdf, 6 (last accessed 8 December 2017).
118. Ibid.
119. Social Watch, "The Arab Region: 30 Years of CEDAW" (2010). Available http://www.socialwatch.org/sites/default/files/B15ArabRegion2010_eng.pdf (last accessed 8 December 2017.
120. Freeman, "Reservations to CEDAW", i.
121. Office of the High Commissioner for Human Rights (OHCHR), "Status of Ratification: Interactive Dashboard". The United Nations: Human Rights. Available http://indicators.ohchr.org (last accessed 8 December 2017).
122. Ibid.
123. Ibid.
124. Human Rights Committee, "List of Issues in Relation to the Third Periodic Report of Kuwait. Addendum: Replies of Kuwait to the List of Issues". UN Doc CCPR/C/KWT/Q/3/Ad. 21 April 2016, [7].
125. Ibid.
126. Ibid.
127. OHCHR, "Status of Ratification".
128. Ali, *Conceptualising Islamic Law*, 86.
129. OHCHR, "Status of Ratification".
130. Mahmuda Islam, "CEDAW and Bangladesh: A Study to Explore the Possibilities of Full Implementation of CEDAW in Bangladesh" in *Conceptualising Islamic Law*, 202.
131. Comm EDAW, "Replies of Pakistan to the List of Issues to be Taken up in Connection with the Consideration of its Fourth Periodic Report", UN Doc CEDAW/C/PAK/Q4/Add.1, 27 November 2012, [7c].
132. Ibid, [2].
133. Ibid, [7c].
134. Ali, *Conceptualising Islamic Law*, 259.
135. Comm EDAW, "Replies of Pakistan to the List of Issues", [22].
136. Ihsan Yilmaz, "Pakistan Federal Shariat Court's Collective Ijtihād on Gender Equality, Women's Rights and the Right to Family Life", *Islam and Christian–Muslim Relations* 25(2) (2014): 186.
137. Yilmaz, "Pakistan Federal Shariat Court's Collective Ijtihād", 187, citing Suo Moto No. 1/K of 2006, *Pakistan Citizenship Act 1951*, Re: Gender Equality, at 23 and 24.
138. Ibid, 187.
139. Ibid.
140. M. Ilyas Khan, "Why Is a Pakistani Bill to Protect Women Unpopular", *BBC News*, 17 March 2016. Available http://www.bbc.com/news/world-asia-35811180 (last accessed 8 December 2017).
141. Zara Jamal, "To Be a Woman in Pakistan: Six Stories of Abuse, Shame and Survival", *The Atlantic*, 9 April 2012. Available http://www.theatlantic.com/international/archive/2012/04/to-be-a-woman-in-pakistan-six-stories-of-abuse-shame-and-survival/255585 (last accessed 8 December 2017).
142. Khan, "Pakistani Bill".
143. Islam, "CEDAW and Bangladesh", 213.
144. Comm EDAW, "Concluding Observations on the Fourth Periodic Report of Pakistan". 27 March 2013. UN Doc CEDAW/C/PAK/CO/4, [21].
145. Islam, "CEDAW and Bangladesh", 205.
146. Ibid, 219.
147. Ibid, 218.
148. Ibid, 218–19.
149. Jamal, "To Be a Woman in Pakistan".
150. Khan, "Pakistani Bill".

151. Comm EDAW, "Concluding Observations of the Committee on the Elimination of Discrimination against Women: Tunisia". 5 November 2010. UN Doc CEDAW/C/TUN/CO/6, [38].
152. Ibid, [36].
153. Ibid, [16].
154. Ibid, [24].
155. Ibid.
156. Ibid, [17].
157. Freeman, "Reservations to CEDAW", 3.
158. Ibid.
159. Ibid, 6.
160. Ibid.
161. Ibid, 26.
162. Ali, *Conceptualising Islamic Law*, 18–19.
163. Shah, "Women's Human Rights", 884.
164. Q. 7:18–26.
165. See Q. 2:35–36; 7:18–26; 20:116–22.
166. Ali, *Conceptualising Islamic Law*, 24.
167. Ibid, 25.
168. Ibid.
169. Asma Barlas, "Amina Wadud's Hermeneutics of the Qur'an: Women Reading Sacred Texts", in *Modern Muslim Intellectuals and the Qur'an*, Suha Taji-Farouki (ed.) (Oxford: Oxford University Press, 2004), 101.
170. Ibid, 101–2.
171. Ibid, 102.
172. Ibid, 101–2.
173. Ibid, 103.
174. Ibid, 110.
175. Amina Wadud, *Qur'an and Woman: Rereading the Sacred Text from a Woman's Perspective* (New York: Oxford University Press, 1999), 3.
176. Ibid, 78.
177. Barlas, "Amina Wadud's Hermeneutics", 107.
178. Wadud, *Qur'an and Woman*, 15.
179. Rachel M. Scott, "A Contextual Approach to Women's Rights in the Qur'an: Readings of 4:34", *The Muslim World* 99 (2009): 74. See Wadud, *Qur'an and Woman*, 63–4.
180. Wadud, *Qur'an and Woman*, 9.
181. Scott, "A Contextual Approach to Women's Rights", 74, citing Wadud, *Qur'an and Woman*, 64.
182. Asma Barlas, *"Believing Women" in Islam: Unreading Patriarchal Interpretations of the Qur'an* (Houston, TX: University of Texas Press, 2002), 15.
183. Barlas, "The Qur'an, Sexual Equality, and Feminism". Speech presented at the University of Toronto on 12 January 2004, 4. Available http://www.asmabarlas.com/TALKS/20040112_UToronto.pdf (last accessed 8 December 2017).
184. Barlas, *"Believing Women"*, 147–8.
185. Ibid, 142–3.
186. Barlas, "The Qur'an, Sexual Equality, and Feminism", 5.
187. Barlas, *"Believing Women"*, 206.
188. Ibid.
189. Asma Barlas, "Does the Qur'an Support Gender Equality? Or, Do I Have the Autonomy to Answer This Question?" Paper delivered at a Workshop on Islam and Autonomy at the University of Groningen, 24 November 2006, 5. Available http://www.asmabarlas.com/TALKS/Groningen_Keynote.pdf, 5 (last accessed 8 December 2017).
190. Asma Barlas, "Muslim Women and Sexual Oppression: Reading Liberation from the Quran", *Macalester International* 10 (2001): 129.
191. Asma Barlas, "Does the Qur'an Support Gender Equality?", 5.

192. Kecia Ali, *Marriage and Slavery in Early Islam* (Cambridge, MA: Harvard University Press, 2010), 3.
193. Ibid.
194. Ibid, 4.
195. Ibid.
196. Ibid.
197. Riffat Hassan, "Muslim Women and Post-Patriarchal Islam", in *After Patriarchy: Feminist Transformations of the World's Religions*, Paula M. Cooey, William R. Eakin and Jay B. McDaniel (eds.) (Maryknoll, NY: Orbis Books, 1991), 41.
198. Ibid, 43.
199. Ibid.
200. Fazlur Rahman, *Islam and Modernity: Transformation of an Intellectual Tradition* (Chicago: University of Chicago Press, 1984), 5.
201. Shah, "Women's Human Rights", 881.
202. Rahman, *Islam and Modernity*, 6.
203. Ibid, 7.
204. Ibid.
205. An-Na'im, "The Rights of Women", 500.
206. Ibid, 501.
207. Ibid.
208. Khaled Abou El Fadl, *Reasoning with God* (Lanham, MA: Rowman & Littlefield, 2014), xxxiii.
209. Ibid.
210. Ibid.
211. Ibid.
212. Khaled Abou El Fadl, "In Recognition of Women" (2011). Available http://www.scholarofthehouse.org/inreofwobykh.html (last accessed 8 December 2017).
213. Warren, "Lifting the Veil" citing Khaled Abou El Fadl, *Speaking in God's Name: Islamic Law, Authority, and Women* (London: Oneworld, 2001), 230.
214. Mashood A. Baderin, *International Human Rights and Islamic Law* (Oxford: Oxford University Press, 2005), 60.
215. Human Rights Committee, "General Comment 28: Article 3 (The Equality of Rights between Men and Women)". 29 March 2000. UN Doc CCPR/C/21/Rev.1/Add.10, [5]. Available http://www.refworld.org/docid/45139c9b4.html (last accessed 8 December 2017).
216. Mashood A. Baderin, *International Human Rights*, 62.
217. Norris and Inglehart, "Islamic Culture and Democracy", 235–36.
218. Human Rights Committee, "General Comment 28", [24].
219. Ruth Gaffney-Rhys, "A Comparison of Child Marriage and Polygamy from a Human Rights Perspective: Are the Arguments Equally Cogent?" *Journal of Social Welfare & Family Law* 34(1) (2012): 53, citing Comm EDAW, "General Recommendation 21 on Equality in Marriage and Family Relations." (1994) UN Doc A/47/38, [14].
220. Amina Wadud, *Qur'an and Woman*, 83.
221. Ibid.
222. Ibid.
223. Ibid.
224. See, for instance, discussion by Niaz A. Shah, "Women's Human Rights in the Koran", 890–91.
225. Venkatraman, "Islamic States", 44.
226. Wadud, *Qur'an and Woman*, 84.
227. Ibid.
228. Ibid.
229. Mashood A. Baderin, *International Human Rights*, 141.
230. Ibid.
231. Bustami Mohamed Khir, "The Right of Women to No-Fault Divorce in Islam and its Application by British Muslims", *Islam and Christian–Muslim Relations* 17(3) (2006): 296.

232. Ibid.
233. Ibid; Baderin, *International Human Rights*, 149.
234. Baderin, *International Human Rights*, 149; Khir, "The Right of Women to No-Fault Divorce", 297.
235. Baderin, *International Human Rights*, 150.
236. Ibid, 149.
237. *CEDAW*, Article 16(1)(c).
238. Human Rights Committee, "General Comment 28", [26].
239. Baderin, *International Human Rights*, 150.
240. Wadud, *Qur'an and Woman*, 79.
241. Ibid, 80.
242. Ibid.
243. Venkatraman, "Islamic States", 2008.
244. John L. Esposito with Natana J. DeLong-Bas, *Women in Muslim Family Law*, 2nd edn. (Syracuse, NY: Syracuse University Press, 2001), 34.
245. Baderin, *International Human Rights*, 151.
246. Ibid.
247. Ibid.
248. Niaz A. Shah, "Women's Human Rights in the Koran", 895.
249. Baderin, *International Human Rights*, 147.
250. Ibid, 146. See Human Rights Committee, "General Comment 28", [26].
251. Wadud, *Qur'an and Woman*, 87.
252. Ibid.
253. Ibid, 88.
254. Venkatraman, "Islamic States", 2008.
255. Baderin, *International Human Rights*, 148.
256. Ibid.
257. Ibid, 62. See Human Rights Committee, "General Comment 28", [5].
258. Barlas, *"Believing Women"*, 73.
259. Ibid.
260. Ibid, 74.
261. Fatema Mernissi, *The Veil and the Male Elite: A Feminist Interpretation of Women's Rights in Islam [Le harem politique]* (New York: Addison-Wesley, 1996), 180.
262. Ibid.
263. Ibid.
264. Barlas, *"Believing Women"*, 75.
265. Ibid.
266. Baderin, *International Human Rights*, 64. See also B.F. Stowasser, *Women in the Qur'an, Traditions, and Interpretation* (New York: Oxford University Press, 1994), 93–4.
267. Baderin, *International Human Rights*, 66.
268. Opened for signature and ratification by General Assembly Resolution 1040 (XI) of 29 January 1957. Entered into force 11 August 1958.
269. Ekaterina Yahyaoui Krivenko, *Women, Islam and International Law within the Context of the Convention on the Elimination of All Forms of Discrimination against Women* (Leiden: Martinus Nijhoff Publishers, 2009), 118 fn. 383.
270. Comm EDAW, "Consideration of State Party Reports, Combined Initial and Second Periodic Report of Malaysia" 2005. UN Doc CEDAW/C/MYS/1-2, [380].
271. http://www.iwraw-ap.org/resources/pdf/Malaysia_SR.pdf.

8. The rights of the child

INTRODUCTION

Islamic tradition has a long history of protecting the rights of children. The Qur'an and the Prophet both emphasise the need to treat vulnerable people in the community, such as the old and very young, with special care and respect.[1] As Kamran Hashemi notes, "[b]ased on this principle ... early Muslims established special arrangements and legal institutions for the care of children".[2]

This chapter first outlines the arrangements and protections established by Islamic law for children. It sets out the norms affirmed by the Qur'an and the Prophet's practice and examines the Islamic human rights instruments that have been developed by Muslim-majority states with provisions to protect children. The chapter then sets out the international framework for protecting children's rights. The Convention on the Rights of the Child is one of the most ratified treaties in the world, so the chapter looks closely at some of its provisions and identifies areas of compatibility and tension with Islamic law. It concludes that, while there are differences in the language and conceptual framework used by Islamic law to protect children, there are strong compatibilities between Islam's fundamental message and the international human rights framework.

THE RIGHTS OF CHILDREN IN ISLAM

The rights of children are an important part of Islamic legal thinking today, and have been since the emergence of Islam almost 1,400 years ago. As Geraldine van Bueren argues, "the very concept that children possess rights has a far older tradition in Islamic law than in international law, where the notion did not emerge until the twentieth century".[3] When Islam emerged, it set out to address a number of tribal customs that were harmful to children. One of the most troubling was the practice of female infanticide by some Arabian tribes. This practice was most likely tied to ideas of tribal honour and shame and the reality of tribal warfare. It was common, at the time, for a winning tribe to enslave the women and children of the defeated tribe. This was a source of shame to be avoided; hence surplus female children were to be put to death in some cases. Another reason for the practice of infanticide was poverty. Children were sacrificed if they were deemed unable to produce wealth in the future, again targeting baby girls who would not be raised to be breadwinners. In response to this cultural practice, the Qur'an very clearly prohibited female infanticide and emphasised that babies of both sexes should be treated with equal care. The banning of female infanticide is regarded as a crucial point in the Islamic discourse on the rights of the child.[4]

There are a wide range of texts in the Qur'an and hadith literature that address the treatment of children and remind parents and society in general of their responsibility towards children,[5] recognising that they are highly vulnerable. Children are considered a fundamental blessing and must be raised with this in mind. The Qur'an and the Prophet therefore developed a wide range of duties and obligations for parents and guardians, addressing their general care, maintenance, and education, as well as specific issues that particularly concern children, such as breast-feeding, adoption, and protection from infanticide.[6]

Islamic views on the rights of children include the idea that parents are responsible for teaching children the necessary ethical, moral, and religious values that make up Islam. The Qur'an acknowledges that both a mother and father are crucial for raising children; however, if a child's parents are unable to do this, the community has the responsibility to provide the necessary support. The Qur'an recognises that children are crucial to the future of society and therefore insists on them being treated with the utmost care and respect. They should be protected from "adult conflicts" because they are "born innocent"[7] and are to be raised with the broader community in mind, suggesting that the welfare of the community and the welfare of the child go hand in hand. Finally, legal guidelines for guardianship and custody have also been established in Islamic law.

Masoud Rajabi-Ardeshiri argues that Islamic law extends the rights of the child to the unborn child. For instance, if a mother miscarries, the foetus must be buried with the same rituals as any other Muslim. In other words, the body of the foetus must be treated with the same dignity and respect granted to any other human person.[8]

In summary, while the Qur'an and hadith do not express the rights of children in the same language as the contemporary human rights discourse, it is possible to tie their fundamental message to the international framework that protects children's rights. Indeed, Abdel Rahim Omran argues that the Qur'an and prophetic precedent establish a set of rights for children. These include the right to life; the right to have a good name; the right to be breastfed and provided with shelter, maintenance and support; the right to education; and the right to equitable treatment irrespective of gender.[9]

THE RIGHTS OF CHILDREN IN ISLAMIC HUMAN RIGHTS INSTRUMENTS

Perhaps recognising the importance of these protections in Islamic tradition, a number of Islamic human rights instruments also contain specific provisions for protecting the rights of children. One of the first formal declarations solely on children's rights was made in 1994 at the Twenty-Second Conference of Foreign Ministers from the Organization of the Islamic Conference (OIC—now Organisation of Islamic Cooperation) in Casablanca, Morocco.[10] Significantly, this declaration calls upon its member states to "sign and ratify the UN 1989 Convention on the Rights of the Child ... and bring their constitutions, laws and practices into conformity with the provisions of the Convention".[11] As Rajabi-Ardeshiri states, the declaration affirms that "the right to lineage, social, health, psychological and cultural care, ownership, and education are among the most important rights considered necessary for children".[12] However, there are also a number of obvious contradictions between the declaration and international human rights standards.[13] For example, Article 8 of the declaration, on the right to education, states:

> While Islam guarantees Man's freedom to voluntarily adopt Islam without compulsion, it prohibits apostasy of a Muslim afterwards, in view of the fact that Islam is the Seal of Religions and, therefore, the Islamic society is committed to ensuring that the sons of Muslims preserve their Islamic nature and Creed and to protecting them against attempts to force them to relinquish their religion.[14]

This statement appears to curtail the principle of freedom of religion that can be found in the Convention on the Rights of the Child (CRC), which will be discussed in more detail below. Article 14 of the CRC declares, "States Parties shall respect the right of the child to freedom of thought, conscience and religion."[15]

The 1981 Universal Islamic Declaration of Human Rights (UIDHR)[16] also makes several references to children, mainly affirming parental responsibility for their upbringing. In addition, Article 19 of the UIDHR declares children's responsibilities towards their parents, stating that "parents are entitled to material support as well as care and protection from their children".[17] Rajabi-Ardeshiri observes that the "emphasis on children's responsibilities towards their parents alongside children's rights represents one of the earliest interventions by Muslim countries in the debate on the rights of the child".[18] The issue of children's duties or responsibilities will be discussed further below.

Article 7 of the Cairo Declaration on Human Rights in Islam (CDHRI) affirms that "every child ... [has the right to] proper nursing, education and material, hygienic and moral care",[19] which parents and society more broadly are responsible for providing. Article 7 of the CDHRI also gives parents or guardians the right to choose their children's form of education: "Parents and those in such like capacity have the right to choose the type of education they desire for their children, provided they take into consideration the interest and future of the children in accordance with ethical values and the principles of the Shariah."[20]

COVENANT ON THE RIGHTS OF THE CHILD IN ISLAM

The Covenant on the Rights of the Child in Islam was drafted by the Organization of the Islamic Conference and adopted at the 32nd Conference of Foreign Ministers in June, 2005.[21] It was preceded by the Dhaka Declaration on Human Rights in Islam (1983), the Cairo Declaration on Human Rights in Islam (1990) and the Declaration on the Rights and Care of the Child in Islam (1994).[22] The Covenant is significant because it is the first binding human rights instrument adopted by the OIC.[23]

The Covenant specifically aims to protect the rights of children, recognising the significant responsibility that Islamic states have towards children as "the vanguard and maker of the future of the Ummah".[24] It acknowledges the special vulnerability of children, who, potentially, "bear the burden of the greater suffering as a result of natural and man-made disasters leading to tragic consequences".[25] As a result, it establishes three state obligations:

> Respect the rights stipulated in this Covenant, and take the necessary steps to enforce it in accordance with their domestic regulations.
>
> Respect the responsibilities and duties of parents, legal guardians or other persons that are legally responsible for the child in accordance with existing domestic regulations as required by the child's interest
>
> End action based on customs, traditions or practices that are in conflict with the rights and duties stipulated in this Covenant.[26]

The Covenant goes on to recognise the following rights and freedoms: the principle of equality; the right to life; the right to identity; the right to family cohesion; the right to certain personal freedoms (expressing personal views; having a personal life); freedom of assembly; the right to a sound upbringing; the right to education and culture; the right to rest and activity times; the right to a suitable standard of living and to some elements of social security; the right to health; special protection for the disabled and children with special needs; the right to justice; and the right to certain protections in the context of child labour, and so on.

According to several commentators, the rights established by the Covenant fall short of international standards for children and of the rights prescribed by the Convention on the Rights of the Child. NGOs describe many of its articles as "brief in nature and weak in terms of strength and enforcement".[27] Other shortcomings include the absence of a definition of a "child" (in terms of specifying an age of maturity); the lack of protection for children in Muslim-majority states who are at risk of terrorism and landmines; and the lack of provisions for children in conflict situations.[28] According to Mosaffa, its position toward child protection is "weaker" than the position of other documents in international humanitarian law[29] when it comes to children in armed conflict.

At the time of writing the number of its signatories is unknown and the status of the Covenant is uncertain.[30] Moreover, it appears that very few member states of the OIC have taken steps to put into place legislative changes or national mechanisms to ensure its provisions are implemented.[31]

THE RIGHTS OF THE CHILD IN INTERNATIONAL LAW

The international framework protecting the rights of the child rests on the principles of equality and non-discrimination, extending those fundamental norms to all human beings, regardless of age. There are also a host of specific provisions which establish special protection for children. Two articles of the Universal Declaration of Human Rights (UDHR) explicitly address their situation, establishing social protection for children (and mothers) and, as part of the right to education, affirming that parents have the right to choose the type of education their children receive. Article 25(b) states "Motherhood and childhood are entitled to special care and assistance. All children, whether born in or out of wedlock, shall enjoy the same social protection."[32]

Article 26(3) states "Parents have a prior right to choose the kind of education that shall be given to their children."[33]

The International Covenant on Civil and Political Rights (ICCPR) addresses the situation of children more extensively, with four articles related to children. Article 18 affirms the freedom of parents and legal guardians "to ensure the religious and moral education of their children in line with their own convictions",[34] and Article 23 emphasises "provision shall be made for the necessary protection of any children" in the case of divorce.[35] Article 24 is the most extensive provision in the ICCPR, recognising children's need for special protection by the family, society, and the state, and establishing this right, regardless of the child's "race, colour, sex, language, religion, national or social origin, property or birth".[36] The article also requires children to be named and their birth registered, and gives them the right to "acquire a nationality".[37]

However, the Human Rights Committee has emphasised that these are not the only rights for children established by the ICCPR. Indeed, all of the civil rights in the Covenant apply to children. Some articles even specify a greater protection for children than for adults.[38] For instance, Article 6, concerning the right to life, disallows the death penalty to be imposed on those under 18 years; whereas it can be imposed on adults in certain circumstances. Likewise, children must be separated from adults in prison and treated according to their age.[39] Importantly, the ICCPR does not specify an "age of majority" but leaves this up to states to determine. Even so, a state "cannot absolve itself from its obligations under the Covenant regarding persons under the age of 18, notwithstanding that they have reached the age of majority under domestic law".[40]

The Convention on the Rights of the Child

Efforts to produce a comprehensive international treaty on children's rights began in the second half of the twentieth century. 1979 was made the International Year of the Child, and this event was used to promote the idea of children's rights, with the aim of establishing them in the mainstream human rights discourse shortly afterwards.[41] Ten years later a convention was formalised.

The International Convention on the Rights of the Child (CRC) was adopted in 1989, and came into force in 1990.[42] Every nation in the world is a party to the convention and has ratified it, except the United States of America, which is only a signatory.[43] This widely accepted convention is the most comprehensive human rights document related to children. Indeed, it has been described as "the most comprehensive single treaty in the human rights field".[44]

The CRC is founded on the principle of the best interests of the child, a norm which "pre-dates the Convention" and can be found in a number of other international and regional instruments and national laws.[45] Article 3(1) specifies that a child's best interests "shall be a primary consideration" in "all actions … whether undertaken by public or private social welfare institutions, courts of law, administrative authorities or legislative bodies".[46] The principle of the child's best interests is also a lens through which "all the rights of the child" are interpreted and implemented.[47]

Article 1 establishes the definition of a child as any human being under the age of eighteen.[48] States are allowed to establish majority at a different age (for example under the age of eighteen) but they are required to justify their position to the treaty's monitoring committee, the Committee on the Rights of the Child.[49]

The remaining forty articles can be divided into various categories. A number of rights ensure that a child's basic needs for survival are met. These rights ensure adequate food, reasonable shelter, clean water, basic health care, and basic education (Article 24). Importantly, these rights all require reasonable resources from the state to be fulfilled. Other rights sit in the category of protective rights. These include the right to be protected from various kinds of child abuse and exploitation (Article 34), cruelty, and neglect, and, in times of war, protection from the effects of war (Article 39). Finally, other rights can be described as participatory rights (Article 12; Article 13; Article 14 and so on). They include the right to express an opinion, the right to be heard, the right to relevant information, and freedom of association. These rights aim to assist the development of the child, to help them become active members of their society, and reach their full potential.

While the CRC provides a wide range of protections for children, there are challenges when it comes to implementation. One of these is that the CRC allows for general agreement on issues associated with the welfare of children, but it also relies on a set of assumptions that may conflict with the values or norms of some cultures. One example is the legal age of majority. Different cultures conceive maturity differently and some may argue that the way childhood is conceptualised in the CRC is based on a "Western" understanding. This is the view of Vanessa Pupavac,[50] who argues that the CRC reflects "Western social policies which emphasise the role of individual causations and professional interventions and de-emphasise the influence of the wider social, economic, political and cultural circumstances".[51] However, Kristina Bentley observes that:

> While it is certainly the case that the CRC reflects this bias, it is also important to note that many of the rights included in the convention are … not specifically *children's* rights [original emphasis], but rather fall under the broader aegis of human rights. The reason these rights are included … in the CRC is … because children are more vulnerable to their abuse.[52]

MUSLIM STATES' RESPONSES TO THE CRC

Since Islamic law sets out a variety of protections for children, Muslim states, in general, are reasonably comfortable with the provisions of the CRC. This is evident in the fact that all Muslim-majority states have ratified it;[53] however, as is the case with other conventions, many states have submitted reservations against various articles. These generally claim that the article(s) conflict with aspects of Islamic law or the Shari'a.[54] Indeed, along with the Convention on the Elimination of All Forms of Discrimination against Women (CEDAW), the CRC has received the most religion-based reservations by Muslim states, either against specific articles or against the convention as a whole.[55]

Qatar, Kuwait, Saudi Arabia, and Iran, for example, have submitted general reservations against the treaty as a whole. When Qatar ratified the CRC on 3 April 1995, it entered a general reservation against "any of its provisions that are inconsistent with the Islamic sharia".[56] Similarly, Kuwait entered "reservations on all provisions of the Convention that are incompatible with the laws of Islamic Shari'a", as well as local statutes in effect.[57] The reservations submitted by Iran and Saudi Arabia are expressed using similar wording. In terms of reservations against specific articles, Iraq has entered a reservation against Article 14 on freedom of religion, stating that "allowing a child to change his or her religion runs counter to the provisions of the Islamic Shariah".[58] Likewise, Jordan has submitted a reservation against Article 14, stating it does not consider itself bound by the article since it is "at variance with the precepts of the tolerant Islamic Shariah".[59] It has also entered reservations against Articles 20 and 21 of the convention, which concern adoption,[60] as have several other Muslim-majority states.[61] Apart from these articles, other problematic articles for some Muslim-majority states include Article 7 (right to birth registration and nationality), Article 13 (freedom of expression), Article 16 (protection against unlawful interference in a child's privacy, family, or correspondence) and Article 17 (access to information). While most of these reservations are made referring to Islamic law, some nations also express reservations against articles that conflict with their national constitution.

The CRC also has two optional protocols. The first prohibits the sale of children, child prostitution, and child pornography, and the second aims to prevent the involvement of children in armed hostilities. With the exception of Somalia, all Muslim-majority states have ratified the First Optional Protocol. Most Muslim-majority states have ratified the Second Optional Protocol, while Pakistan, Iran, and Somalia have only signed it.[62] Mauritania has not signed or ratified the second Protocol.[63]

TENSIONS BETWEEN THE CRC AND ISLAMIC NOTIONS OF CHILDREN'S RIGHTS

As we have seen, special protection for children and their rights has a long history in Islamic tradition; it is not a purely modern concept. However, the main area that Islamic tradition emphasises that is not part of the contemporary human rights discourse is the child's obligations to his or her parents. That is to say, Islam also places obligations on children; most notably, that it is the responsibility of the child to look after their parents when they are older and in need of support. Two key verses in the Qur'an address the issue of the child's care of their parents:

> Your Lord has commanded that you should worship none but Him, and that you be kind to your parents. If either or both of them reach old age with you, say no word that shows impatience with them, and do not be harsh with them, but speak to them respectfully. (Q. 17:23)

and

> Lower your wing in humility towards them in kindness and say, "Lord, have mercy on them, just as they cared for me when I was little". (Q. 17:24)

The Qur'an, the Prophet's practice, and Islamic law make it clear that children and parents have mutual obligations toward each other and reciprocal rights to care for one another. These are so important that some "contemporary Muslim scholars argue that rights of the parents come next after [the] rights of God and disobeying the parents is regarded as a major, unforgivable sin".[64]

There are a number of key differences between Islamic and international conceptions of children's rights. As noted above, some argue that the notion of childhood the CRC protects is largely a Western ideal. It depicts childhood as "a time of play and training" where children "should be protected from the adult world".[65] Bentley argues that this notion of childhood sees children as "passive objects of duties".[66] It does not allow them "any significant levels of autonomy nor does it require of them responsibility for … decisions".[67]

The concept of the legal age of adulthood is also a sticking point because traditional Islamic law does not consider the transition from childhood to adulthood as associated only with age. Instead, it is connected with "maturity" (*bulugh*).[68] When a child reaches maturity, according to Islamic law, there are a whole range of duties and responsibilities that he or she must bear. One example is criminal responsibility. For example, today in Iran, criminal responsibility is based upon "maturity".[69] For girls, the age of maturity is usually significantly lower than for boys, a considerable difference with international law. The Iranian Penal Code states "Article 147: The age[s] of maturity for girls and boys are, respectively, a full nine and fifteen lunar years."[70]

Islamic law also grants certain rights upon adulthood, such as the right to deal with property or to decide on matters of marriage.[71] The age of maturity also affects a child's marriageable age. In some Muslim-majority states the marriageable age for girls is sixteen (in Indonesia, for example),[72] while in others it is seventeen or eighteen.[73] The marriageable age for boys is usually older. In general, in Islamic law, when a child reaches the age of maturity they can make decisions about marriage. However, before a child reaches this age, in some cases their father or guardian has the right to marry the child to another, sometimes without their consent, although the child may repudiate the marriage upon attaining puberty according to some scholars.[74] Some of these rules reflect tribal traditions at the time when Islamic law emerged.[75] Although the CRC does not explicitly address the issue of child marriage, the Committee on the Rights of the Child has interpreted other articles as having a bearing on this issue (such as Article 2 on non-discrimination, Article 3 on the best interests of the child, and Article 6 on providing maximum support for a child's survival and development).[76]

The CEDAW and CRC have also issued a joint recommendation on harmful practices that explicitly addresses child marriage. This document defines child marriage as a union "where at least one of the parties is under 18 years of age".[77] In their view, child marriage is equivalent to "forced marriage" because, having not obtained adulthood, "one and/or both parties have not expressed full, free and informed consent"[78] and may not be "physically and psychologically" mature enough for the responsibilities of marriage.[79]

The Committee has also expressed concern about such practices in its periodic review of state party reports.[80] For instance, in its review of the fourth and fifth periodic reports of the Maldives (2016), the Committee expressed concern that the "legal minimum age for sexual consent", which is expected to occur within the union of marriage, is thirteen years of age.[81] With respect to the third and fourth periodic reports of Saudi Arabia (2016), the Committee also noted with concern that the age of majority in the state is established at the discretion of the courts, which means that girls are often given legal sanction to marry at the age of puberty,[82] well before the age of eighteen. Moreover, the country's most authoritative Islamic leader has publicly supported marriage for girls "as young as 9 years old".[83] Bahrain has also been chastised for establishing different legal marital ages for boys and girls, with the age for girls set three years younger than for boys and below the age of eighteen.[84]

In addition, Article 16(2) of CEDAW states that "the betrothal and the marriage of a child shall have no legal effect",[85] although the article does not clearly state a minimum age for marriage. A UN General Assembly recommendation has, however, established that the minimum age of marriage should not be less than fifteen.[86]

There are also tensions between international and Islamic law when it comes to the criminalisation of sexual relations outside marriage. In Pakistan, for instance, the Hudood laws prohibit and criminalise such relations.[87] As Hashemi points out, this code, if applied to children under eighteen years of age, conflicts with Articles 37(a) and 37(b) of the CRC.[88] In Saudi Arabia a girl can be arrested for "*khalwa* or mingling (*ikhtilat*)" and potentially be tried as an adult in court.[89]

For children born out of wedlock, there is also a potential conflict between Islamic law and the CRC.[90] Islamic law does not generally permit such children from receiving any share of inheritance from their father.[91] Hashemi notes that legislative changes have been made in many Muslim-majority countries (for example in Egypt, Indonesia, Syria, Iran, and Tunisia) to protect children in such cases.[92] Nevertheless, Islamic law continues to hold its position.

Capital punishment is a crucial issue that is addressed in the CRC. The CRC prohibits capital punishment for children below the age of eighteen; however, a younger age of criminal responsibility in traditional Islamic law means that those under eighteen can be considered adults and punished by the state accordingly. For crimes that carry the death penalty, this theoretically places Islamic law in conflict with Article 37 of the CRC.[93] Interestingly, however, no Muslim state has made a specific reservation against this article of the CRC. In fact, the majority of Muslim-majority states have expressly confirmed, in their periodic reports, their commitment to Article 37.[94] Iran, however, is one exception, and in relation to the state's combined third and fourth periodic report (2016), the Committee expressed grave concern about the death penalty being carried out on those less than eighteen years old.[95] The

Committee also expressed concern in the context of Yemen's fourth periodic report (2014) about numerous cases of children being sentenced to death, including a fifteen year old girl.[96]

Care and custody are also areas of contention. Generally speaking, the financial responsibility for the care of children lies primarily with the father in Islamic law. The father is responsible for maintaining his children—in his absence, this responsibility falls to the child's male relatives.[97] Because of this, fathers have the most control over the lives of their children, or, as Hashemi puts it, "an open hand to interfere in various aspects of [their] children's lives".[98]

An illustrative case occurred in Malaysia in 2007. The parties were both Hindu and had two children. After some years their marriage became "rocky"; and in 2006 the wife received a letter from the Syariah High Court, Kuala Lumpur, stating that her husband had applied to the court for custody of their eldest son. From the document the wife deduced that her husband "had converted himself and the elder son to Islam ... without her knowledge and consent".[99] The wife petitioned the High Court to stop her husband from "(1) converting either child of the marriage to Islam; and (2) commencing or continuing with any proceedings in any Syariah Court with regard to the marriage or the children of the marriage";[100] but the appeal failed.[101] In Malaysia, it appears that this was not an isolated case. Indeed, a husband "often turns the Syariah court as a court of convenience. His conversion and the immediate conversion of the child provides the easiest and fastest route to gaining full custody of the child easily defeating the wife's similar claim in the civil court [*sic*]".[102]

There are specific rules and regulations that govern custody under Islamic law. Usually if the children are very young, say, up to the age of seven, the mother gets custody. Nasrin Mosaffa cites an example of where Islamic law might grant a child's father sole custody, which would curtail a child's right to access his or her mother, enshrined in Article 8(3) of the CRC.[103] Also, in the case of Pakistan, the Committee on the Rights of the Child recommended "that the State party review its current legislation concerning custody in order to ensure that the principle of the best interests of the child is a primary consideration", rather than a child's gender or age.[104]

Adoption, at least in some of its forms, is another area where there is potential for conflict between Islamic law and the CRC.[105] In traditional Islamic law, adoption is a system of guardianship called *kafala*, which provides care for children. "Closed adoption", where the biological parents' identity is kept secret, is legal in many Western countries today, but is not permissible according to Islamic law, which emphasises protection of lineage.[106] The Qur'an is very clear that adoptive parents cannot be treated identically to biological parents, and the adoptive family can never be considered blood relatives of the child.[107] Thus, an adopted child may not inherit from his or her adoptive parents.

Child labour is another issue that is problematic. Article 32 of the CRC provides that children have the right "to be protected from economic exploitation and from performing any work that is likely to be hazardous or to interfere with the child's education, or to be harmful to the child's health or physical, mental, spiritual, moral, or social development".[108] As Bentley notes, however, the CRC "gives no hint as to *what* the minimum age(s) [or] working conditions [for children] should be" [original emphasis].[109] Thus, Pakistan, which has many child workers under the age of ten,[110] could claim to be complying with the CRC, "as long as [the relevant] age limits and conditions were regulated by law".[111]

Finally, there are also tensions in the area of religious freedom. The main concern of Muslim-majority states with regard to a child's freedom to choose or change their religion relates to the application of family law. According to Islamic law, if a child changes their religion applicable family law may also change, particularly those laws that concern inheritance and marriage. Laws criminalising apostasy may also come into play in some Muslim states if a child changes their religion. Under international law, Sylvie Langlaude notes that a religious child has the right to be protected against intervention by the state into their religion.[112] This includes protection of the child's involvement in "practices, festivals, classes, [as well as] the transmission of parental beliefs to the child and religious education".[113] The child thus has a right to "flourish as a religious being".[114] However, as Langlaude points out, this right does not necessarily protect the parents' choice of religion for the child indefinitely. International law also requires that "the state must not interfere with the child's right to choose another religion, and ... must protect the child against the family and religious community if necessary", as well as provide safeguards against "harmful practices" by the religious community.[115]

POSSIBILITIES FOR HARMONISATION

In summary, while "Musljm States generally believe that 'the provisions set forth in [the Children's] Convention are in conformity with the teachings of Islamic law concerning the need to fully respect the human rights of the child'",[116] there are, as mentioned, a number of areas where Islamic law or current Muslim-majority states' practice conflict with the international framework protecting the rights of children. For those areas of tension that are simply a matter of state practice, rather than the prescriptions of Islamic law per se, these can be addressed by the monitoring committees of the CRC or the ICCPR as they engage with the relevant state parties. For instance, the practice of child labour in Pakistan stems from social and economic factors,[117] rather than from Qur'anic prescriptions, and may be addressed through the UN's technical assistance programme or other forms of aid.

Likewise, difficulties around the issue of adoption can be resolved. Article 20 of the CRC specifies that if a child is "temporarily or permanently deprived of his or her family environment, or in whose own best interests cannot be allowed to remain in that environment",[118] they can be placed into an alternative care arrangement, such as "foster placement, kafalah of Islamic law, adoption or if necessary placement in suitable institutions".[119] Since *kafala* is acknowledged as a legitimate option for children in this situation, Article 20 poses no difficulties for Muslim-majority states. Likewise, Article 21 on adoption only applies to "States Parties that recognize and/or permit the system of adoption".[120]

The issue of child custody or care is perhaps more difficult to reconcile with international human rights law. Article 18 of the CRC emphasises that state parties must take steps to ensure realisation of the principle that "both parents have common responsibilities for the upbringing and development of the child".[121] Moreover, states must ensure that "a child shall not be separated from his or her parents against their will", except if it is determined that this is in the best interests of the child.[122] However, in the case of divorce, Islamic law establishes rules for the custody (*hadana*) and guardianship (*wilaya*) of a child that are prescribed by gender and age. In general, mothers are awarded custody of infants and young children; while fathers are considered the "natural guardian of both the person and property".[123] Guardians have authority over marriage, education, and discipline, and can undertake legal transactions on a child's behalf.[124] This changes, however, as the child becomes older: "once the child attains a certain age the mother loses this automatic right [to custody]".[125] The rules here differ according to the relevant school of Islamic law. According to the Hanafi school, "a mother retains the right of custody till the age of 7 years for boys and puberty[126] for girls".[127] For the Maliki school, a mother has custody of a son until puberty and of a daughter until she is wedded.[128] For the Hanbali school, a son can choose who he wishes to live with once he reaches an appropriate age, usually seven,[129] while a daughter will go to her father once she is seven years old.[130] These juristic prescriptions are of concern when it comes to international human rights law because they may not be in the best interests of the child, which is the standard set out in the CRC. In practice, they may also curtail the rights and responsibilities of the other parent in terms of access or input into the child's life and upbringing.

Tunisia is one Muslim-majority country that has adopted more progressive laws when it comes to guardianship and custody. In its reply to the list of issues raised by the Committee on the Elimination of All Forms of Discrimination against Women in relation to its fifth and sixth periodic report, the state set out its laws regarding guardianship and custody:

Article 67 of the Personal Status Code states that:

> if a marriage is dissolved by death, custody shall be granted to the surviving parent. If a marriage is dissolved during the lifetime of the spouses, custody shall be granted to either of them or to a third party. The decision shall be at the discretion of the judge, taking into account the interests of the child. Should custody be granted to the mother, she shall enjoy all the prerogatives of guardianship with respect to the travel and education of the child and management of his or her financial accounts.[131]

With respect to custody, article 57 of the Personal Status Code provides that "custody of children during marriage is held by both the father and the mother".[132]

According to Shabnam Ishaque and Muhammad Khan, in Pakistan, this issue has also been proactively addressed by its higher courts. The principle of the best interests of the child has been taken into account in a number of cases, including in custody disputes.[133] Courts are also using *ijtihad* to promote the principle of the child's welfare and to evolve the law.[134] According to Ishaque and Khan, "Pakistani Superior Courts have in almost every judgment stressed that the ultimate criterion remains the best interests of the child".[135] In a number of cases, decisions have been made contrary to traditional juristic prescriptions. For instance, in one case the High Court "granted custody to the father, with visitation [rights] to the mother against the presumption of a mother's right to hadanah because the child seemed well-adjusted, confident, happy, healthy, and emotionally stable and handing custody to the mother would risk traumatising the child".[136] Other commentators agree that "[s]tudies of Pakistani case law show that courts have preferred a case by case consideration of the fact rather than rigidly applying the principles of established Muslim Jurisprudence" with respect to the rights of the child.[137] This jurisprudence could serve as a model for other Muslim-majority states, removing the tension with the relevant articles of the CRC.

CONCLUSION

The rights of children have a prominent place in Islamic law and tradition. Recognising children's special vulnerability, Islamic law established a number of rights and protections for children long before the emergence of contemporary human rights law. Many of these are compatible with instruments such as the CRC, and pose no difficulty for Muslim-majority states attempting to apply international human rights standards for children within their jurisdiction. However, there are some areas of tension. While Islamic law establishes rights for children, it also emphasises their obligations, especially towards their parents. Many Muslim-majority states also define maturity at younger than eighteen years, which imposes obligations or responsibilities that international law does not necessarily envisage for children. Adoption is also a significant difficulty for Muslim-majority states since Islamic law only permits a form of guardianship or trusteeship that is less encompassing than modern adoption practices. Nevertheless, the emphasis on children's rights in Islam provides an important basis for dialogue and engagement with the international community, with the well-being of children a common concern for both legal regimes.

* * *

LOOKING AT AN ISSUE CLOSELY: PRESIDENTIAL DECREE NO. 1083: "CODE OF MUSLIM PERSONAL LAWS OF THE PHILIPPINES"

Presidential Decree No. 1083. *Code of Muslim Personal Laws of the Philippines.* 4 February 1977. Available http://www.lawphil.net/statutes/presdecs/pd1977/pd_1083_1977.html (last accessed 8 December 2017).

This case contains extracts from the Code of Muslim Personal Laws of the Philippines. It shows how Islamic teachings about children are codified as part of Muslim personal status laws and how issues such as custody, guardianship, legitimacy, and the rights and responsibilities of children are approached in the context of Muslims in Philippines.

A Decree to Ordain and Promulgate a Code Recognizing the System of Filipino Muslim Laws, Codifying Muslim Personal Laws, and Providing for its Administration and for Other Purposes.

…

TITLE III
Paternity and Filiation

Article 58. *Legitimacy, how established.* Legitimacy of filiation is established by evidence of valid marriage between the father and the mother at the time of the conception of the child.

Article 59. *Legitimate children.*

(1) Children conceived in lawful wedlock shall be presumed to be legitimate. Whoever claims illegitimacy of or impugns such filiation must prove his allegation.

(2) Children born after six months following the consummation of marriage or with[in] two years after the dissolution of the marriage shall be presumed to be legitimate. Against this presumption no evidence shall be admitted other than that of the physical impossibility of access between the parents at or about the time of the conception of the child.

Article 60. *Children of subsequent marriage.* Should the marriage be dissolved and the wife contracts another marriage after the expiration of her 'IDDA, the child born within six months from the dissolution of the prior marriage shall be presumed to have been conceived during the former marriage, and if born thereafter, during the latter.

Article 61. *Pregnancy after dissolution.* If, after the dissolution of marriage, the wife believes that she is pregnant by her former husband, she shall, within thirty days from the time she became aware of her pregnancy, notify the former husband or his heirs of that fact. The husband or his heirs may ask the court to take measures to prevent a simulation of birth.

Article 62. *Rights of legitimate child.* A legitimate child shall have the right:

(a) To bear the surnames of the father and of the mother;

(b) To receive support from the father or, in his default, from his heirs in accordance with Articles 65 and 68; and

(c) To share in the legitimate (furud) and other successional rights which this Code recognises in his favour.

Article 63. *Acknowledgment by father.* Acknowledgment (igrar) of a child by the father shall establish paternity and confer upon each the right [to] inherit from the other exclusively in accordance with Article 94, provided the following conditions are complied with:

(a) The acknowledgment is manifested by the father's acceptance in public that he is the father of the child who does not impugn it; and

(b) The relations [*sic*] does not appear impossible by reason of disparity in age.

Article 64. *Adoption.* No adoption in any form shall confer upon any person the status and rights of a legitimate child under Muslim law, except that said person may receive a gift (hiba).

…

TITLE V
Parental Authority

Chapter One
Nature and Effects

Article 71. *Who exercises.*

(1) The father and the mother shall jointly exercise just and reasonable parental authority and fulfill their responsibility over their legitimate and acknowledged children. In case of disagreement, the father's decision shall prevail unless there is a judicial order to the contrary.

(2) The mother shall exercise parental authority over her children born out of wedlock, but the court may, when the best interests of the children so require, appoint a general guardian.

Article 72. *Duty to parents.*

(1) Children shall respect, revere, and obey their parents always unless the latter cast them into disbelief.

(2) Grandparents are likewise entitled to respect and reverence, and shall be consulted whenever practicable by all members of the family on all important questions.

Article 73. *Duty to children.* Every parent and every person exercising parental authority shall see to it that the rights of the children are respected, and their duties complied with, and shall particularly by precept and example, imbue them with religious and civic attachment to the ideal of permanent world peace.

Article 74. *Effects upon person of children.* The parents have, with respect to their unemancipated children:

(a) The duty to support them, have them in their company, educate and instruct them in keeping with their means and represent them in all actions which shall redound to their benefits; and

(b) The power to correct, discipline, and punish them moderately.

Article 75. *Effects upon property of children.*

(1) The father, or in his absence the mother, shall be the legal administrator of the property of the child under parental authority. If the property is worth more than five thousand pesos, the father or the mother shall give a bond to be approved by the court.

(2) The court may appoint a guardian (wasi) in the absence of one who is natural or testamentary.

Article 76. *Parental authority non-transferable.* Parental authority can neither be renounced nor transferred except as otherwise provided in this Code and the general principles of Islamic law.

Article 77. *Extinguishment of parental authority.*

(1) Parental authority terminates upon the death of the parents or the child, or upon emancipation.

(2) Subject to Article 78, the widowed mother who contracts a subsequent marriage shall lose parental authority and custody over all children by the deceased husband, unless the second husband is related to them within the prohibited degrees of consanguinity.

(3) The court may deprive a person of parental authority or suspend the exercise thereof if he treats his children with excessive harshness, gives them corrupting or immoral orders and counsel, or abandons them.

Chapter Two
Custody and Guardianship

Article 78. *Care and custody.*
(1) The care and custody of children below seven years of age whose parents are divorced shall belong to the mother or, in her absence, to the maternal grandmother, the paternal grandmother, the sister and aunts. In their default, it shall devolve upon the father and the nearest paternal relatives. The minor above seven years of age but below the age of puberty may choose the parent with whom he wants to stay.

(2) The unmarried daughter who has reached the age of puberty shall stay with the father; the son, under the same circumstances, shall stay with the mother.

Article 79. *Guardian for marriage (wali).* The following persons shall have authority to act as guardian for marriage (wali) in the order of precedence:

(a) Father;

(b) Paternal grandfather;

(c) Brother and other paternal relatives;

(d) Paternal grandfather's executor or nominee; or

(e) The court.

Article 80. *Guardian of minor's property.* The following persons shall exercise guardianship over the property of minors in the order of precedence:

(a) Father;

(b) Father's executor or nominee;

(c) Paternal grandfather;

(d) Paternal grandfather's nominee; or

(e) The court.

NOTES

1. Kamran Hashemi, "Religious Legal Traditions, Muslim States and the Convention on the Rights of the Child: An Essay on the Relevant UN Documentation", *Human Rights Quarterly* 29(1) (2007): 197.
2. Ibid. See generally J. Nasir, *The Islamic Law of Personal Status* (Leiden: Brill, 1990) 56, 189–90.
3. Geraldine van Bueren, *The Best Interests of the Child: International Co-operation on Child Abduction* (London: British Institute of Human Rights, n.d.), 51.
4. Masoud Rajabi-Ardeshiri, "The Rights of the Child in the Islamic Context: The Challenges of the Local and the Global", *International Journal of Children's Rights* 17 (2009): 478.
5. Baderin, *International Human Rights*, 154.
6. Ibid, 154–5.
7. Ibid, 154.
8. Rajabi-Ardeshiri, "The Rights of the Child", 478–9.
9. See Abdel Rahim Omran, *Family Planning in the Legacy of Islam* (London: Routledge, 1992), 32–7.
10. Rajabi-Ardeshiri, "The Rights of the Child", 484; Organisation of Islamic Cooperation, "Resolutions on Islamic and Cultural Affairs Adopted by the Twenty-Second Islamic Conference of Foreign Ministers, Casablanca, Kingdom of Morocco, 8–10 Rajab, 1415 H (10–12 December, 1994)", "Resolution No. 16/22-C on Child Care and Protection in the Islamic World". Available http://ww1.oic-oci.org/english/conf/fm/22/Resolution22-C.htm (last accessed 20 December 2017).
11. OIC, "Resolution No. 16/22-C."
12. Rajabi-Ardeshiri, "The Rights of the Child", 484.
13. Ibid.
14. Rajabi-Ardeshiri, "The Rights of the Child", 484–5.
15. United Nations General Assembly, *Convention on the Rights of the Child (CRC)*. 20 November 1989. United Nations, Treaty Series, vol. 1577, p. 3, art. 14. Available http://www.refworld.org/docid/3ae6b38f0.html (last accessed 8 December 2017).
16. See Chapter 3 for a discussion of the background to this declaration.
17. Islamic Council of Europe, *Universal Islamic Declaration of Human Rights*. 19 September 1981/21 Dhul Qaidah 1401, art. 19. Available http://hrlibrary.umn.edu/instree/islamic_declaration_HR.html (last accessed 2 December 2017).
18. Rajabi-Ardeshiri, "The Rights of the Child", 482.
19. Organization of the Islamic Conference, *Cairo Declaration on Human Rights in Islam*. 5 August 1990. UN Doc A/CONF.157/PC/62/Add.18. Available https://www1.umn.edu/humanrts/instree/cairodeclaration.html (last accessed 8 December 2017).
20. Rajabi-Ardeshiri, "The Rights of the Child", 483.
21. Organization of the Islamic Conference, *Covenant on the Rights of the Child in Islam*. Adopted by the 32nd Islamic Conference of Foreign Ministers in Sana'a, Republic of Yemen, June 2005. OIC/9-IGGE/HRI/2004/Rep.Final. Available http://www.refworld.org/docid/44eaf0e4a.html (last accessed 12 January 2018).
22. *Covenant on the Rights of the Child in Islam*, Preamble.
23. Nasrin Mosaffa, "Does the Covenant on the Rights of the Child in Islam Provide Adequate Protection for Children Affected by Armed Conflicts?", *Muslim World Journal of Human Rights* 8(1) (2011): 1.
24. *Covenant on the Rights of the Child in Islam*, Preamble.
25. Ibid.
26. *Covenant on the Rights of the Child in Islam*, art. 4.
27. The Danish Institute for Human Rights, "The OIC, Children's Rights and Islam" (2015). Available https://www.humanrights.dk/publications/oic-childrens-rights-islam (last accessed 20 December 2017), 12.
28. Ibid, 13.

29. Mosaffa, "Does the Covenant", 15.
30. The Danish Institute for Human Rights, "Children's Rights and Islam", 13.
31. Ibid, 14 (specifically referring to the example of Iran).
32. *Universal Declaration of Human Rights*, art. 25.
33. Ibid, art. 26.
34. *ICCPR*, art. 18.
35. Ibid, art. 23.
36. Ibid, art. 24.
37. Ibid.
38. Human Rights Committee, "General Comment No. 17: Article 24 (Rights of the child)". 7 April 1989, [2].
39. Ibid.
40. Ibid, [4].
41. Kristina Anne Bentley, "Can There Be Any Universal Children's Rights?", *International Journal of Human Rights* 9(1) (2005): 109.
42. *CRC*.
43. Office of the High Commissioner for Human Rights (OHCHR), "Status of Ratification: Interactive Dashboard". Available http://indicators.ohchr.org (last accessed 8 December 2017).
44. Bentley, "Universal Children's Rights?", 109.
45. Committee on the Rights of the Child, "General Comment No. 14 (2013) on the Right of the Child to have His or Her Best Interests Taken as a Primary Consideration (art. 3, para. 1)". 29 May 2013. UN Doc CRC/C/GC/14, [1]
46. *CRC*, Article 3(1).
47. Committee on the Rights of the Child, "General Comment No. 14 [1] citing the Committee's General Comment No. 5 (2003) on the General Measures of Implementation of the Convention on the Rights of the Child, para. 12; and No. 12 (2009) on the Right of the Child to be Heard, para. 2.
48. *CRC*, art. 1.
49. Bentley, "Universal Children's Rights?", 109.
50. Ibid, 110.
51. Ibid, citing Vanessa Pupavac, "The Infantilization of the South and the UN Convention on the Rights of the Child", in *International Human Rights in Context*, 2nd edn., Henry J. Steiner and Philip Alston (eds.), (Oxford: Oxford University Press, 2000) 517.
52. Bentley, "Universal Children's Rights?", 110.
53. Hashemi, "Religious Legal Traditions", 225.
54. L.J. Leblanc, "Reservations to the Convention on the Rights of the Child: A Macroscopic View of State Practice", *International Journal of Children's Rights* 4 (1996): 368.
55. Hashemi, "Religious Legal Traditions", 194.
56. OHCHR, "Status of Ratification".
57. Ibid.
58. Ibid.
59. Ibid.
60. Ibid.
61. See Leblanc, "Reservations to the CRC", 369.
62. OHCHR, "Status of Ratification".
63. Ibid.
64. Rajabi-Ardeshiri, "The Rights of the Child", 479, citing A. Hussain, *Muslim Parents, their Rights and Duties* (New Delhi: Adam Publishers, 2003).
65. Bentley, "Universal Children's Rights?", 117.
66. Ibid.
67. Ibid.
68. Hashemi, "Religious Legal Traditions", 199.

69. *Islamic Penal Code of 2013 of the Islamic Republic of Iran*, Book 1. Available http://www.iranhrdc.org/english/human-rights-documents/iranian-codes/1000000455-english-translation-of-books-1-and-2-of-the-new-islamic-penal-code.html#1, Article 146 (last accessed 8 December 2017).
70. Ibid, Article 147.
71. Hashemi, "Religious Legal Traditions", 199.
72. Girlsnotbrides, "Child Marriage around the World: Indonesia" (2016). Available http://www.girlsnotbrides.org/child-marriage/indonesia (last accessed 8 December 2017), citing the 1974 Marriage Law.
73. Hashemi, "Religious Legal Traditions", 212.
74. Ibid, 200.
75. Ibid.
76. UNICEF, "Child Marriage and the Law", *Legislative Reform Initiative Paper Series* (2008). Available http://www.unicef.org/policyanalysis/files/Child_Marriage_and_the_Law(1).pdf, 5 (last accessed 8 December 2017).
77. Committee on the Elimination of All forms of Discrimination against Women (Comm EDAW) and Committee on the Rights of the Child, "Joint General Recommendation No. 31 of the Committee on the Elimination of Discrimination against Women/General Comment No. 18 of the Committee on the Rights of the Child on harmful practices". 14 November 2014. UN Doc CEDAW/C/GC/31-CRC/C/GC/18, [20].
78. Ibid.
79. Ibid, [21].
80. UNICEF, "Child Marriage and the Law", 6.
81. Committee on the Rights of the Child, "Concluding Observations on the Combined Fourth and Fifth Periodic Reports of Maldives". 14 March 2016. UN Doc CRC/C/MDV/CO/4-5, [44].
82. Committee on the Rights of the Child, "Concluding Observations on the Combined Third and Fourth Periodic Reports of Saudi Arabia". 25 October 2016. UN Doc CRC/C/SAU/CO/3-4, [13].
83. Ibid.
84. Committee on the Rights of the Child, "Consideration of Reports Submitted by States Parties under Article 44 of the Convention". 3 August 2011. UN Doc CRC/C/BHR/CO/2-3, [28].
85. Hashemi, "Religious Legal Traditions", 201.
86. Ibid, 201, citing United Nations General Assembly, "Recommendation on Consent to Marriage, Minimum Age for Marriage and Registration of Marriages". 1 November 1965. G.A. Res. 2018 (XX), 20 UN GAOR Supp. (No. 14) at 36. UN Doc A/60141.
87. *Hudood Laws*. Available http://www.pakistani.org/pakistan/legislation/hudood.html (last accessed 8 December 2017). The crime of sexual relations outside marriage is enacted in *The Offence of Zina (Enforcement of Hudood) Ordinance, 1979*. Ordinance No. VII of 1979, 9 February 1979. Available http://www.pakistani.org/pakistan/legislation/zia_po_1979/ord7_1979.html (last accessed 8 December 2017).
88. Hashemi, "Religious Legal Traditions", 203.
89. Committee on the Rights of the Child, "Concluding Observations on the Combined Third and Fourth Periodic Reports of Saudi Arabia", [43].
90. Baderin, *International Human Rights*, 155.
91. Hashemi, "Religious Legal Traditions", 208.
92. Ibid, 209.
93. Ibid, 199.
94. Ibid, 205.
95. Committee on the Rights of the Child, " Concluding Observations on the Combined Third and Fourth Periodic Reports of the Islamic Republic of Iran". 14 March 2016. UN Doc CRC/C/IRN/CO/3-4, [35].
96. Committee on the Rights of the Child, "Concluding Observations on the Fourth Periodic Report of Yemen". 25 February 2014. UN Doc CRC/C/YEM/CO/4, [33].

97. Hashemi, "Religious Legal Traditions," 212–13.
98. Ibid, 213.
99. [2007] 2 MLJ *Saravanan a/l Thangathoray v Subashini a/p Rajasingam*, 706.
100. Ibid.
101. Ibid, 745.
102. Norman Fernandez, "OPINION: Subashini case—Worrying Implications for Non-Muslim Spouse". *Malaysian Bar* 30 March 2007. Available http://www.malaysianbar.org.my/members_opinions_and_comments/opinion_subashini_case_worrying_implications_for_non_muslim_spouse.html (last accessed 20 December 2017).
103. Nasrin Mosaffa, "Does the Covenant", 8.
104. Committee on the Rights of the Child, "Consideration of Reports Submitted by States Parties under Article 44 of the Convention. Concluding Observations: Pakistan". 27 October 2003. UN Doc CRC/C/15/Add.217, [45].
105. Baderin, *International Human Rights*, 155.
106. Faisal Kutty, "Islamic Law, Adoptions and Kafalah", *Jurist* (2012). Available http://www.jurist.org/forum/2012/11/faisal-kutty-adoption-kafalah.php (last accessed 8 December 2017).
107. Q. 33:4–5.
108. *CRC*, art. 32.
109. Bentley, "Universal Children's Rights?", 111.
110. See ibid.
111. Ibid.
112. Sylvie Langlaude, "Children and Religion under Article 14 UNCRC: A Critical Analysis", *International Journal of Children's Rights* 16 (2008): 480.
113. Ibid.
114. Ibid.
115. Ibid, 480.
116. Baderin, *International Human Rights and Islamic Law*, 155.
117. Serena Chaudhry, "Millions Pushed into Child Labor in Pakistan". *Reuters* 7 February 2012. Available http://www.reuters.com/article/us-pakistan-childlabour-idUSTRE8160LA20120207 (last accessed 8 December 2017).
118. *CRC*, Article 20(1).
119. Ibid, art. 20(3).
120. Ibid, art. 21.
121. Ibid, art. 18.
122. Ibid, art. 9.
123. Shabnam Ishaque and Muhammad Mustafa Khan, "The Best Interests of the Child: A Prevailing Consideration within Islamic Principles and a Governing Principle in Child Custody Cases in Pakistan", *International Journal of Law, Policy and the Family* 29 (2015): 80.
124. Ibid.
125. Ibid, 82.
126. Ibid.
127. Ibid.
128. Ibid.
129. Ibid.
130. Ibid.
131. Comm EDAW, "Written Replies from the Government of Tunisia to the List of Issues and Questions (CEDAW/C/TUN/Q/6) with Regard to the Consideration of the Combined Fifth and Sixth Periodic Reports (CEDAW/C/TUN/5-6) Tunisia". 18 August 2010. UN Doc CEDAW/C/TUN/Q/6/Add.1, [366(5)].
132. Comm EDAW, "Written Replies from the Government of Tunisia", [366(6)].
133. Ishaque and Khan, "The Best Interests of the Child", 89, citing *Muhammad Zaman v Ameer Hamza* 2009 CLC 230 [Shariat Court (AJ&K)].
134. Ishaque and Khan, "The Best Interests of the Child", 89.

135. Ibid.
136. Ibid, 90.
137. Aayesha Rafiq, "Child Custody in Classical Islamic Law and Laws of Contemporary Muslim World (An Analysis)", *International Journal of Humanities and Social Science* 4(5) (2014): 272, citing Cassandra Balchin, *A Handbook on Family Laws in Pakistan* (Lahore: Shirkatgah, 1994) 164.

9. Freedom of expression

Along with freedom of religion, freedom of expression is one of the most fundamental human rights protected by international human rights law. It is closely associated with other rights, such as freedom of association and freedom of the press, and it is regarded as an essential element of democracy. But what does Islamic law say about this right, and how do these prescriptions compare to the freedom established by international human rights law? This chapter will compare Islamic and international articulations of the right to freedom of expression. It will reflect on what is considered permissible speech under each legal regime, and what kinds of limitations frame the right. It will also look at recent controversies where different understandings of the right have come into conflict. It concludes by suggesting ways that Islamic and international approaches to freedom of expression may be reconciled.

THE MEANING OF FREEDOM OF EXPRESSION

In many liberal democratic societies freedom of expression is one of the most highly held values. In these societies, the state puts as few limitations or restrictions on people's expression as possible. This is because freedom of expression is considered beneficial for society as a whole. While there may be negative consequences from allowing this kind of freedom, it could be argued that the benefits far outweigh them.

In international human rights law, the right to freedom of expression is established by Article 19 of the UDHR. All other human rights instruments that prescribe freedom of expression stem from this Article, which states "Everyone has the right to freedom of opinion and expression; this right includes freedom to hold opinions without interference and to seek, receive and impart information and ideas through any media and regardless of frontiers."[1]

Based on this article, Article 19 of the ICCPR states:

1. Everyone shall have the right to hold opinions without interference.
2. Everyone shall have the right to freedom of expression; this right shall include freedom to seek, receive and impart information and ideas of all

kinds, regardless of frontiers, either orally, in writing or in print, in the form of art, or through any other media of his choice.

3. The exercise of the rights provided for in paragraph 2 of this article carries with it special duties and responsibilities. It may therefore be subject to certain restrictions, but these shall only be such as are provided by law and are necessary:

   (a) For respect of the rights or reputations of others;
   (b) For the protection of national security or of public order (*ordre public*), or of public health or morals.[2]

As expressed in these two articles, freedom of expression is a fundamental right that every individual may lay claim to. The UN Human Rights Committee has expressed the view that freedom of opinion and expression is considered one of the most important conditions for a person to reach their full development and to participate as a free individual member of society.[3] Freedom of expression is also extremely important at a community or societal level; along with freedom of opinion, it is regarded as the foundation of every free and democratic society. Accordingly, they are closely related, with "freedom of expression providing the vehicle for the exchange and development of opinions".[4] Without freedom of expression there can be no meaningful communication of information or opinions. Instead, one dominant position or belief system will structure or dictate to society and subordinate all others.

Article 19 of the ICCPR draws attention to a number of issues. Firstly, it affirms that individuals are free "to hold opinions without interference".[5] Such opinions can be of a religious nature, or indeed of any other kind, such as political, moral, or scientific. Accordingly, opinions of any category cannot be restricted. No individual or law can penalise a person for holding opinions. The Human Rights Committee notes that it is at odds with Article 19(1) "to criminalise the holding of an opinion".[6] Likewise, to harass, intimidate, or stigmatise a person for their opinion, or to order their arrest, detention, trial, or imprisonment for that reason, constitutes a violation of the article.[7]

Secondly, Article 19 of the ICCPR "requires states to guarantee the right to freedom of expression",[8] which includes the right "to seek, receive and impart information and ideas of all kinds".[9] The Human Rights Committee points out that this right includes "even expression that may be regarded as deeply offensive, although such expression may be restricted in accordance with the provisions of article 19, paragraph 3 and article 20".[10] Article 19(2) goes on to safeguard "all forms of expression and the means of their dissemination".[11]

Thirdly, while Article 19 sets out broad parameters for freedom of expression, it recognises that the right must be exercised in a way that is sensitive to the "rights or reputations of others", as well as the protection of "national security", "public order", or "public health or morals".[12] The Human Rights Committee notes that any restrictions imposed must not "put in jeopardy the right itself".[13] Restrictions must be governed by law, and any breach of such restrictions must be responded to in legal and proportionate ways.[14] This aspect of the article is an attempt to balance the right of individual expression with the rights of others.

Importantly, the Human Rights Committee does not view disrespect towards religion to be grounds for restricting freedom of expression. Accordingly, prohibiting the expression of "lack of respect for a religion or other belief system, including blasphemy laws", is considered incompatible with Article 19, "except in the … circumstances envisaged by Article 20(2)".[15] Any restrictions imposed in this regard must "comply with the strict requirements of Article 19, paragraph 3"—referring to necessity and proportionality—as well as other relevant articles of the ICCPR, such as the prohibition on discrimination. This means, for instance, that "it would be impermissible for any such [restrictions] to discriminate in favour of or against" a particular religion or belief system.[16] "Nor would it be permissible for such [restrictions] to be used to prevent or punish criticism of religious leaders or commentary on religious doctrine" or other aspects of faith.[17] This point is a source of significant tension. Many Muslims argue that lack of respect for Islam should be prohibited because it touches on the most fundamental aspect of their identity; that is their religious identity.

Indeed, one of the most notable controversies in the area of freedom of expression is whether Article 19 allows what some refer to as the "defamation of religion", or whether such "defamation" should be considered a permissible restriction of the right to freedom of expression.[18]

Since 2008, the UN's Human Rights Council (formerly Commission on Human Rights) has had to consider a range of resolutions in relation to this matter. In Resolution 7/19 (2008), for instance, the Council urged states to "take actions to prohibit the dissemination, including through political institutions and organisations, of racist and xenophobic ideas and material aimed at any religion or its followers that constitute incitement to racial and religious hatred, hostility or violence".[19]

This resolution followed a number of resolutions on the issue of defamation of religions that were presented to the General Assembly, the Human Rights Council, and its predecessor.[20] These resolutions, put forward mainly by Muslim states, primarily concern negative portrayals of religion, particularly Islam. The Human Rights Council refers in its 2008 report to these states' concern about

> the association of Islam with violence and terrorism in the aftermath of the 2001 terrorist attacks in the United States of America, the dissemination of ideas based on superiority, discriminatory laws, policies and practices that have targeted minority religious groups, and physical attacks on individuals and communities and their properties and places and symbols of worship.[21]

These resolutions argue that negative portrayals of Islam and Muslims have a significant negative impact on Muslims around the world, to such an extent that it must be kept in check by international law. However, the Council notes that "while these resolutions make reference to 'defamation of religions,' it appears that they often use the term [defamation] in [the] generic sense to describe some of the above phenomena ... rather than in the strict legal sense".[22] The resolutions describe defamation "in conjunction with the need to combat hatred, discrimination, intimidation, coercion, etc"[23] rather than as the act of damaging the reputation of a particular individual.

The issue of the defamation of religions is a controversial one in terms of international law. While many Muslim-majority states argue that this form of "defamation" should be prohibited, European countries, the United States, and many others argue otherwise, protesting that defamation is an issue concerning the rights of individuals, not institutions or religions. As a legal term, defamation refers to "an inaccurate statement (oral [or] written) that is published through various means of communication (printed, audio-visual, [or] electronic) and is intended to or actually causes harm to a person's reputation".[24] Furthermore, defamation of individuals is usually an issue for individual states, not international law.

There are many uncertainties surrounding the "defamation" of religions, most of which centre on the tension between defamation as an individual offence or as an experience of disrespect through identification with a certain community or religion, such as Islam. Certain individuals may express views about Islam that are hurtful to Muslims, but these views are not necessarily directed towards individuals. Paul Marshall observes that "an additional problem is that there is no clarity about what specific forms of expression the [Muslim-majority] countries seek to limit".[25] Similarly, there is "no common practice regarding blasphemy crimes" among the Muslim-majority states that have advocated for this issue.[26] Marshall notes that many of these countries do not have codified definitions of the crime.[27] The Human Rights Council thus observes that "in the framework of international human rights law, the combination of 'defamation' with 'religion' remains unclear".[28]

There are other arguments against the prohibition of defamation of religion through international law. One is that discrimination and incitement to violence against Muslims or people of any faith are already regulated by other laws.[29] Another is that to prevent "defamation" states would have to regulate the beliefs of individuals and arbitrate between various belief systems. This may generate state-imposed limitations on the right to freedom of expression. It would also curtail the freedom to critically examine belief systems or religions, significantly impacting vital debates that need to take place within and between religious communities as they attempt to preserve or reform existing ideas, values, norms, and practices.

In general, as expressed by the Human Rights Council, "further clarity is needed" to demarcate the line "between freedom of expression and incitement to religious hatred".[30] In addition, "to protect individuals and groups, a better understanding of the permissible limitations to freedom of expression in accordance with international human rights law needs to be developed".[31]

THE DANISH CARTOON CONTROVERSY

In 2005, a Danish newspaper called *Jyllands-Posten* printed a number of satirical cartoons featuring the Prophet Muhammad, which were later republished by a number of other European newspapers. The cartoons were considered by most Muslims to be mocking and offensive, with one depicting the Prophet wearing headwear that apparently contained a bomb. Their publication caused a public outcry among Muslims in many countries of the world.[32]

As Nazeem Goolam explains, the outcry against these pictures from Muslims stemmed from a number of concerns. Firstly, that "images of the Prophet ... are strictly prohibited in Islam".[33] They are considered disrespectful and "may lead to distortion"[34] of Muhammad's person or characteristics. Further, "the greatest reverence is ... accorded to God's last Prophet", whom the cartoons were seen as disrespecting.[35] Thirdly, as Muhammad is "considered the greatest role model" for Muslims around the world,[36] any mockery of him "is seen as a mocking of all those who follow and revere him".[37]

One commentator describes the controversy as essentially

> a clash between two opposed views of freedom of expression. One, put forward by *Jyllands Posten* and its supporters, is that what occurred was simply an exercise of a right of freedom of expression that is central to the effective working of democratic society. The other, as expressed by the Muslim opponents of the publication of the cartoons, is that there are limits to freedom of expression, [including] the denigration of religion and ... the insulting ... of religious people. The central concern, then, is the question whether there are [permissible] limits to freedom of expression.[38]

Goolam points out that "in most European countries freedom of expression, like all other human rights, is limited. These limitations are in respect of libel, hate speech, invasion of privacy, communication of national secrets, blasphemy and anti-Semitism".[39] Thus, the right to freedom of expression, even in countries that are widely regarded as allowing significant freedom in this area, is not unfettered. Goolam argues that "nearly everyone agrees that [the] law ought to prevent harm" that can be "inflicted through words or pictures".[40] However, a balance must be struck between all important (and often competing) values in a democratic society.[41]

International human rights law and Islamic law are in agreement that freedom of expression is permissible but with certain limitations. As noted above, Article 19(3) of the ICCPR permits limitations on the rights recognised in Article 19(2), but those limitations must be:

(1) provided by law, and
(2) necessary for respect of the rights or reputations of others, for the protection of national security, public order, or public health or morals.[42] Under Islamic law, there are many more limits.

FREEDOM OF EXPRESSION IN ISLAM

There is no explicit Qur'anic statement or set of statements that affirm or deny freedom of expression. Qur'anic references that can support a broad understanding of freedom of expression, as well as possible limitations to such freedom, are not specific in their treatment of the issues. Therefore, interpretive judgement is critical for understanding what Islam teaches in relation to this issue.

Mohammad Hashim Kamali observes that in Islam, freedom of expression can be considered "an extension of ... the freedom of conscience and belief, which the *Shari'ah* has validated and upholds".[43] Accordingly, freedom of expression can be understood as a privilege under Islamic law. This is supported by Q. 55:1-4, which states: "It is the Lord of

Mercy who taught the Qur'an. He created man and taught him to communicate." He argues that "the concept of free expression in Islam can only be fully understood in the context of the *Qur'anic* principle of *hisbah*".[44] Indeed, freedom of expression is the most essential element of *hisba*.[45]

The Qur'an does not seem to suggest that a Muslim is bound by the views, opinions, and ideas held by other members of the community. Instead, Muslims have the ability and the right to put forward ideas that may conflict with majority opinions. A key example of this is the Qur'an's teachings on belief and disbelief. A believer has the right to put forward ideas or opinions in support of their beliefs. Accordingly, others may object to or reject these, but both parties have the fundamental right to put forward the ideas. Encounters between believers and disbelievers are a recurrent theme that runs through the Qur'an. The Qur'an in many cases presents the opposing views and opinions of both individuals and groups, even if the opposing views are not acceptable from its point of view. Freedom to express oneself is therefore not limited only to the believers but given to their opponents as well.

The Qur'an also affirms the freedom of individuals to speak according to their convictions, requiring people to stand up for the truth, decency, and justice.[46] Although the Qur'an denounces a variety of opinions, for example about theological matters, the Qur'an does not prohibit people from expressing them. The Qur'an also suggests that it is necessary for both sides of a debate to be heard, but also that ultimately the truth will prevail. Truth can only prevail if untruth is also expressed. It is by bringing these two opposing sides into the arena that what is true can be revealed. The practice of the Prophet Muhammad also supports elements of freedom of expression. For instance, in a hadith the Prophet is reported to advocate restraint and gentleness in response to the harsh words of others.[47]

There are also a number of references within Islamic law which suggest that human beings are free to express their views, opinions, and ideas, even though these ideas may not be acceptable to other individuals or to society more broadly. According to Kamali, Islamic law allows a range of forms of public expression, including freedom to express an opinion publicly, speak in line with one's convictions, critique speech or conduct that is contrary to justice and truth, and stand up for decency.[48] According to Abul Ala Maududi, "decent intellectual debate and religious discussions are permitted in Islam".[49] Kamali notes further that individuals have the right to "point out … shortcomings of government employees, people's representatives in national assemblies, and anyone engaged in public services", as well as to publicly question or criticise political leaders.[50] Historical narrations from the Prophet Muhammad's lifetime and the time of the first four caliphs (rulers) in Islam also suggest that, as Baderin argues, "freedom of speech and expression [has been] an acknowledged right from the inception of Islamic law".[51] The freedom to express views or opinions contrary to the majority was tolerated within certain bounds. Historically, many prominent scholars, theologians, and jurists stood up against governments that they deemed were promoting injustice. Examples of such scholars include Abu Hanifa (d. 150/767) and Ahmad b. Hanbal (d. 241/855), both "founders" of schools of Islamic law. In sum, there is some support in Islamic tradition for a broad understanding of freedom of expression but there are also significant restrictions.

RESTRICTIONS TO FREEDOM OF EXPRESSION IN ISLAMIC LAW

Much like international human rights law, Islamic tradition also recognises that there must be limitations to freedom of expression. However, the exact extent of these restrictions is unclear because many of the relevant Qur'anic verses and hadith texts require interpretation, which can vary enormously.

Baderin argues that "under the *Shari'ah*, the main objective of this right [of freedom of expression] is the discovery of truth and upholding human dignity".[52] According to him, Islamic law attempts to maintain both of these objectives. It does not allow "the spread of evil or obscenity" under the banner of freedom of expression, nor does it permit the spread of "gossip or scandal" (Q. 24:19). Further, "while the Qur'an affirms that God gave [hu]mankind the power and freedom of expression", it also instructs people to use the freedom appropriately (as seen in Q. 4:148, quoted above).[53] Thus, as Baderin argues, "freedom of expression under Islamic law is also not absolute" but limited to "apposite speech and expressions".[54]

Within Islamic tradition there are certain kinds of speech and expression that are highly problematic. Kamali notes that "public opinion determines, to a large extent, the acceptable limits of … freedom [of speech]".[55] Such limits also come from positive ethical teachings that encourage qualities like compassion and respect for the rights of others.[56] Kamali describes two categories of constraints that can curtail free expression, namely: moral and legal.[57] Moral restraints have no particular legal consequences, and include lying and all kinds of rancorous disputes. Legal constraints, on the other hand, include public slander, hurtful speech, libel, insult, blasphemy, and sedition.[58]

Public Utterance of Evil Speech

Based on the Qur'anic verse "God does not love the public utterance of evil speech except by one who has been wronged" (Q. 4:148),[59] some scholars argue that the public expression of evil speech is prohibited in Islamic law.[60] The verse can also be read as God does not love the "broadcasting" of something that is "evil" or "hurtful".[61] Thus the prohibition as stated in the verse could cover any "evil" speech that is expressed in public. Kamali gives the examples of finding fault in others or attributing misdeeds to them, obscene literature, or "indulgent speech concerning evil deeds committed by oneself".[62] Commentary on this verse suggests that all evil and hurtful speech is prohibited, even if it contains some truth, or supposedly has a good purpose.[63] The only exception is stated in the verse: if someone has been wronged, in their "quest for justice" they are given greater scope for public expression.[64] Kamali points out the general nature of the addressees of this verse and that it includes both Muslims and non-Muslims.[65]

Insult and Blasphemy

In Islamic law, insulting or humiliating another person is unacceptable. Depending on the severity of the insult there could be legal consequences. The key idea here is that each person has dignity and they should be allowed to maintain that dignity and be protected from insult and humiliation.[66] Although expressions of insult or humiliation could be covered by the notion of evil or hurtful speech,[67] insults are considered a separate offence under Islamic law and carry separate penalties.[68] According to Kamali, the penalty for insults should be determined by considering "the nature of the offence and ... the circumstances".[69] This suggests that what is considered insulting speech in one time and in one context might be considered acceptable speech in another.[70] Forms of insult include finding faults, using bad names, and other types of abuse.[71] Insulting God or the Prophet is an offence of a much higher class. Muslim jurists considered the use of expressions that are offensive to God and the Prophet as blasphemy, which is prohibited under Islamic law.[72]

Baderin notes that "the *Encyclopaedia of Religion and Ethics* defines blasphemy in Islam broadly as 'all utterances expressive of contempt for Allah [God] Himself, for His Names, attributes, laws, commands or prohibitions ... [and] all scoffing at Muhammad or any other prophets or apostles of Allah [God]'".[73] Under Islamic law, blasphemy falls under the concepts of *sabb Allah* (reviling God) or *sabb al-rasul* (reviling the Messenger).[74] Goolam explains that insulting Prophet Muhammad could take "either an explicit [form]", such as speech "attacking his personal integrity", or an "implicit form", such as "mockery or disrespect".[75] Language that is contemptuous or hostile to the fundamentals of Islam or that "outrage[d] the religious sensibilities of believers … such as throwing the Holy Qur'an on a heap of rubbish"[76] could also be considered blasphemy. As a religious law, Kamali suggests that the prohibition of blasphemy was designed "to defend the dogma and belief-structure of Islam".[77]

Importantly, insults against God and the Prophet respectively were considered two different kinds of insults, and consequently attracted different punishments.[78] Goolam points out that this distinction was based on "the division of rights in Islam into the rights of God and the rights of man".[79] Reviling God is considered a violation of the rights of God, which God could pardon. However, an insult against the Prophet is considered a violation of the personal rights and honour of the Prophet, and, in the Hanafi and Maliki schools of law, is only pardonable by the Prophet.[80] This is based on the idea that the right to pardon existed only when the Prophet was alive.[81] Most jurists held that this offence attracts the death penalty. Nevertheless, there is disagreement as to whether a person who insulted the Prophet could be allowed to repent and "whether such repentance could absolve the offender from punishment".[82] Kamali's position is that "after the passing of the Prophet the offence of *sabb al-Rasul* should be no different to *sabb Allah* since both … violate the right of God".[83] The crime of blasphemy was also closely connected to that of apostasy, in that blasphemy could be considered an indication of apostasy in certain circumstances. As such, "classical Islamic jurists often paired the two together … and prescribed the death penalty for both".[84] Blasphemy, however, was still distinct from apostasy because it could be committed by a non-Muslim.[85]

Today blasphemy laws still exist in many Muslim-majority countries, and are often used by governments to suppress unorthodox religious views or opponents of the government, under the guise of protecting religion. Kuwait is one country where blasphemy laws are actively applied. While reviewing its third periodic report in 2016, the Human Rights Committee expressed concern that "defamation and blasphemy [laws]" are used against "activists, journalists, bloggers and other individuals for expressing critical views or views deemed to 'insult' the Emir or undermine his authority, defame religion or threaten the national security of Kuwait or the country's relations with other States".[86]

In Indonesia, blasphemy and "defamation of religion" laws are used to uphold and protect the doctrines of the state's recognised religions.[87] The Human Rights Committee has therefore urged the state to repeal laws, such as Law No. 1 of 1965,[88] because

> Prohibitions of displays of lack of respect for a religion or other belief system, including blasphemy laws, are incompatible with the Covenant, except in the specific circumstances envisaged in article 20, paragraph 2, of the Covenant ... Thus, for instance, it would be impermissible for any such laws to discriminate in favour of or against one or certain religions or belief systems, or their adherents over another, or religious believers over non-believers. Nor would it be permissible for such prohibitions to be used to prevent or punish criticism of religious leaders or commentary on religious doctrine and tenets of faith.[89]

In a number of countries around the world cases of blasphemy have been tried in court, most notably in Bangladesh, Egypt, and Saudi Arabia. In a 2009 case in Egypt, the Court of Administrative Justice revoked the licence of the magazine *Ibda'a* for publishing a poem it deemed "an offensive image of the Lord".[90] In its reasoning the Court explained its position on the offence:

> The magazine is the tool used to commit this crime against God and the sacred beliefs of this nation, regardless of who the perpetrator is; it is the means by which this heinous crime was committed. Moreover, the contempt shown for the Creator is eminently clear, an offense to God which is hidden from no one. It is inconceivable that this work was published by mistake, without having been seen by those who evaluate such works for publication. This indicates that some of these people have the conviction and willingness to publish insolent slights against the Lord.[91]

The Court also noted that while magazines and other publications do have the right to freedom of expression, this cannot be at the expense of society's core values, such as "the family, religion, morals, patriotism and motherhood".[92]

Even if blasphemy laws do not formally exist in a state, there have been cases where individuals have taken the law into their own hands and murdered accused blasphemers for their apparent violation. For instance in 2017, Pakistani student Mashal Khan was accused of blasphemy and killed by fellow students after a debate in which he raised sensitive theological questions.[93] NGOs in the country estimate 65 people have been killed extrajudicially in Pakistan since 1990 after being accused of blasphemy.[94]

POSSIBILITIES FOR HARMONISATION

There is much common ground between understandings of freedom of expression in international human rights law and Islamic law. In both, there is significant freedom for individuals to express their opinions, even if these ideas are not in line with dominant political or religious views. In both areas of law, individuals are given the right to freely express themselves but, at the same time, they are asked to respect others. Thus the right brings with it certain obligations. The Qur'anic position on freedom of expression offers much room for interpretation. There is therefore the possibility of using Qur'anic teachings to either expand or constrain the scope of permissible expression.

Unlike international human rights law and the Qur'an, traditional Islamic law has formalised a range of exceptions to the right to freedom of expression. One of these is blasphemy, which aims to "[protect] the sensibilities and beliefs of the Muslim community in particular and that of other faiths in general".[95] As far as reconciliation with international human rights law is concerned, the Human Rights Committee has determined that blasphemy laws can only be compatible with the ICCPR when the public expression that is limited is that described in Article 20(2) of the ICCPR: "advocacy of national, racial or religious hatred that constitutes incitement to discrimination, hostility or violence".[96] These are forms of speech that can be legitimately prohibited by law. For Muslims (and indeed people of other religious traditions) this stipulation allows some scope for protecting their religious sensibilities.

In terms of the punishment for blasphemy, the tension between Islamic law and international human rights law is much clearer when it comes to the death penalty. The Human Rights Council has unequivocally stated that blasphemy cannot be defined as one of the "most serious crimes"[97] for which the death penalty may be applied. However, there may be room to retain the notion of blasphemy in Islamic tradition but remove its traditional punishment. The death penalty can be set aside because there is no Qur'anic instruction or hadith which demands clearly that this should be the punishment for blasphemy. Moreover, since there is no clear definition of blasphemy in the Qur'an or hadith, and the offence (and its punishment) were the product of *ijtihad*, this creates space for contemporary Muslim scholars to use reason to generate new ideas about blasphemy. In this way, traditional understandings of blasphemy could be brought to some extent in line with contemporary understandings of freedom of expression.

The rethinking of the punishment for blasphemy should be seen as a critically important task for Muslim scholars today, given that blasphemy laws in Muslim-majority states are often abused and used to curtail legitimate freedom of expression. This in turn is having a negative impact on the expression of creativity, scholarship, and critical thought in these states. Given the difficulties many Muslim societies face because of restrictions to freedom of expression, it makes sense to open up this issue for further debate and discussion, perhaps eventually coming to terms with a more expansive view of freedom of expression that is compatible with international standards.

CONCLUSION

As freedom of expression is such a fundamental human right, clarifying the notion of blasphemy and its corresponding punishment should be seen as a critically important task for Muslim scholars today. Scholars can draw on the flexibility that the Qur'an offers in terms of its position on freedom of expression to reconsider the traditional constraints established by Islamic law. This will remove many of the difficulties that Muslim-majority states face in coming to terms with Article 19 of the UDHR and the ICCPR. Continuing to curtail freedom of expression will only have negative effects on those societies where such restrictions are enforced. Societies where people are not free to speak, debate, or criticise publicly cannot progress intellectually or socially.

* * *

LOOKING AT AN ISSUE CLOSELY: POSSIBLE MISUSE OF BLASPHEMY LAWS

Human Rights Watch, "Saudi Arabia: Poet Sentenced to Death for Apostasy Reverses Earlier Ruling of 4 Years, 800 Lashes" (2015). Available https://www.hrw.org/news/2015/11/23/saudi-arabia-poet-sentenced-death-apostasy.

This case concerns the application of blasphemy laws in Saudi Arabia. It shows the close connection between charges of blasphemy and apostasy and how blasphemy laws can be used for personal agendas (rather than strictly for regulating freedom of expression).

A Saudi court sentenced a Palestinian man to death for apostasy on November 17, 2015, for alleged blasphemous statements during a discussion group and in a book of his poetry.

The accused, Ashraf Fayadh, 35, denies the charges and claims that another man made false accusations to the country's religious police following a personal dispute. …

The trial documents, which Human Rights Watch reviewed, indicate that members of Saudi Arabia's Committee on the Promotion of Virtue and Prevention of Vice, or religious police, arrested Fayadh at a café in Abha, in southern Saudi Arabia, in August 2013. The religious police went to the café after a man reported that Fayadh had made obscene comments about God, the Prophet Muhammad, and the Saudi state. The man also alleged that Fayadh passed around a book he wrote that allegedly promoted atheism and unbelief.

After Fayadh was arrested, the court documents indicate, the religious police discovered on his phone photos of Fayadh with several women, whom Fayadh said he met at an art gallery.

The religious police held him for a day, then released him, but authorities re-arrested him on January 1, 2014. Prosecutors charged him with a host of blasphemy-related charges, including: blaspheming "the divine self" and the Prophet Muhammad; spreading atheism and promoting it among the youth in public places; mocking the verses of God and the prophets; refuting the Quran; denying the day of resurrection; objecting to fate and [the] divine decree; and having an illicit relationship with women and storing their pictures in his phone.

During the trial, which consisted of six hearings between February and May 2014, Fayadh denied the charges, and called three witnesses contesting the testimony of the man who reported him to the religious police. The defence witnesses said that the man reported Fayadh following a personal dispute, and that they had never heard blasphemous statements from Fayadh. Fayadh also said that his book, *Instructions Within*, published a decade before, consists of love poems and was not written with the intention of insulting religion.

During the last session, Fayadh expressed repentance for anything in the book that religious authorities may have deemed insulting, stating, according to trial documents, "I am repentant to God most high and I am innocent of what appeared in my book mentioned in this case".

On May 26, 2014, the General Court of Abha convicted Fayadh and sentenced him to four years in prison and 800 lashes. The court rejected a prosecution request for a death sentence for apostasy due to trial testimony indicating "hostility" between Fayadh and the man who reported him, as well as Fayadh's repentance.

The prosecutor appealed the ruling. Human Rights Watch was not able obtain a copy of the appeals ruling on the initial verdict, but the case was eventually sent back to the lower court. On November 17, 2015, a new judge with the General Court of Abha reversed the previous sentence and sentenced Fayadh to death for apostasy.

According to the judge's ruling, he dismissed the testimony of the defence witnesses in the initial trial and ruled that Fayadh's repentance was not enough to avoid the death sentence.

"Repentance is a work of the heart relevant to [the] matter of the judiciary of the hereafter; it is not the focus of the earthly judiciary", the ruling said.

The case moves next to the appeals court. The sentence must be approved by the appeals court and the Supreme Court.[98]

NOTES

1. United Nations General Assembly, *Universal Declaration of Human Rights*, 10 December 1948, 217 A (III). Available http://www.refworld.org/docid/3ae6b3712c.html, Article 19 (last accessed 8 December 2017).
2. United Nations General Assembly, *International Covenant on Civil and Political Rights* (*ICCPR*), 16 December 1966, United Nations, Treaty Series, vol. 999, p. 171. Available http://www.refworld.org/docid/3ae6b3aa0.html, Article 19 (last accessed 8 December 2017).
3. Human Rights Committee, General Comment No. 34 (Article 19: Freedoms of Opinion and Expression). Adopted 21 July 2011. UN Doc CCPR/C/GC/34, [2].
4. Ibid.
5. *ICCPR* art. 19(1).
6. Human Rights Committee, "General Comment 34", [9]. See Communication No. 550/93, *Faurisson v France*, views adopted on 8 November 1996.
7. Ibid.
8. Ibid, [11].
9. *ICCPR* art. 19(2).
10. Human Rights Committee, "General Comment No. 34", [11].
11. Ibid, [12].
12. *ICCPR*, art. 19(3).
13. Human Rights Committee, "General Comment No. 34", [21].
14. Ibid, [22].
15. Ibid, [48].
16. Ibid.
17. Ibid.

18. See Human Rights Council (HRC), *Annual Report of the United Nations High Commissioner for Human Rights and Reports of the Office of the High Commissioner and the Secretary-General: Study of the United Nations High Commissioner for Human Rights Compiling Existing Legislations and Jurisprudence Concerning Defamation of and Contempt for Religions*. 5 September 2008. Document No. A/HRC/9/25.
19. HRC, *Annual Report Concerning Defamation of and Contempt for Religions*, [1] (p. 3).
20. Ibid, [6] (p. 3).
21. Ibid, [6] (pp. 3–4).
22. Ibid, [7] (p. 4).
23. Ibid, [7] (p. 4).
24. Ibid, [8] (p. 4).
25. Paul Marshall, "Exporting Blasphemy Restrictions: The Organisation of the Islamic Conference and the United Nations", *The Review of Faith & International Affairs* (2011): 61. Marshall's article concentrates on OIC member countries.
26. Ibid.
27. Ibid.
28. Ibid.
29. Ibid.
30. HRC, *Annual Report Concerning Defamation of and Contempt for Religions*, 18.
31. Ibid.
32. Nazeem MI Goolam, "The Cartoon Controversy: A Note on Freedom of Expression, Hate Speech and Blasphemy", *The Comparative and International Law Journal of Southern Africa* 39(2) (2006): 333.
33. Ibid, 334.
34. Ibid.
35. Ibid.
36. Ibid.
37. Ibid.
38. Paul Sturges, "Limits to Freedom of Expression? Considerations Arising from the Danish Cartoons Affair", *IFLA* 32 (2006), 181–2.
39. Goolam, "The Cartoon Controversy", 334.
40. Ibid, 339, citing W. Sadurski, *Freedom of Speech and its Limits* (London: Kluwer Academic, 1999), 41, and R. Delgado "Words that Wound: A Tort Action for Racial Insults, Epithets, and Name-Calling", *Harvard Civil Rights Civil Liberties Law Review* (1982): 133.
41. Goolam, "The Cartoon Controversy", 340.
42. https://www.humanrights.gov.au/publications/background-paper-human-rights-cyberspace/4-permissible-limitations-iccpr-right-freedom.
43. Baderin, *International Human Rights*, 127.
44. Goolam, "The Cartoon Controversy", 341.
45. Ibid, 342.
46. See Q. 3:104, 4:9, 4:135, 4:171, 5:107, 17:80–81.
47. *al-Bukhari, Sahih al-Bukhari*, Kitab istitabat al-murtaddin wa-l-mu'anidin wa-qitalihim, No. 6927.
48. M.H. Kamali, *Freedom of Expression in Islam* (Kuala Lumpur: Berita Publishing, 1994), 243.
49. Baderin, *International Human Rights*, 129.
50. Kamali, *Freedom of Expression in Islam*, 164.
51. Baderin, *International Human Rights*, 127. See M.S. Chaudhry, *Islam's Charter of Fundamental Rights and Civil Liberties* (1995), 31–3.
52. Baderin, *International Human Rights*, 127.
53. Ibid.
54. Ibid.
55. Kamali, *Freedom of Expression in Islam*, 15.
56. Ibid, 243.

57. Baderin, *International Human Rights*, 127.
58. Ibid.
59. The Arabic phrase that Kamali translates as "the public utterance of evil speech" is *al-jahr bi-l-su' min al-qawl*. M.A.S. Abdel Haleem translates it as "bad words to be made public", while Abdullah Yusuf Ali gives it as "that evil should be noised abroad in public speech". A.J. Arberry gives "the shouting of evil words". Refer to the translation of the verse in relevant translations.
60. Kamali, *Freedom of Expression in Islam*, 162. Given the importance of Kamali's work in this area, I will rely heavily on him in the following.
61. Ibid.
62. Ibid.
63. Ibid.
64. Ibid, 162–3.
65. Ibid, 164.
66. Ibid, 166.
67. Ibid, 163.
68. Insults, if proven, could be punished with a *ta'zir* (discretionary) punishment. See ibid, 172.
69. Kamali, *Freedom of Expression in Islam*, 172.
70. Ibid, 173.
71. Ibid, 173.
72. Kamali, Sultanhussein Tabandeh, and Mashood Baderin all agree on this point. Kamali also affirms there is a great deal of consensus among the four leading Islamic law schools on blasphemy, with the differences related to issues about whether the perpetrator should be given the opportunity to repent. See Kamali, *Freedom of Expression in Islam*, 211.
73. Baderin, *International Human Rights*, 128, *Encyclopaedia of Religion and Ethics* vol. 2, J. Hastings (ed.) (1909), 672.
74. Baderin, *International Human Rights*, 128.
75. Goolam, "The Cartoon Controversy", 343.
76. Ibid.
77. Baderin, *International Human Rights*, 128.
78. Goolam, "The Cartoon Controversy", 343.
79. Ibid.
80. Ibid, 343–4.
81. Ibid, 344.
82. Ibid, 343.
83. Ibid, 344.
84. Baderin, *International Human Rights*, 128.
85. Ibid.
86. Human Rights Committee, "Concluding Observations on the Third Periodic Report of Kuwait", UN Doc CCPR/C/KWT/CO/3. 11 August 2016, [40].
87. Human Rights Committee, "Concluding Observations on the Initial Report of Indonesia", 21 August 2013. UN Doc CCPR/C/IDN/CO/1, [25].
88. Ibid.
89. Ibid.
90. Freedom of Religion and Belief Program Egyptian Initiative for Personal Rights, "Freedom of Religion and Belief in Egypt Quarterly Report: April to June 2009" (2009). Available https://eipr.org/en/file/331/download?token=ItksLz-5, 6 (last accessed 8 December 2017). Referring to Case No. 21751/61, ruling handed down 7 April 2009.
91. Freedom of Religion and Belief Program Egyptian Initiative for Personal Rights, "Freedom of Religion and Belief in Egypt Quarterly Report: April to June 2009" (2009).
92. Ibid.
93. Jibran Ahmed, "Dorm Debate Led to Death in Pakistan 'Blasphemy Killing' – Witnesses" (2017) *Reuters* 14 April 2017. Available http://in.reuters.com/article/pakistan-blasphemy-idINKBN17G1DI (last accessed 8 December 2017).

94. Ibid.
95. Baderin, *International Human Rights*, 128.
96. See Human Rights Committee, "General Comment 34", [48] with reference to Article 20(2) of the ICCPR.
97. Human Rights Council, *Question of the Death Penalty: Report of the Secretary-General* (2014). 30 June 2014 UN Doc A/HRC/27/23, [35], citing CCPR/C/79/Add.85, [8].
98. Human Rights Watch, "Saudi Arabia: Poet Sentenced to Death for Apostasy Reverses Earlier Ruling of 4 Years, 800 Lashes" (2015). Available https://www.hrw.org/news/2015/11/23/saudi-arabia-poet-sentenced-death-apostasy (last accessed 8 December 2017).

10. Islam and religious freedom

INTRODUCTION

In this chapter we will explore one of the most important human rights today: religious freedom. The practice of religion has been one of the most observable features of human history. Belief and ritual are important elements of life and each of us wishes to function in line with what our conscience demands. This is something essential to our psyche, regardless of the religion that we follow, or how we define religion. Given its importance, it is understandable that debate about freedom of religion and belief has occurred since the earliest times, generated by theologians, philosophers, religious traditions, and governments.

This interest in religious freedom has not waned over time. Despite modernisation, religion remains one of the most prevalent aspects of life across the globe. Religion brings people together around common issues and provides a way to create a meaningful and collective identity. In the contemporary period religion affects us all, regardless of whether or not we actually believe in a particular religion or consider ourselves "religious", and despite the fact that some political and philosophical trends have attempted to marginalise it.

Religion can unify communities by providing a common value system. However, religion can also be destructive. It can create tension and conflict in a society, especially if multiple religions or belief systems are present. People of different religious traditions and even from the same tradition can easily come into conflict over competing beliefs. This has led to war and the destruction of whole societies, and many parts of the world today are burdened by religious conflict. Given that most people live in multi-religious societies today, freedom of religion has an important role to play in maintaining community harmony and allowing different faith groups to co-exist peacefully. In this chapter we will explore how religious freedom is understood in international human rights law and in Islamic tradition, the kinds of restrictions on religious freedom that exist in some Muslim-majority countries, the resources and ideas that exist within Islamic tradition to support religious freedom as it is understood today, and how religious freedom functioned in Muslim societies in some key periods of Islamic history.

WHAT IS RELIGIOUS FREEDOM?

Religious freedom has a number of elements. It concerns beliefs and theology, the manifestation of practices (such as rituals), and broader socio-cultural issues. Theologically, religious freedom involves the right of an individual to hold a certain set of beliefs. These beliefs may be about God, the nature of the universe, accountability, salvation, or life after death. These matters of belief are not necessarily manifest; rather, they are internal to the believer. In this sense the right to hold internal and personal beliefs, according to one's conscience, is an absolute right—it cannot be restricted in any way.

However, belief is also demonstrated or made evident through ritual or other practices, such as prayer, chanting, recitation of sacred texts, or the visiting of holy places. While the holding of beliefs cannot be restricted in any way, the observable practice of religion can be. Here, society may impose regulations about the extent to which religion can be practised, particularly in public. This is important in societies made up of different religious traditions or competing understandings of the one tradition. In these contexts, constraints on religious practice are arguably required to ensure the smooth functioning of society. Restrictions are accepted in most societies as part of the necessary balancing of rights within society, where the interests of all are treated with equal importance.

Religion can also structure social relations, including the forming of families, marriage, and divorce, as well as relations between parents and children, husbands and wives, and men and women more broadly. State restrictions can be applied to these aspects of religious practice. Since most socio-cultural contexts are religiously diverse, with each religion providing its own (potentially conflicting) teachings and guidelines, it is the duty of the state to ensure that these practices do not lead to conflict and tension within society. This is generally considered acceptable, given the pluralistic make-up of most modern societies today.

RELIGIOUS FREEDOM IN INTERNATIONAL LAW

In international human rights law, the right to freedom of religion is expressed in Article 18 of the UDHR: "Everyone has the right to freedom of thought, conscience and religion; this right includes freedom to change his religion or belief and freedom, either alone or in community with others and in public or private to manifest his religion or belief in teaching, practice, worship and observance."[1]

This article affirms that religious freedom is a basic human right. While it is not directly binding on states, most of its elements have been incorporated into other binding treaties. For example, the ICCPR, which is monitored by the Human Rights Committee, and the 1965 International Convention on the Elimination of All Forms of Racial Discrimination (ICERD), both "follow in the direction set by the [UDHR]", although they "do not explicitly restate the right to change religion".[2]

Article 18 of the ICCPR on freedom of religion states:

> 1. Everyone shall have the right to freedom of thought, conscience and religion. This right shall include freedom to have or to adopt a religion or belief of his choice, and freedom, either individually or in community with others and in public or private, to manifest his religion or belief in worship, observance, practice and teaching.
>
> 2. No one shall be subject to coercion which would impair his freedom to have or to adopt a religion or belief of his choice.
>
> 3. Freedom to manifest one's religion or beliefs may be subject only to such limitations as are prescribed by law and are necessary to protect public safety, order, health, or morals or the fundamental rights and freedoms of others.[3]

This provision has broad implications. It comprises an individual's freedom to hold views, beliefs or opinions on "all matters"; the convictions a person may hold; and their personal commitment to "religion or belief", as well as its public outworking.[4] Recognising the importance of this freedom, General Comment 22 of the Human Rights Committee specifies that this article "cannot be derogated from, even in time of public emergency".[5]

State parties to the ICCPR therefore have "the positive obligation of ensuring the freedom of religion or belief of [all] persons on ... [their] territory and under ... [their] jurisdiction".[6] States must ensure that individuals from all religious traditions can practise their religion or beliefs without coercion or fear. UN Special Rapporteur Asma Jahangir notes in a 2005 report to the UN General Assembly that "if non-state actors interfere with this freedom ... the State ... [must] investigate, bring the perpetrators to justice and compensate the victims".[7] More recently, Special Rapporteur Heiner Bielefeldt also makes the point that while a state religion is not prohibited under international law per se, states must "ensure that this [practice] does not lead to ... discrimination [against the] members of other religions and beliefs. The burden of proof in this regard falls on the State".[8]

Like Article 18 of the UDHR, Article 18 of the ICCPR identifies a number of elements of freedom of religion. Firstly, the right of an individual to adopt a religion or belief of his or her choice.

Freedom to Adopt a Religion or Belief

The first paragraph of Article 18 of the ICCPR, concerning freedom to adopt a religion or belief, was only agreed upon after significant debate in the former Human Rights Committee and the General Assembly's Third Committee. Some states objected strongly to the initial wording proposed during the drafting process, that—"Everyone should have the freedom to maintain or to change his religion"—on the grounds that it would potentially encourage proselytism. Eventually, an alternative formulation—"have or to adopt a religion or belief of his choice"—was adopted unanimously instead. But "This final version of the provision was undoubtedly intended to include the right to convert from one religion or belief to another."[9]

According to General Comment No. 22,

> the freedom to "have or to adopt" a religion or belief necessarily entails the freedom to choose a religion or belief, including, *inter alia*, the right to replace one's current religion or belief with another or to adopt atheistic views, as well as the right to retain one's religion or belief.[10]

Indeed, as Special Rapporteur Abdelfattah Amor notes in his 1996 report to the United Nations Economic and Social Council, "it is now established that religious freedom cannot be dissociated from the freedom to change religion".[11] He cites Elisabeth Odio Bénito, a prominent lawyer and human rights advocate, who wrote that although the UDHR and ICCPR "var[y] slightly in wording, [they mean] precisely the same thing: that everyone ha[s] the right to leave [their] religion or belief and to adopt another, or to remain without any at all".[12] He concludes that "the right to change religion ... [is an] essential aspect of religious freedom".[13]

An individual's right to freely adopt a religion or belief of their choice means that they cannot be compelled or coerced to adopt a particular religion or belief. Article 18(2) of the ICCPR prohibits any action that may curtail an individual's freedom in this regard. For example, the state may not use the "threat of physical force or penal sanctions to compel believers or non-believers to adhere to their religious beliefs and congregations, to recant their religion or belief or to convert".[14] In countries such as Egypt, Saudi Arabia and Turkmenistan (among others),[15] individuals have been "arrested, tried or otherwise challenged" because they have adopted another religion, held particular beliefs, or the state has "attempt[ed] to force them to renounce or abandon their faith".[16] Punishment for changing one's religion can also include being tried for the offence of "apostasy", a prison sentence, or even the death penalty.[17] In other instances it can include civil consequences like "the suspension of all contracts and inheritance rights, the annulment of marriages, loss of property or the removal of children".[18] Such actions are, according to the Special Rapporteur, contrary to the right to freedom of religion.[19] Likewise, the state is not allowed to offer any form of incentive to encourage an individual to convert to another religion or to prevent them from doing so.[20]

This point is particularly pertinent for Muslim-majority nations, many of which have significant difficulties in accepting the right of an individual to change their religion. This is deemed apostasy and punishable by death in traditional Islamic law. There is an impasse between Muslim governments which believe that punishing apostasy is justifiable, and those who affirm the right to change one's religion, a fundamental part of the right to freedom of religion under international law.

The Death Penalty

The death penalty is not actually prohibited under international law. The ICCPR addresses the matter of the death penalty under Article 6 on the right to life. This article affirms that life cannot be arbitrary taken;[21] however the death penalty can be judicially imposed "for the most serious crimes" and "pursuant to a final judgement rendered by a competent court",[22] although not on children, nor on pregnant women.[23] Indeed, the imposition of the death penalty on persons below 18 years of age was a key concern for the Human Rights Committee when reviewing the fifth periodic report of Yemen in 2012.[24]

The legitimacy of a death sentence, according to international law, depends (in part) on whether the crime it is being imposed for can be considered a "most serious crime". This threshold has been elaborated over time. For the Human Rights Committee, the death penalty can only be prescribed as an "exceptional measure".[25] In the 1984 instrument *Safeguards Guaranteeing Protection of the Rights of Those Facing the Death Penalty*, the General Assembly affirmed that the most serious crimes include "intentional crimes with lethal or other extremely grave consequences".[26] "[N]on-violent financial crimes ... non-violent religious practices or expressions of conscience, and sexual relations between consenting adults", do not meet this threshold,[27] nor do "economic offences (including embezzlement by officials), drug-related offences, political offences, robbery, abduction not resulting in death, and apostasy, illicit sex ... and theft by force".[28] The Human Rights Committee has also raised objections to the death penalty being imposed for political or security-related crimes,[29] or as a mandatory penalty (without any judicial discretion).[30] While reviewing the third periodic report of Iran (2011), the Committee reiterated that the death penalty can only be imposed in a very limited way for the "most serious crimes",[31] and expressed concern about the wide range of offences that currently attract a capital sentence.[32]

Freedom to Manifest One's Religion

Article 18 affirms an individual's right to manifest his or her religion or belief, either alone or with others, and both publicly and privately.[33] This freedom "encompasses a broad range" of expressions:[34] from being able to participate in rituals and ceremonies; to the "building of places of worship" and display of religious symbols; to being allowed to recognise days of special religious significance, follow particular dietary restrictions, wear certain religious clothing; and "freedom to choose ... religious leaders, priests and teachers, the freedom to establish seminaries or religious schools and the freedom to prepare and distribute religious texts or publications".[35] According to the Human Rights Committee, the freedom to manifest one's religion also includes freedom to proselytise.[36] Similarly, the Special Rapporteur on Freedom of Religion has opined that "constitutional provisions prohibiting proselytism ... [are] inconsistent with the 1981 Declaration [on the Elimination of All Forms of Intolerance and of Discrimination Based on Religion or Belief]".[37]

Unlike an individual's right to freely adopt a religion or belief, an individual's freedom to manifest their religion can be permissibly restricted in certain circumstances. Article 18(3) elaborates that such limitations must be "prescribed by law" and "necessary to protect public safety, order, health, or morals or the fundamental rights and freedoms of others".[38] When applying such limitations, states must keep in mind other relevant rights, such as "the right to equality and non-discrimination"[39] and not impose limitations for reasons outside those specified in the article.[40]

The majority of Muslim states have signed and ratified the ICCPR without qualification,[41] acknowledging, at least in a legal sense, that they support the right to freedom of religion. However, a number of states have entered reservations against Article 18, expressing their disagreement with some or all of the wording of the article. For instance, Bahrain is a state party to the ICCPR but has entered a reservation stating that the government "interprets the provisions of Article … 18 … as not affecting in any way the prescriptions of the Islamic Shariah".[42] Mauritania's reservation has similar wording: that interpretation of the Article "shall be without prejudice to the Islamic Shariah".[43] Similarly, the Maldives states that "the application of the principles set out in Article 18 of the Covenant 'shall be without prejudice to the Constitution of the Republic of Maldives'",[44] which establishes Islam as the state religion and affirms that Islam is one of the bases of all its laws.[45]

RESTRICTIONS BY MUSLIM-MAJORITY STATES ON RELIGIOUS FREEDOM

Many Muslim-majority states today do restrict various aspects of the right to religious freedom to a significant extent, which creates conflict with the standards established by international human rights law. Specific problematic restrictions include: blasphemy laws, apostasy laws, and severe limitations to the religious practices of religious minorities.

Some of these restrictions apply particularly to Muslims; for instance, apostasy laws, limitations on religious and social practices, and even restrictions on beliefs that can be held internally. Iraq is one country that applies apostasy laws and the Human Rights Committee has expressed concern that such provisions "adversely affect the exercise of the right to freedom of religion or belief enshrined in article 18 of the Covenant".[46] Egypt applies similar restrictions and the courts have upheld the prohibition on a Muslim changing their religion. For instance, the Court of Administrative Justice discussed the issue of apostasy in cases 53717/62 and 22566/63 (2009) in relation to a Muslim individual who had decided to change his religious affiliation to Christianity and was petitioning the Ministry of the Interior to have this change recognised. The Court refused his claim,[47] affirming that "converts of Muslim origin are prohibited from converting from Islam".[48] While the Court acknowledged that Egypt's Constitution recognises freedom of religion, this right, according to it, "is not absolute".[49] Freedom of religion, as articulated in Article 18 of the ICCPR, runs counter to this position. In Jordan, a Muslim's decision to leave Islam has various civil consequences that, in effect, work as restrictions to religious freedom.[50] While there are no criminal penalties for apostasy,[51] the apostate can be denied inheritance, for example.[52]

Other restrictions particularly apply to non-Muslims. Common restrictions include limitations on where and whether new places of worship can be built and bans on the public ringing of church bells, the importation of religious literature and proselytism amongst Muslims. Kuwait is one country that applies "a series of administrative and organizational steps" before a new place of worship can be built.[53] "Compliance with the procedures is obligatory and cannot be circumvented".[54] However, the Human Rights Committee has noted that the processes for granting a licence are "discriminatory" towards religious minorities and "adversely affect the exercise of the right to freedom of thought, conscience and religion".[55]

Many of these restrictions are rooted in traditional Islamic law, unfolding from traditional apostasy laws and from the interpretation of specific Qur'anic and hadith texts. Some political and religious establishments in Muslim-majority countries argue that these traditional Islamic norms must be maintained. According to this position, it is imperative to maintain traditional understandings of apostasy (especially its criminality) because if it is diluted or the punishment is not applied as a deterrent, this could lead to the unravelling of the religion of Islam itself. This perspective comes from certain sayings attributed to the Prophet that seem to suggest that converts from Islam should be punished with death. Perhaps the most important in this regard is the hadith: "Whoever changes his religion, kill him",[56] which seems to give explicit permission for Muslims to kill anyone who leaves Islam.

These narrations were used in the early centuries of Islam to develop what is now known as the law of apostasy and its associated punishment—the death penalty. In Islamic legal texts written during the first four centuries of Islam, almost all jurists from the surviving Islamic schools of law argued that an apostate should be put to death.[57] Thus, there are claims of "consensus" among Muslims on the death penalty for apostasy. Naturally, these claims of consensus ignore the views of those that did not support this punishment.

Furthermore, although widely considered reliable, a number of scholars argue that hadith such as the one cited above do not reach the level of certainty that is required from textual evidence to justify the death penalty.[58] Indeed, some argue that there is no strong textual evidence in the Qur'an or hadith that clearly supports apostasy laws and the death penalty associated with them.[59] Accordingly, I argue these laws may not be part of the fundamentals of Islam; they were developed from legal or political interpretations that are not inherent to the religion and which do not carry enough authority in themselves to justify such restrictions to religious freedom. Given the absence of a clear basis for many of these restrictions particularly in the Qur'an, it is possible to develop an understanding of religious freedom that is both in line with the spirit of the Qur'an and compatible with international human rights standards.

SUPPORT IN ISLAMIC SOURCES FOR RELIGIOUS FREEDOM

In the Qur'an there is ample support for the right to freedom of thought, conscience, and religion. The key principles upon which these ideas can be developed are human dignity, personal responsibility, non-coercion, the prevention of religious hypocrisy, and persuasion.

Human Dignity

The first principle that can be used to support a modern conception of religious freedom is that of human dignity. The Qur'an emphasises that human beings have inherent worth and dignity. God created humans "in the finest state" (Q. 95:4) and in doing so honoured humanity and granted it special favours (Q. 17:70). Kamali argues that "a person's dignity is intimately related to his or her [ability to exercise personal] freedom—particularly freedom of conscience".[60] Indeed, God gave human beings the ability and the intellect to discern between right and wrong on the basis of their conscience (Q. 17:15 and 6:104). For Kamali, freedom in Islam is inherently individualistic in the sense that it was designed to protect the basic dignity of a person against imposition by state or society. Thus, "freedom of belief, like all other freedoms, operates as a safeguard against the possible menace of oppression that emanates from superior sources of power".[61]

Personal Responsibility

From a Qur'anic point of view, belief is something that is left to individual conscience and personal reflection. On the Day of Judgement individuals will stand before God and be questioned about what they did (or failed to do) and what they did to others (Q. 6:164). Accountability is therefore very closely connected to the individual and their personal responsibility to make choices. It is individuals who will be saved or damned. The Qur'an does not see the question of belief as a collective or a community matter.[62]

Non-coercion

In a well-known verse, the Qur'an says, "There is no compulsion in religion" (Q. 2:256). While there are some debates about the precise meaning and legal implications of this verse, many Muslims today argue that it sets out the most important principle when it comes to matters of faith and religion: that there be no coercion in matters of faith. As Shah argues, "this verse has two implications: first … no one is compelled to adopt Islam as … [a] religion[,] and secondly, that once someone embraces Islam, h/she should not be forced to follow what others believe".[63] Abdolkarim Soroush, an influential Iranian thinker, argues that "genuine acceptance of religion requires freedom of conscience",[64] which cannot be achieved through coercion. Maududi, another influential Islamist thinker from Pakistan, further emphasises that "people should accept Islam through their own free will", not by force. Therefore "Muslims must avoid placing political or social pressure on [people] to convert. Rather, Muslims are obligated to acknowledge and respect their decision" in matters of faith.[65]

Many Muslim scholars today argue that Muslims should follow the practice of the Prophet Muhammad, who was "not allowed to coerce people into believing in Islam".[66] Indeed, Q. 2:256 "serve[s] as a reminder that God does not sanction religious compulsion".[67]

Prevention of Religious Hypocrisy

The Qur'an considers religious hypocrisy (*nifaq*) to be a major moral and religious problem. It therefore condemns hypocrisy and hypocrites in many verses, encouraging sincerity in all human dealings (Q. 61:2–3). This is particularly important in matters of faith. Forced belief does not result in sincere faith, which is an essential element of all religious traditions, including Islam. Indeed, sincerity in belief and practice is an essential part of what it means to be Muslim.[68]

Persuasion

Finally, the Qur'an emphasises gentle persuasion in communicating matters of faith and religion. In Q. 16:125, it says: "[Prophet], call [people] to the way of your Lord with wisdom and good teaching. Argue with them in the most courteous way." This precludes the use of compulsion.[69] It also states: "Say, 'Now the truth has come from your Lord: let those who wish to believe in it do so, and let those who wish to reject it do so'" (Q. 18:29).

RESTRICTIONS TO RELIGIOUS FREEDOM IN ISLAM

Despite the Qur'anic and Prophetic instructions regarding freedom of religion, Islamic law developed a range of rules and regulations to restrict religious freedom in Muslim societies. The most critical restriction and important challenge for contemporary understandings of religious freedom is the issue of apostasy, discussed above. While Muslim jurists and thinkers in the past and present are generally comfortable with the idea that non-Muslims under Muslim rule should not be coerced or forced to accept Islam, this does not extend to Muslims who wish to leave Islam. As there is nearly unanimous agreement among pre-modern Muslim jurists that apostasy should be punished by death, it is very difficult for many Muslims today to move beyond this legal position, at least theoretically.

Another key example here relates to the treatment of non-Muslims under Muslim rule in the past. They were typically considered unequal citizens. Much of the classical jurists' thinking on this issue was based on the interpretation of certain Qur'anic and hadith texts, as well as precedents from the practice of various Muslim rulers in the early centuries of Islam, not to mention the prevailing idea among Muslims that Islam was superior to all other religious traditions. Citizenship rights in many parts of the world at that time were usually accorded based on affiliation with a dominant religion or ethnicity, and similar practices were followed in Muslim states too. For example, when it came to building or renovating places of worship, giving evidence in certain types of court cases, and intermarriage, Muslim jurists did not see Muslims and non-Muslims as equal. These practices differed from state to state according to the composition of communities and the political issues faced at the time. In many cases the extent of the restriction was probably only theoretical, rather than actually applied, depending on the temperament of rulers and the pressures being exerted on Muslim states. In any case, equal citizenship rights is a relatively modern concept and Muslims, like others, had to wait for centuries for the concept to emerge.

Another key restriction propagated by traditional Islamic law was on the proselytisation of Muslims by people of other faiths. This issue is still controversial, not only in traditional Islamic law but also in the modern period. Under Islamic law, acts of proselytisation that target Muslims in a Muslim-majority society have been considered unacceptable. More recently, the maintenance of social harmony in a number of countries has required that religious minorities mind their own business in religious matters and not attempt to recruit from the majority.

HISTORICAL PRACTICE OF RELIGIOUS FREEDOM IN MUSLIM SOCIETIES[70]

Historical evidence suggests that early Muslim states actually maintained a relatively high degree of religious freedom for both Muslims and non-Muslims in a number of different ways. From then, the concept of freedom of religion evolved progressively (and not always more tolerantly) throughout various historical periods.

The Prophetic Period (610–32 CE)

The first era of Islamic thought—the Prophetic period—consisted of two periods: the Meccan period and the Medinan period. The first period (610–22 CE) was when the Prophet lived in Mecca. At this time Islam had relatively few followers and Muslims were a persecuted minority. However, the period is crucial to Islamic thought: it was during this time that many Qur'anic revelations relating to religious freedom occurred, and the Prophet Muhammad gave the instructions that provided a textual basis for Muslim thinking on freedom of religion today.

In Mecca, the Qur'an made it clear that individuals were free to follow (or not) the Prophet and his teachings.[71] It also strongly emphasised that individuals should not be compelled to believe in Islam. The Qur'an reminded the Prophet that he did not have the power to force people to convert to Islam.[72] His only responsibility was to communicate the messages he received from God, allowing his listeners the freedom to make decisions about what to believe.[73]

In Medina, after the Prophet's migration there in 622 CE, the Prophet continued the same message of individual freedom concerning belief. Unlike in Mecca, his teachings spread rapidly and soon he was able to establish a visible Muslim community. Even so, he maintained the principle that no one should be forced to convert to Islam, including the Jewish communities that were living in the city when he arrived. The terms of the agreement he established with these communities suggest that he considered the Jewish people an essential part of the community of Medina. Despite religious differences, all parties were considered on a par with each other and treated without discrimination. For instance, one of the agreement's provisions affirms: "The Jews of Banu Awf are a community [*umma*] with the Believers; the Jews have their religion/law [*din*] and the Muslims have their religion/law."[74]

Under the leadership of the Prophet Muhammad, the Muslim community in Medina gradually strengthened politically and numerically, enabling it to withstand a range of military attacks by the Prophet's opponents. The Prophet's preaching also gradually expanded the message of Islam to neighbouring tribes. In the last two years of the Prophet's life (631–32 CE), a number of Qur'anic verses urged Muslims and the Prophet to go to war if necessary to end the aggression of their opponents and to bring them under the control of the state, politically and militarily.[75] These texts have been read by some Muslims and non-Muslims as an end to the message of religious freedom that was so emphasised in Mecca and the early period of Medina. However, in the context of the political developments that were taking place, it can be seen that these texts were not about limiting religious freedom, but about bringing opponents of the emerging Muslim state under its political control and subduing hardliners.[76] In this context, the anticipated outcome of the conflict was not that opponents would convert to Islam, or that they would be theologically or religiously quashed, but they would be controlled politically and militarily. Therefore, we can conclude that the basic idea of freedom of religion, in terms of allowing individuals and communities to maintain their religious beliefs and to be free from coercion, was consistently maintained in the Prophetic period.

Post-Prophetic Period

The relatively permissive attitude of the Qur'an and the Prophet towards religious freedom continued in the post-Prophetic period. One of the best examples of this is the attitude of the first Muslim state in Medina towards the religious freedom of those non-Muslims who came under its political and military control during its expansion into the Middle East and North Africa. As the Muslim state expanded, agreements were concluded with the peoples of the various towns and cities that came under Muslim rule. In general, these people were able to maintain their own religions, often in exchange for paying a tax to the Muslim state. Conversion by force was not practised.

As Islamic law evolved, Muslim jurists developed their understanding of religious freedom based on the guidance of the Qur'an, the practice of Prophet Muhammad, and early Muslim governments, particularly during the first century of Islam. In general, the emerging legal discourse recognised that the principles of religious freedom and non-coercion needed to be maintained.[77] Non-Muslims under Muslim rule were to be allowed to keep their religions and religious traditions. This legal position has largely remained throughout Muslim history. For example, under the Ottoman empire (1299–1924) what was known as the *millet* system was instituted, allowing religious communities to function with relative freedom and to apply their own norms and values.[78] The Ottoman Empire managed its significant religious diversity by allowing non-Muslims a high degree of religious freedom, and this often prevented religious uprisings and conflict. Although the dominance of the Muslim state was seen as necessary, there was no requirement for non-Muslims to give up their religious traditions and become Muslims.

The Modern Period

Generally, these historical examples show that Muslims were not expected to force non-Muslims to convert to Islam. Non-Muslims received protection from the state, and legally they had their own religious institutions and were free to believe in and practise their traditions. Rachel Scott observes that in general, "coercion was condemned" and faith was seen as "a voluntary act", although there were "rare incidents of forced conversion".[79] However this position of non-coercion was widely held and maintained by Islamic law, which meant that pre-modern Muslim societies encompassed a significant level of religious tolerance.

In the latter part of the twentieth century, as the global discourse on human rights gathered momentum, many Muslim scholars, politicians, and influential members of the community have debated the issue of religious freedom in Muslim societies. In this debate, particular attention has been paid to the law of apostasy. Many scholars argue that while the Qur'an and the Prophet's practice support the idea of religious freedom, traditional Islamic law maintains that apostasy is a crime and therefore Muslims must maintain this restriction. Opposition to this restriction has gradually increased; however, very few Muslims have tried to counter this publicly until recently. Those that have done so, in their individual capacities or as members of activist organisations, have lacked the necessary influence to change political and religious opinion in Muslim-majority states so far. The debate on apostasy and freedom of religion has instead been couched in terms of defending Muslims' right to reject proselytisation in their societies. The claim is made that this proselytisation is being driven by major powers, especially Christian or Western powers. The question of apostasy has therefore been often framed as Muslim/Christian competition for the saving of souls, where Christians have the upper hand politically, militarily, and economically. Thus, newly independent Muslim states, particularly in the post-war period, have reacted very defensively to this debate.

While there are still many Muslim voices that object to the idea of giving complete freedom to Muslims to convert from Islam, by and large the idea of religious freedom, as articulated by international human rights instruments, is also becoming more accepted. Indeed, it can be argued with significant textual support that the Qur'an emphasises freedom of religion and does not support the death penalty for Muslims who convert from Islam. The Qur'an contains many verses that affirm the right to freedom of religion from both the Meccan and Medinan periods. Nevertheless, the Qur'an views conversion from Islam with dismay and criticises it. On a number of occasions the Qur'an declares that those who move away from the true path of God and the Prophet will be condemned and punished with hellfire after death.[80] However, in line with its position of individual and personal responsibility for matters of belief and religion, it does not force Muslims to remain Muslims if they choose to convert. From the Qur'an's point of view, a Muslim who leaves Islam commits a grave sin that warrants punishment in the life to come. Despite this the Qur'an envisages a natural death for such a person. No verse of the Qur'an specifies any worldly punishment for converting from Islam, let alone death.[81] Similarly, there is no evidence to indicate that the Prophet Muhammad himself ever imposed the death penalty on an apostate for the simple act of conversion from Islam.[82]

While some Muslim-majority countries have entered reservations against Article 18 of the ICCPR, they are still in the minority. Many of these states tend to pay lip service to the traditional Islamic legal position on apostasy, but at the same time are distancing themselves from that position in practice. In fact, only some Muslim-majority countries today, like Saudi Arabia, Iran, and Malaysia, still apply apostasy laws. Not all of these implement the death penalty as punishment. Some, like Malaysia, instead implement measures of compulsory religious "rehabilitation".

Importantly, more recently, a number of new trends in Muslim societies have become apparent that are moving towards religious freedom for both Muslims and non-Muslims. A growing number of Muslims do not support punishment for apostasy, and see the need for all people to have freedom to choose their religion. For them, this right should be respected because the Qur'an and the Prophet's practice support this position.

POSSIBILITIES FOR HARMONISATION

Today, criminalisation of apostasy remains one of the greatest challenges when it comes to reconciling Islamic law and international human rights norms in the area of religious freedom. While only a few Muslim-majority states are applying the death penalty for apostasy in practice, and many contemporary Muslim scholars and jurists have challenged the criminalisation of changing one's religion,[83] the traditional position on apostasy remains and has not been overturned.[84] Apostasy remains "politically and legally salient"[85] because apostasy laws are notoriously open to abuse in some Muslim-majority states. There are many examples of these laws being used to stifle political opponents, curtail legitimate debate and discussion of religiously or politically sensitive issues, harass intellectuals, or encourage private acts of violence against individuals.[86] From the perspective of the Human Rights Committee, apostasy laws are indeed incompatible with states' obligations under Article 18 of the ICCPR.[87]

However, as noted above, there are considerable resources in the Qur'an and hadith to affirm an understanding of freedom of religion that is compatible with international human rights law. As this thinking develops and Muslim scholars engage in the discourse on religious freedom, it is possible that many restrictions surrounding religious freedom may be dismantled through *ijtihad*. This will resolve the current tension that exists between international human rights law and Islamic law.

Another stream of scholarship is challenging the death penalty. Scholars such as Mohamed El-Awa and Mohammad Hashim Kamali argue that apostasy is not an offense that attracts a prescribed punishment (*hadd*),[88] referring to the position of the Maliki jurist Abu al-Walid al-Baji (d. 474/1081), who stated that apostasy is "a sin for which there is no *hadd* punishment".[89] El-Awa notes that "the Qur'an prescribes no punishment in this life for apostasy, [and] the Prophet never sentenced a man to death for it, [but] some of the companions of the Prophet recognised apostasy as a sin for which there was a *ta'zir* [discretionary] punishment".[90] Baderin notes that this "placed the matter within the legislative discretion of the Islamic State".[91] Challenging the view that the death penalty is a prescribed penalty for apostasy will certainly go a considerable way towards reducing the tension between Islamic law and international human rights law, which only allows the death penalty to be applied "for the most serious crimes".[92]

CONCLUSION

Despite the uphill battle of countering the traditional Islamic legal position on freedom of religion and apostasy, there is definitely room for

Muslims today to rethink the restrictions on religious freedom. We certainly have the Qur'an, hadith and other legal texts at our service. In the modern period, Muslim scholars should therefore be arguing for a notion of religious freedom that accommodates Article 18 of both the UDHR and ICCPR. Indeed, the fact that Muslim scholars are prepared to engage in the discourse on religious freedom is an important development, and it is possible that many restrictions surrounding religious freedom may be dismantled. A number of Muslim-majority nations have already moved in this direction, and there is every chance that the idea of religious freedom, as articulated by international law, may soon become the norm for many more.

* * *

LOOKING AT AN ISSUE CLOSELY: HASAN YOUSEFI ESHKEVARI AND APOSTASY LAWS IN IRAN

Iran Human Rights Documentation Centre, "Apostasy in the Islamic Republic of Iran" (2014). Available http://www.iranhrdc.org/english/publications/reports/1000000512-apostasy-in-the-Islamic-Republic-of-Iran.html#3.1.1. Extract*

This case concerns the high profile case of Hasan Yousefi Eshkevari, a religious leader who was charged with apostasy in Iran, although he did not explicitly renounce Islam or change his religion. It shows how apostasy laws can be used by regimes to uphold their versions of Islamic orthodoxy and to curtail religious freedom.

Hasan Yousefi Eshkevari was charged with apostasy after attending a controversial conference in Berlin in 2000.[93] Eshkevari's case is among the best-known apostasy cases in Iran due to his position as a cleric and the political aftermath of the Berlin conference. …

… The text of his indictment, which is dated September 13, 2000 and is published on his website, listed his charges as follows:

> Insulting sacred Islamic beliefs, denying and repudiating basic tenets of the enlightening religion of Islam and everlasting laws of the Qur'an through

---

* See Iran Human rights Documentation Centre. www.iranhrdc.org. 129 Church Street Suite 423, New Haven, Connecticut 06510 U.S.A. Phone: 1 (203) 745 4247.

> giving a speech against the Islamic veil and Islamic penal laws, giving interviews to foreign radio stations and denying the everlasting nature of Islamic and Qur'anic laws (addressed in the first discussion of the chapter ["A]postasy["] in Imam Khomeini's *Tahrīr al-Vasīlah* as well as in Article 513 of the Book of *Ta'zirat*).
>
> Waging war on God, sowing corruption on earth, and acting against national security through participation in and leadership of a group that acted with the slogan of changing the religious government, taking part in the shameful Berlin conference, giving speeches against the Islamic Republic, participating in the meeting of the People's Fedaian Organisation (majority branch) in Berlin, and other similar acts while abroad (related to Articles 186 and 498 of the Islamic Penal Code).
>
> Propaganda against the Islamic Republic and disseminating falsehoods through speeches, writing articles, and giving interviews to foreign publications and radio stations (related to Articles 500 and 698 of the Islamic Penal Code).
>
> Insulting and making false accusations against Imam Khomeini by attributing false statements to him (related to Articles 514 and 697 of the Islamic Penal Code).
>
> Seriously insulting the clergy by engaging in the above.[94]

The charge of apostasy mentioned in the first count of the indictment was not predicated on an explicit rejection of Islam by Eshkevari, nor was it based on him swearing at the Prophet. Rather, the claim in the indictment was that Eshkevari had become an apostate through rejecting and denying basic Islamic precepts. …

Turning to Eshkevari's alleged repudiation of Islamic precepts, the indictment quoted Eshkevari as saying that virtually all Islamic laws are "social laws", and, as such, they are subject to change, even if they have been mentioned in the Qur'an.[95] In particular, Eshkevari had allegedly included "eternal" Islamic laws such as the veiling of women, the amputation of a thief's hand, judgeship of women and inheritance laws among provisions that could be changed. The indictment quoted Eshkevari as saying that Islamic laws revealed to Prophet Mohammad were not meant to be eternal, but that they were revealed to solve a particular issue at the time.[96]

Eshkevari was not notified of his trial date. Rather, on a day in which he was brought to the court to visit his family, he was informed that his trial was to take place right away.[97] … Eshkevari's trial was not open to the public, and even his relatives were not allowed to observe the proceedings.[98]

Defending the apostasy charge in his trial before Judge Mohammad Salimi, Eshkevari stated that he had not repudiated Islamic laws. Rather, he argued, he had only made the point that Islamic laws could be viewed as temporary solutions and not immutable dictates governing society.[99] Citing examples from Islamic history and even that of the Islamic Republic itself, Eshkevari maintained that he had not said anything new.[100] …

On October 18, 2000, while Eshkevari was in prison, he saw the news of his conviction on state-run television.[101] …

On November 21, 2000 Eshkevari was taken to the prosecutor's office at the Special Court for the Clergy, and he was informed that his verdict was issued. … Eshkevari was found guilty on all charges except the fourth charge, which involved insulting Ayatollah Khomeini.[102] Accordingly, he was sentenced to death and two years of imprisonment, and he was permanently defrocked.[103]

Eshkevari filed an appeal to the Special Court for the Clergy's appellate court.[104] The appeal process took approximately two years, during which Eshkevari remained in prison. After two years, the appeals court quashed Eshkevari's conviction and ordered a new trial.[105] In the new trial, which was held in the summer of 2002, the charges of apostasy, waging war against God, and sowing corruption on earth were dropped.[106] While no official reason was given for dropping the charges, Eshkevari states that Supreme Leader Khamenei had been opposed to his death sentence.[107]

Eshkevari was, nevertheless, found guilty of insulting sacred Islamic beliefs on the basis of questioning whether the veil could be compulsory.[108] Eshkevari was sentenced to four years of imprisonment for this charge. In addition, he was sentenced to two years of imprisonment for disseminating falsehoods and one year of imprisonment for participating in the Berlin conference.[109] Eshkevari was eventually released on February 6, 2005 after serving four and a half years of his sentence, in accordance with Article 38 of the previous Islamic Penal Code.

NOTES

1. United Nations General Assembly, *Universal Declaration of Human Rights*. 10 December 1948, 217 A (III). Available http://www.refworld.org/docid/3ae6b3712c.html, Article 18 (last accessed 9 December 2017).
2. Office of the High Commissioner for Human Rights (OHCHR). 'Rapporteur's Digest on Freedom of Religion or Belief: Excerpts of the Reports from 1986 to 2011 by the Special Rapporteur on Freedom of Religion or Belief Arranged by Topics of the Framework for Communications' (2011) Available http://www.ohchr.org/EN/Issues/FreedomReligion/Pages/FreedomReligionIndex.aspx, 6 (last accessed 9 December 2017).
3. United Nations General Assembly, *International Covenant on Civil and Political Rights (ICCPR)*. 16 December 1966. United Nations, Treaty Series, vol. 999, p. 171. Available http://www.refworld.org/docid/3ae6b3aa0.html, Article 18 (last accessed 9 December 2017).
4. Human Rights Committee, "General Comment No. 22: art. 18 (Freedom of Thought, Conscience or Religion)". 30 July 1993. UN Doc CCPR/C/21/Rev.1/Add.4, [1].
5. Ibid.
6. OHCHR, 'Rapporteur's Digest on Freedom of Religion', 13.
7. United Nations General Assembly, *Report of the Special Rapporteur of the Commission on Human Rights on Freedom of Religion or Belief, Asma Jahangir*. 30 September 2005. UN Doc A/60/399, [53] (p. 16).
8. United Nations General Assembly, *Report of the Special Rapporteur on freedom of religion or belief, Heiner Bielefeldt*. 20 December 2011. UN Doc A/HRC/19/60, [64] (pp. 17–18).
9. OHCHR, "International Standards – Freedom of Religion or Belief: Excerpts of Relevant Paragraphs of 25 Years Mandate Reporting Practice [Special Rapporteur on Freedom of Religion or Belief]" (1986–2011). UN Doc A/60/399, [48].
10. Human Rights Committee, "General Comment No. 22", [5] (p. 2).
11. United Nations Economic and Social Council, *Implementation of the Declaration on the Elimination of All Forms of Intolerance and of Discrimination Based on Religion or Belief: Report Submitted by Mr. Abdelfattah Amor, Special Rapporteur, in Accordance with Commission on Human Rights Resolution 1996/23*. 30 December 1996. UN Doc E/CN.4/1997/91, [77] (p. 16).
12. Ibid, [78] (p. 16).
13. Ibid, [80] (p. 16).
14. Human Rights Committee, "General Comment No. 22", [5] (p. 2).
15. OHCHR, "International Standards", [45].
16. Ibid.
17. Ibid, [43].
18. Ibid.
19. Ibid, [46].
20. Ibid, [50].
21. *ICCPR* Article 6(1).
22. *ICCPR* Article 6(2).
23. *ICCPR* Article 6(5).
24. Human Rights Committee, "Concluding Observations of the Human Rights Committee: Yemen". 23 April 2012. UN Doc CCPR/C/YEM/CO/5, [14].
25. Amnesty International, "Death Penalty Only for 'Most Serious Crimes'?" (2011). Available https://www.amnesty.org.hk/en/our-work/abolish-death-penalty/death-penalty-only-for-most-serious-crimes (last accessed 9 December 2017).
26. Ibid.
27. Ibid.
28. Ibid.
29. Ibid.
30. Ibid.

31. Human Rights Committee, "Concluding Observations of the Human Rights Committee: Islamic Republic of Iran". 29 November 2011. UN Doc CCPR/C/IRN/CO/3, [12].
32. Ibid.
33. *ICCPR* art. 18(1).
34. Human Rights Committee, "General Comment No. 22", [4].
35. Ibid.
36. OHCHR, "International Standards", [59].
37. Ibid, citing UN Doc A/RES/36/55, adopted 25 November 1981.
38. *ICCPR* art. 18(3).
39. Human Rights Committee, "General Comment No. 22", [8].
40. Ibid.
41. Saudi Arabia, Oman, Qatar, Malaysia, Brunei and the United Arab Emirates are not state parties to the ICCPR: OHCHR, "Status of Ratification: Interactive Dashboard". Available http://indicators.ohchr.org (last accessed 9 December 2017).
42. OHCHR, "Status of Ratification: Interactive Dashboard".
43. Ibid.
44. Ibid.
45. *Constitution of the Republic of Maldives 2008*. Available http://www.presidencymaldives.gov.mv/Documents/ConstitutionOfMaldives.pdf (last accessed 9 December 2017).
46. Human Rights Committee, "Concluding Observations on the Fifth Periodic Report of Iraq". 3 December 2015. UN Doc CCPR/C/IRQ/CO/5, [37].
47. Moataz Ahmed El Fegiery, "Islamic Law and Freedom of Religion: The Case of Apostasy and its Legal Implications in Egypt", *Muslim World Journal of Human Rights* 10(1) (2013): 17.
48. Ibid.
49. Ibid.
50. Human Rights Committee, "Consideration of Reports Submitted by States Parties under Article 40 of the Covenant. Concluding Observations of the Human Rights Committee: Jordan". 18 November 2010. UN Doc CCPR/C/JOR/CO/4, [13].
51. Ibid.
52. Ibid
53. Human Rights Committee, "List of Issues in Relation to the Third Periodic Report of Kuwait. Addendum: Replies of Kuwait to the List of Issues". 21 April 2016. UN Doc CCPR/C/KWT/Q/3/Ad., 21.
54. Ibid.
55. Human Rights Committee, "Concluding Observations on the Third Periodic Report of Kuwait". 11 August 2016. UN Doc CCPR/C/KWT/CO/3, [38].
56. *al-Bukhari, Sahih al-Bukhari*, Kitab istitabat al-murtaddin wa-l-mu'anidin wa qitalihim, No. 6922.
57. Abdullah Saeed and Hassan Saeed, *Freedom of Religion Apostasy and Islam* (Burlington, VT: Ashgate Publishing, 2004), 51.
58. See Mohammad Hashim Kamali, *Freedom of Expression in Islam*, 91.
59. See, for instance, S.A. Rahman, *Punishment of Apostasy in Islam*, 2nd edn (Lahore, Pakistan: Institute of Islamic Culture, 1978), 54.
60. Ibid, 99.
61. Mohammad Hashim Kamali, "Freedom of Religion in Islamic Law", *Capital University Law Review* 21 (1992): 64.
62. See also Abdullah Saeed, "Limitations on Religious Freedom in Islam: The Witness of the Qur'an and Prophetic Traditions", *ABC Religion and Ethics*, 23 May 2014. Available http://www.abc.net.au/religion/articles/2014/05/23/4010689.htm (last accessed 9 December 2017).
63. Niaz A. Shah, "Freedom of Religion: Koranic and Human Rights Perspectives", *Asia-Pacific Journal on Human Rights and the Law* 1 & 2 (2005): 71.
64. Irene Oh, *The Rights of God: Islam, Human Rights and Comparative Ethics* (Washington DC: Georgetown University Press, 2007), 83.

65. Ibid, 76.
66. Shah, "Freedom of Religion", 72.
67. Oh, *The Rights of God*, 75.
68. See also Saeed, "Limitations on Religious Freedom in Islam".
69. Kamali, *Freedom of Expression in Islam*, 100.
70. This section relies heavily on the author's paper, Abdullah Saeed, *Islam and Belief: At Home with Religious Freedom* (Palo Alto, CA: Zephyr Institute, 2014).
71. Q. 18:29: "Say, 'Now the truth has come from your Lord: let those who wish to believe in it do so, and let those who wish to reject it do so.'"
72. Q. 24:54: "Say, 'Obey God; obey the Messenger. If you turn away, [know that] he is responsible for the duty placed upon him, and you are responsible for the duty placed upon you. If you obey him, you will be rightly guided, but the Messenger's duty is only to deliver the message clearly.'"
73. Q. 88:21: "So [Prophet] warn them: your only task is to give warning." See also Q. 10:108 and 27:92.
74. Fred M. Donner, *Muhammad and the Believers: At the Origins of Islam* (Cambridge, MA: Belknap Press of Harvard University Press, 2010), 230.
75. See Q. 9, which is believed to be among the final revelations received by the Prophet Muhammad.
76. See Q. 9:5, 9:12, 9:14, and 9:29.
77. See A. Hourani, *Minorities in the Arab World* (Oxford: Oxford University Press, 1947), 18.
78. Rachel M. Scott, "Contextual Citizenship in Modern Islamic Thought", *Islam and Muslim–Christian Relations* 18(1) (2007): 3.
79. Ibid, 4.
80. Q. 4:115, 72:23.
81. Mohammad Hashim Kamali, *Islamic Law in Malaysia: Issues and Developments* (Kuala Lumpur: Ilmiah Publishers, 2000), 209.
82. Kamali, *Freedom of Expression in Islam*, 91.
83. Mohammad H. Fadel, "Public Reason as a Strategy for Principled Reconciliation: The Case of Islamic Law and International Human Rights Law", *Chicago Journal of International Law* 8(1) (2007): 19.
84. Ibid.
85. Ibid, 18.
86. See Saeed and Saeed, *Freedom of Religion*.
87. See, for instance, the Committee's concluding remarks with respect to the fourth periodic report of Sudan (9 July 2014). Available http://www.ohchr.org/EN/NewsEvents/Pages/DisplayNews.aspx?NewsID=14841&LangID=E (last accessed 9 December 2017).
88. Baderin, *International Human Rights*, 123. See M.S. El-Awa, *Punishment in Islamic Law: A Comparative Study* (Indianapolis: American Trust Publications, 1982) pp. 50–56 and Kamali, *Freedom of Expression in Islam*, pp. 87–107.
89. Baderin, *International Human Rights*, 123.
90. Ibid, 124.
91. Ibid.
92. *ICCPR*, art. 6(2).
93. For an account of another individual arrested and imprisoned for his involvement in the Berlin conference, see Iran Human Rights Documentation Center, "Witness Statement of Ali Afshari" (2008). Available http://www.iranhrdc.org/english/publications/witness-testimony/3175-witness-statement-ali-afshari.html#.U3Fo5oFdXyI (last accessed 9 December 2017).
94. Hasan Yousefi Eshkevari, *Asnādi Dādgāhi Kunfirānsi Birlīn-Muqaddami (Qismati Duvvum)*, Yousefieshkevari.com (19 March 2011). Available http://yousefieshkevari.com/?p=1791 (last accessed 9 December 2017).
95. Ibid.
96. Ibid.

97. Ibid.
98. IHRDC Interview with Hasan Yousefi Eshkevari (25 April 2014) (on file with IHRDC). Article 165 of the Iranian Constitution states, "Trials are to be held openly and members of the public may attend without any restriction; unless the court determines that an open trial would be detrimental to public morality or discipline, or if in case of private disputes, both the parties request not to hold an open hearing." Despite this constitutional guarantee, the right to public trial is routinely violated in Iran.
99. Eshkevari, *Asnādi Dādgāhi Kunfirānsi Birlīn-Lāyihiyi Defā ʿAz Ittihāmāti Kiyfarkhāst*. Available http://yousefieshkevari.com/?p=1816 (last accessed 9 December 2017).
100. Ibid.
101. IHRDC Interview with Hasan Yousefi Eshkevari. Prisoners in many Iranian prisons such as Evin and Rajaee Shahr have access to Iran's state-run television programming. There is no access to television when a prisoner is in a solitary ward and undergoing interrogation.
102. Hasan Yousefi Eshkevari, *Asnādi Dādgāhi Kunfirānsi Birlīn-Ḥukmi Dādgāhi Badvī*. 9 May 2011. Available http://yousefieshkevari.com/?p=1824 (last accessed 9 December 2017).
103. Ibid.
104. IHRDC Interview with Hasan Yousefi Eshkevari.
105. Ibid.
106. Ibid.
107. Ibid, [88].
108. Ibid.
109. Ḥasan Yūsifī Ishkivarī Āzād Shud, *BBC Persian*. 6 February 2005. Available http://www.bbc.co.uk/persian/iran/story/2005/02/050206_a_eshkevari.shtml (last accessed 9 December 2017).

11. Human rights and war

INTRODUCTION

At a time when militant groups around the world are using the notion of so-called "jihad" to justify their involvement in violent armed conflict and the atrocities they commit, it is worth revisiting the regulations that govern war and the use of armed force. This chapter examines briefly the rules that determine whether a war is ethically justifiable, and how it should be conducted from the perspectives of international law and Islamic law. Although there is a common perception that war allows freedom to act without restraint against an enemy, there are in fact strict rules that regulate when and how armed conflict should be conducted. This chapter considers whether there are commonalities between the rules of war in international law and Islamic law and, where there are tensions, how these may be resolved. It also examines the notion of jihad, how it emerged, and the contextual factors that governed its interpretation, with the aim of dispelling some of the misunderstandings surrounding its use.

INTERNATIONAL HUMANITARIAN LAW

The area of international law that specifically regulates violent armed conflict is called international humanitarian law. International humanitarian law (IHL) is the body of rules and norms that aims to limit, as far as possible, the human impact of warfare.[1] It applies to those persons directly participating in an armed conflict and those in the immediate vicinity of the conflict who are not participants (for instance civilians, other non-combatants or medical personnel), as well as to "the means and methods of warfare".[2] IHL comes from "customary rules",[3] and international treaties such as the Geneva Conventions and their Additional Protocols, the Hague Conventions, and other treaties that address ways of waging war; for instance "those banning blinding laser weapons, landmines and chemical and biological weapons".[4]

RELATIONSHIP BETWEEN HUMAN RIGHTS AND HUMANITARIAN LAW

Before examining the rules that govern war and the use of armed force from an international and Islamic perspective, it is important to firstly consider how international human rights law and IHL apply and interact when there is an armed conflict. Commentators have noted that IHL and international human rights law are "distinct" yet "complementary"[5] legal regimes. They have elements in common in that they both aim to protect human dignity and life, but IHL only applies in situations of violent armed conflict, while "human rights law applies at all times, in peace and in war".[6] On the other hand, elements of human rights law can be suspended at particular times (for instance, if the country declares a state of emergency), whereas "IHL cannot be suspended (except as provided in Article 5 to the Fourth Geneva Convention)".[7] Nevertheless, states have a legal obligation of applying IHL and international human rights law where and when they apply.[8]

HISTORICAL DEVELOPMENT OF INTERNATIONAL HUMANITARIAN LAW AND INTERNATIONAL HUMAN RIGHTS LAW

Historically, international human rights law and IHL developed as distinct areas of law. Human rights law was developed to protect citizens from the state's unfettered power and its potential abuse during times of peace, while IHL evolved to protect those involved in state to state conflict by focusing on the actions of military combatants.[9] This meant that each area of law was historically considered "mutually exclusive".[10]

However, after the Second World War this began to change, as Patrick Knäble explains:

> After the experience of the Second World War, HR [human rights] and HL [humanitarian law] began influencing each other's development and increasingly converged. HR in part grew out of HL, particularly the Nuremberg trials.[11] The acknowledgement by the international community that crimes against humanity existed in customary international law suggested the recognition of corresponding fundamental HR for the individual.[12] On the other hand, the Universal Declaration of Human Rights,[13] drafted in the aftermath of the Nuremberg judgements, had some influence on the development of HL through the preparation and adoption of the 1949 Geneva Conventions …[14] In 1968 the United Nations (UN), for the first time, acknowledged the convergence of the two legal bodies.[15]

Today, there is general acknowledgment that both bodies of law support and mutually reinforce each other: "Each body of law offers in some areas, greater protection than the other[16] and has important and constructive contributions to make towards closing gaps with respect to the enjoyment of fundamental rights."[17]

A BRIEF LOOK AT JUST WAR THEORY

Historically, societies have always imposed restrictions on the use of violence, including violence in its "institutionalised form"—what we commonly refer to as "war".[18] Under international law, when and how warfare is used has been influenced by what is called "just war theory", a doctrine that seeks to address what is (or is not) morally justifiable on the battlefield and before entering into conflict. At its most basic, just war theory argues that the use of force must always be justified, and conducted in a way that is morally acceptable.

Many elements of just war theory have been incorporated into international legal instruments, such as the United Nations Charter and the Hague and Geneva Conventions.[19] These laws, some of which come under the banner of IHL, are commonly divided into three categories: (1) *jus ad bellum* or the justifications for entering into armed conflict; (2) *jus in bello* or the rules governing conduct in war; and (3) *jus post bellum* or the rules governing peace agreements and the termination of a conflict.[20] The first two categories of rules will be looked at in this chapter.

Jus ad Bellum or the Justification for Armed Conflict

Before considering the use of armed force to achieve a particular end, there is a need to ensure that a number of key requirements are met.[21] These can be summarised as follows:

1. There must be a just cause for engaging in armed conflict. This may include defence of the community or the state from external aggression, or the defence of defenceless people from oppressive regimes.
2. The state initiating armed conflict must do so with the right intention, that is, it must intend to achieve a just cause and not some other hidden objective.
3. The state must have the proper authority to go to war. It must go through the relevant official procedures that are recognised by law and its people.

4. Armed conflict must be a last resort. All other possible peaceful avenues must first be exhausted.
5. Armed conflict must hold potential for success. The state must consider whether it is possible to achieve its goals through warfare. If there is no hope of success, war cannot be an option.
6. The use of force must be proportional. That is, a state must weigh the "good" expected to come from engaging in armed conflict against the evils that will result, such as death and injury.[22]

These six requirements must be met to satisfy the rules of *jus ad bellum* and to justify the resort to military force.

***Jus in Bello* or Rules of Engagement**

Once hostilities have commenced, IHL also governs how armed conflict can be conducted. Indeed, war does not justify the wanton or unrestricted use of violence against an opponent, no matter how grave an enemy they are. The principles of *jus in bello* govern the rules of engagement for combatants. They can be summarised as follows:[23]

1. Discrimination: a distinction must be made between civilian and military targets; non-combatants must not be targeted.
2. Proportionality: combatants must only use force in proportion to the military end they are striving for.
3. Necessity: weapons or methods that are considered inherently evil, such as rape, genocide, or ethnic cleansing, must not be used by combatants.
4. Those combatants who have surrendered must be treated humanely. They must not be tortured, raped, starved, or killed.

These ideas stem from just war theory and most have been translated into international legal instruments for governing military conflict. The most important international instruments to set out these rules of engagement are the four Geneva Conventions and their additional protocols. These govern armed conflicts between states and armed conflict within states (or internal armed conflict).[24] Some of the most fundamental principles to come from these instruments include:

1. People who are not directly involved in military conflict should not be harmed, but protected.

2. An enemy who surrenders must not be harmed or killed. Similarly, an enemy who is sick or injured must not be harmed or killed.
3. The sick and wounded must be tended to. Medical and other personnel who care for the sick and wounded must also be protected from harm.
4. Prisoners of war must not be harmed, tortured, or subject to inhumane treatment, and they have certain rights: the right to food, basic care, and the ability to contact their families.
5. No one should be subjected to torture or other cruel, inhumane or unusual treatment, held responsible for an act they have not committed, or denied basic judicial guarantees.
6. Armed force must be proportional. Unnecessary force leading to excessive suffering is prohibited.
7. The civilian population must not be targeted, nor should their property. There must be a clear distinction between civilian and military populations and targets.

In addition to the legal regime of IHL, certain provisions of international human rights law also apply to armed conflict. For instance, Article 20 of the ICCPR prohibits using propaganda to incite war, or any advocacy of "racial or religious hatred that constitutes incitement to discrimination, hostility or violence".[25] In practice, this means that an individual's right to freedom of expression cannot be used to spark hostility, violence or armed conflict. The UN Human Rights Committee has also affirmed that Article 20 "extends to all forms of propaganda threatening or resulting in an act of aggression or breach of the peace contrary to the Charter of the United Nations".[26]

As we will see in the next section, many of the rules discussed above are similar to the Islamic norms surrounding legitimate warfare, which can be traced back to the time of the Prophet himself.

ISLAMIC LAW, WAR, AND PEACE

Most of the Islamic norms and rules that govern armed conflict come from the Qur'an, the practice of the Prophet Muhammad, and the conduct of the early Muslims in the first century of Islam. These fundamental texts and historical precedents have had significant influence on contemporary Muslim thinking on the conduct of war and peace.

Many of the customs and practices that existed in pre-Islamic Arabia concerning armed conflict were adopted by the early Muslims. This means that Islam's approach to warfare was influenced to some extent by the prevailing socio-political context; however, the Qur'an and the Prophet's practice also modified certain norms, as did some of the practices of the Muslims in the first century of Islam. Abdullahi An-Na'im points out that in pre-Islamic Arabia, "intertribal relations were heavily ... dependent on the use or threat of violent force" to claim any right.[27] This was

> the norm among the various entities or polities of the region ... Thus, when the first Muslim state was established ... force was the basic method of conducting what is known today as international relations. It was therefore inevitable that Islam should endorse the use of force in Muslim relations with non-Muslims. In doing so, however, Shari'a [also] introduced new norms to control the reasons for going to war as well as its actual practice.[28]

Clearly, there is no outright rejection of armed conflict in the Qur'an. In those verses dating from the Meccan period there is no encouragement for Muslims to engage in the use of armed force. However, this changes in Medina, where several verses of the Qur'an revealed then supported the use of war. These texts can be understood in light of the socio-political context the Muslims were facing at the time, and the growing need to defend Islam and the burgeoning Muslim community from external aggression.

Developments after the Prophet's Death

Muslim scholars, theologians, and jurists eventually developed what could be referred to as a "just war theory" within an Islamic framework, based on their understanding of related Qur'anic verses, Prophetic advice, and the conduct of war during the first century of Islam.[29] Muslim jurists argued that the use of force was justified in two contexts: the propagation of Islam and the defence of the community against outside aggression.[30] The propagation of Islam did not refer to the conversion of non-Muslims; rather, force was permitted to meet the requirements of territorial expansion and to facilitate the political submission of non-Muslims within the newly captured Muslim territories.[31] In other words, as long as non-Muslims were prepared to submit to Muslim rulers they were left in peace. Peace treaties conducted with non-Muslim states or towns were also negotiated on this basis, ensuring that no hostile force would be directed towards the Muslim state.

There were a number of key principles that underpinned the Islamic notion of "just war". Firstly, only the state or governing ruler could declare war or justify the use of force. There also needed to be a just cause for a declaration of war: either a real threat against the Muslim community or state that justified self-defence, or a need to propagate the religion. In both cases the objective of war was not material gain but what the Qur'an calls "God's cause" (Q. 2:190). There were also a number of important rules of engagement: certain weapons could not be used; only combatants could be targeted; prisoners of war had to be treated with respect; and the wanton destruction of land and property was prohibited. These rules of engagement will be elaborated further below.

Dar al-Islam and Dar al-Harb

Early Muslim jurists divided the world into two: on the one hand, the abode of Islam (*dar al-islam*), and on the other, the abode of war (*dar al-harb*), also known as the abode of disbelief (*dar al-kufr*), or of polytheism (*dar al-shirk*).[32] As Hamid Mavani points out, "this world-view, conceived at a time when Muslims were the dominant power, eventually had to be modified to accommodate other scenarios, such as religious diversity or Muslims being in the minority".[33]

The term *dar al-islam*, or "the whole territory in which the law of Islam prevails",[34] is not found in the Qur'an; rather, it is a juristic doctrine.[35] Meanwhile, *dar al-harb* was any land not encompassed by *dar al-islam*, or "any contested or contestable territory which was not under Islamic rule".[36] As Manoucher Parvin and Maurie Sommer point out, "[t]he distinction was … essentially a juridical one: any territory not under Muslim jurisdiction was *dar al-harb*"; however, *dar al-harb* could also refer to "that territory that might fall from Muslim jurisdiction".[37] However, as An-Na'im points out, "the theoretically permanent state of war between Muslims and non-Muslims" that was fundamental to this worldview did not always mean that there was violence or fighting between the parties, although it did mean there was a concerted effort to bring the *dar al-harb* within the *dar al-islam*, "whether through active fighting or other means".[38] However, Muslims could conclude peace treaties (*sulh* or *ahd*), albeit only on a temporary basis, to suspend hostilities with non-Muslim polities.[39]

THE DOCTRINE OF JIHAD

The juristic discussions on armed conflict fall within the legal category of jihad, which is the most commonly used Islamic term for the use of force in international relations.[40] Jihad's literal Qur'anic meaning is to strive to achieve a specific objective or to make an effort towards something, but this does not necessarily only apply to exertion in war.[41] The term is also used to refer to attaining perfect faith, defending Islam with words, helping the disadvantaged, using money to support the Muslim community, as well as the use of force against an enemy who threatens the Muslim community. Thus, the concept of jihad can be understood on a continuum—from an inward spiritual struggle; to jihad by the tongue; jihad by the hand (in actions); jihad in wealth; and jihad by "the sword".

The development of the concept of jihad was inextricably tied to the time of the Prophet and his followers' experiences in the first century of Islam. It was to be understood within this socio-historical context.[42] In Mecca, Muslims were a persecuted minority that could not militarily challenge the hostile Meccan majority. During this period, both the Qur'an and the Prophet emphasised the non-violent nature of Islam, as well as the importance of patience in the face of adversity. Even when extreme violence was used against the Muslims, they were specifically commanded not to retaliate. Thus, jihad did not incorporate ideas of violence at this time. It referred to non-violent resistance and aimed to safeguard the new community and contribute to its welfare. According to many contemporary scholars, this is jihad's core meaning, to which later understandings were then added.

From 622 to 632 CE, a religious and political community was established in Medina, bringing together people from different tribes. Medina became the place where the burgeoning Muslim community established and consolidated its identity, one based on religious rather than tribal affiliation. When the community was threatened by a number of outside tribes (mostly from Mecca), it took up arms to defend itself and its land and the Qur'an gave it permission for this defence. It was in this context that the Qur'an allowed Muslims to engage in warfare. Among the early Qur'anic verses that permit Muslims to use force against others are 2:190–93 and 22:39:[43]

> Fight in God's cause against those who fight you, but do not overstep the limits: God does not love those who overstep the limits (Q. 2:190).
>
> Those who have been attacked are permitted to take up arms because they have been wronged—God has the power to help them (Q. 22:39).

The Qur'an also permitted warfare to combat oppression and injustice (Q. 4:75). Over a period of ten years, the Qur'an's initial permission to use force to defend Medina expanded to allow a military response to the perceived hostile intentions of various powerful enemies elsewhere in Arabia. If tribes were prepared to act in a hostile fashion against the Muslims or were not willing to enter into peace agreements, the Qur'an sanctioned the use of force against them.

During the Prophet's lifetime, jihad was largely used as a means of self-defence and, to a limited extent, for the propagation of the new religion. After the Prophet's death the situation changed to some extent, however, and jihad became closely connected to the idea of territorial expansion. The initial Muslim conquests of the Middle East and North Africa were governed by two main objectives: to open up the region for the propagation of Islam and to expand the territories of the Muslim caliphate or state. Both these objectives were achieved to a large extent through warfare or threat of the possible use of force, though not always. From these events, which occurred during the first 150 years or so of Islam, territorial expansion became essential to the notion of jihad in Islamic thought. Importantly, it was during this time that Muslim jurists began to formulate the legal theory of jihad. Today, much of the law on warfare and the use of force has its roots in this period.

From around the beginning of the tenth century CE the Muslim caliphate fragmented. Muslim territorial power gradually weakened over the centuries and disintegrated into competing entities. The concept of jihad thus changed to accommodate these circumstances, putting less emphasis on the use of armed force for offensive jihad and greater emphasis on defensive jihad. Other concepts also started to emerge in understandings of jihad, such as Sufi ideas about inner spiritual struggle. However, as Said Mahmoudi observes, "the concept of *jihad* as a just and legitimate war survived [until] the early twentieth century".[44]

In sum, the concept of jihad in Islamic thought has not remained static since its emergence in the Prophetic period. As the political situation of Muslims fluctuated over time and the strength or weakness of the Muslim community (vis-à-vis their enemies) changed, so too have different understandings of jihad. At various points in time key texts and traditions were interpreted differently, which eventually led to different rulings and opinions on jihad. This means that the concept of jihad is best understood as an evolving, rather than established, doctrine.

Defensive and Offensive Jihad

In the doctrine of jihad we can find the basic ideas that govern what could be described as an Islamic "just war theory". Here, two different kinds of jihad were conceptualised: defensive and offensive. The notion of defensive jihad was an extension of the early Islamic understanding of armed conflict as self-defence. Jurists who emphasised that jihad should only be used as a means of self-defence referred to Q. 2:190–91. They also emphasised the importance of peace and texts such as Q. 59:23, which states: "God … [is the] Source of Peace and the Granter of

Security", and Q. 7:56, which warns: "Do not corrupt the earth after it has been set right". They also referred to verses such as Q. 109:6, which states: "You have your religion and I have mine", in effect "arguing that [the use of] force against non-Muslims" is only justified when they "threaten[ed] Muslims or interfere[d] with their religious practice".[45]

In contrast, the notion of offensive jihad was tied to the propagation of religion, territorial expansion, and the pre-emption of challenges to state power. Interpretations that sanctioned offensive jihad came from texts in the Qur'an that "directly or indirectly prescribe fighting against or killing apostates and non-believers".[46] A key verse in this regard is Qur'an 22:39–40, which gives permission for Muslims to fight against oppression and persecution. There are also other verses that are stronger in tone and directed at the enemies of the state. However, these verses use the term *qital*—the Arabic word "to fight"—not the word jihad. Nevertheless, according to Karima Bennoune, the position which maintains that jihad does not extend to offensive warfare is the "most firmly established today and ... has the most supporters".[47]

What Was Acceptable in Jihad in Classical Times

In classical Islamic legal thought, certain principles curtailed the wanton use of force and guided the conduct of both offensive and defensive jihad. These included the principle that only the state or its legitimate ruler can declare armed conflict and that it must have a just cause; for example, the eradication of oppression or the defence of the community. There were also constraints on how force could be used. The Muslims' opponents must first be given an opportunity to embrace Islam, or at least to accept the political authority of the Muslim state, under which they would be given the status of a protected minority (*dhimmi*).[48] However, if they refused, Muslim jurists believed the use of force was permitted.[49]

Rules of engagement also specified that force could only be directed against combatants, not civilians.[50] Other requirements from the Prophet's teachings included the prohibition on treachery, mutilation, and the killing of non-combatants, minors, women, and those devoted to religion.[51] Other Muslim leaders, such as the caliphs Abu Bakr (d. 13/634) and Umar b. al-Khattab (d. 23/644), also prohibited wanton destruction.[52] If the Muslims were victorious they were allowed to enslave the enemy and take their property; however, there were rules about how the spoils of war (or what the Qur'an calls *al-anfal*) should be distributed.

COMPATIBILITIES BETWEEN INTERNATIONAL HUMANITARIAN LAW AND ISLAMIC LAW

Bennoune argues that Islamic law was one of the earliest legal regimes to attempt to "institutionalise humanitarian limitations on the conduct of military conflict".[53] There are many parallels between just war theory, which underpins IHL, and the Islamic rules and norms of war. For instance, Islamic law attempts to limit the scope and severity of war. It also provides guidelines for the ceasing of hostilities. Other similarities include the distinction between civilians and combatants in war; the prohibition on killing or disrespecting prisoners of war; the emphasis on preventing unnecessary destruction; and the need to care for the sick and wounded. In what follows I will discuss some of the more important similarities in more detail.

Proportionality

Like just war theory, Islamic law recognises the notion of proportionality. The Qur'an states: "Fight in God's cause against those who fight you, but do not overstep the limits: God does not love those who overstep the limits" (Q. 2:190). Some early Muslim jurists prohibited certain kinds of weapons—for example, poisoned arrows—because the suffering they inflicted far outweighed the ends achieved.[54] The Prophet is reported to have prohibited burning or drowning the enemy because these caused unnecessary suffering.[55] Bennoune notes that "women, children, and other non-combatants were recognised as a separate category of persons entitled to various degrees of immunity from attack", which she argues is a "development which may be seen as the birth of the 'civilian'".[56] The assumption that combatants were usually men meant that there was a general prohibition against the killing of women. The same reasoning extended this rule to prohibit the killing of the very old, the very young, and those who devoted themselves to their religion. Moreover, houses and other buildings could only be destroyed when it was justified by military necessity.[57]

Prisoners of War

Although there have been a wide range of opinions on the rules governing the treatment of prisoners of war, Bennoune argues that "there is a general scholarly consensus that Islamic teachings" were "enlightened" for that era.[58] Although prisoners of war could still be captured and enslaved under Islamic law, various Prophetic instructions state that prisoners of war who were enslaved should be treated humanely. For example, the Prophet reportedly said regarding slaves:

> They are your brothers. God has put them in your hands; so whosoever has his brother in his hands, let him feed him out of what he himself eats and let him clothe him out of what he himself wears, and do not burden them with what will be too much for them. If you do burden them in this way, help them to carry it out.[59]

Ultimately, significant discretionary power was given to the Muslim state: for example, to determine whether prisoners could be freed without any conditions or held for ransom. If prisoners were enslaved, however, Islamic law followed the Prophet's ruling that "captive mothers and children were not to be separated".[60]

SOME TENSIONS

Some scholars argue that there is significant incompatibility between Islamic law and IHL when it comes to the rules of armed conflict, and in some areas this is certainly the case. Below I discuss some of the most important areas of tension.

Permanent State of War with Non-Muslims

One of the key areas of incompatibility centres on an element of traditional Islamic law that claims there is a permanent state of war between Muslims and non-Muslim states. In this context An-Na'im states:

> [The] Shari'a is in direct conflict with the Charter of the United Nations because, whereas that charter prohibits the use of force in international relations except in self-defence, [the] Shari'a sanctions the use of force to propagate Islam or to uphold its integrity in another Muslim country. Moreover, [the] Shari'a's underlying theme of a permanent state of war with, and non-recognition of, non-Muslim states repudiates the entire basis of modern international law.[61]

Thus, according to this idea, if non-Muslim states have not signed peace treaties with the Muslim state, then they could be considered a threat and thus a legitimate target for armed conflict. Certainly, the principles of international law today would not accept this pre-modern idea; however, in my view neither would most Muslims.

Self-Defence

The traditional Islamic notion of self-defence as a justification for jihad also conflicts with the conceptualisation of self-defence in international law. Article 51 of the United Nations Charter allows the right to self-defence and the use of force towards that defence. In the case of traditional Islamic notions of jihad, defensive jihad does not always require an armed attack by the enemy. It is not limited to the defence of one's country or community, but can be broadened to include an individual's life, family, property, honour, religion, or belief. In other words, as Mahmoudi points out, the notion of defensive jihad is much broader in scope than the right to self-defence in international law.[62] Moreover, defensive jihad in Islamic law does not need to be authorised by any recognised, overarching organ, such as the UN Security Council, as is the case under international law.[63]

CONCLUSION AND POSSIBILITIES FOR HARMONISATION

For many scholars, there is a reasonable degree of compatibility between Islamic law and international law as far as the laws of war are concerned, particularly with the developments in Islamic thought in this area today. Bennoune observes similarly that modernist interpretations of Islamic law, which emphasise that the state must "refrain from engaging in wars prompted by differences in religious belief or for exploitation of other peoples' resources", pose no conflict with IHL.[64]

While the traditional Islamic notion of jihad in self-defence is broader than that envisioned by international law, Manisuli Ssenyonjo suggests a methodology for reconciling the tension. Since member states of the OIC have, by ratifying the OIC's Charter, confirmed their commitment to upholding the principles of the United Nations' Charter,[65] they are therefore required to abide by Article 51 of the latter, which establishes the rules for states' use of force in self-defence. Thus "the concept of jihad should be considered in light of those obligations", which require "the application of military jihad under Sharia in a manner compatible with international law".[66]

Moreover, if the concept of offensive jihad was discarded, this would see the goal of the propagation of religion as a justification for armed conflict also being set aside, leaving only the aim of maintaining territorial integrity as a basis for the use of force. An-Na'im argues that "since the use of force was justified by the historical context of violent intercommunal and international relations, it must cease to be so justified in the present context, in which peaceable coexistence has become a vital necessity for the survival of humanity".[67] Since the Muslim community is now divided into nation-states, international conflicts "should be governed by the ... rules of international law".[68] This kind of Islamic articulation of just war today would then sit in harmony with international law.

In summary, while traditional conceptions of jihad remain part of the body of Islamic law, there is increasing evidence that Muslim-majority states are—in practice—conducting international relations in a way that is mindful of the "normative order of secular international law".[69] Even strictly "Islamic" states such as Saudi Arabia tend to conduct international matters according to secular standards.[70] Moreover, Qur'anic norms that encourage "peaceful negotiation and dialogue"[71] mean that Islamic states may be persuaded to use international systems or processes that are available to facilitate "amicable compromises between all nations"[72] for the resolution of conflicts, rather than resorting to the use of armed force at all. Thus the tensions between Islamic and international law in this area can largely be resolved.

* * *

LOOKING AT AN ISSUE CLOSELY: MODERN UNDERSTANDINGS OF THE DOCTRINE OF JIHAD

Elsayed M.A. Amin, *Reclaiming Jihad: A Qur'anic Critique of Terrorism* (Markfield, UK: The Islamic Foundation, 2014). pp. 105–9. Extract*

This case examines the views of three contemporary Muslim scholars on the doctrine of jihad. Their perspectives challenge the common misperception that Islam advocates armed violence against non-Muslims and that jihad should be understood primarily as offensive or military aggression. Instead, there is significant evidence for peace being the norm in Muslim and non-Muslim external relations.

Among the modern scholars who view peace as the basic principle which marks external relations between Muslims and non-Muslims is [Egyptian scholar Muhammad] Abu Zahrah (1898–1974). According to him, military jihad is permitted only to remove aggression (*ʿudwan*) and religious persecution (*fitnah*) against Muslims. He further states that 4:94 and 22:39–40 establish this principle, adding that the scholars who state that military jihad is the basic principle between Muslims and non-Muslims derive their view from the reality they experienced rather than from the texts of the Qur'an and the Sunnah. The rulings arrived at by the classical scholars, Abu Zahrah argues, are related only to the historical period in which they lived, and therefore cannot be considered as definitive and binding rulings. Instead, military jihad is legislated to establish justice and fend off aggression. He considers the Qur'anic verses that call for peace as the basic norm in Muslim and non-Muslim external relations. For Abu Zahrah, the historical context cannot be underestimated, something which is uncommon in classical exegetical interpretations.[73]

[Syrian scholar Muhammad Sa'id Ramadan] al-Buti (1929–2013) stresses, like Abu Zahrah, the intrinsic connection between peace and justice. He maintains that "any genuine call for peace necessitates a genuine call for justice", arguing that justice, which is one of the main causes behind the legislation of jihad, is the only principle that can lead to peace. If the equilibrium between peace and justice is evenly balanced, al-Buti maintains, then not only will Muslims and non-Muslims enjoy permanent peaceful relations (*sulh da'im*), but all peoples will enjoy the same consequence regardless of their faith or ethnicity. However, al-Buti sets two conditions for this permanent peace to be achieved: (1) Muslims should be free to propagate their faith without restriction; and (2) there should be no occupation of *dar al-Islam*. Included in the meaning of occupation which may lead to fighting and put an end to peace, according to al-Buti, is when the enemies of Muslims confiscate, usurp and reside illegally in the land of *dar al-Islam*.[74]

On the unrestricted propagation of Islam, al-Buti does not identify the precise means of doing so that would help define and constitute it. His wording "without hindrance or restriction" (*duna ihrajin aw tadyiqin*) refers to his belief in all possible options, including military action, if the propagation of Islam encounters restrictive measures that may stem its tide. Although al-Buti penned his *Al-Jihad fi al-Islam* in the late 1990s, his handling of the issue considers military jihad an option, even though the information revolution removes all obstacles to the propagation of any religion or ideology including the religion of Islam.[75] Contrary to what al-Buti's statement may indicate, Muslims nowadays enjoy full freedom to propagate their religion in majority non-Muslim countries, in contrast to the "restricted" freedom they enjoy in many majority-Muslim countries. Undoubtedly, modern technology has globalised many aspects of our lives, including the propagation of Islam, so the hindrance and restriction posited by al-Buti is no longer the norm and if it does exist it does so in rare and limited circumstances. Moreover, al-Buti's borrowing of *dar al-Islam*[76] from the classical jurists does not mean that he necessarily follows their lead. On the contrary, his support for maintaining permanent peace expressed above may indicate that the man is an outstanding pacifist. However, he remains adamant in his utter rejection of all forms of illegal confiscation and usurpation of Muslim lands.

The [last] modern scholar whose views stand in total contrast to the offensive jihad narrative is [the Syrian jurist] Wahbah al-Zuhayli, who strongly advocates that peace is the underlying principle of relations between Muslims and non-Muslims. Al-Zuhayli maintains that this view is supported by 8:61, as well as 2:208 and 4:94 that establish the principle of international peace. For him, Muslims should be committed to peace and security (on the basis of 4:90 and 60:8).[77] Al-Zuhayli further argues that considering military jihad to be the norm in relations between Muslims and non-Muslims opposes what the jurists have actually agreed upon, which is that "permissibility is the underlying principle" (*al-asl fi al-ashya' al-ibahah*). He argues, if this legal maxim and others similar to it constitute basic principles, then why do some jurists not consider military jihad to be the original rule in Muslim–non-Muslim relations?[78] Consequently, al-Zuhayli takes the view that "the original rule in international relations is peace" (*al-asl fi al-'alaqat al-dawliyyah al-silm*).[79]

The above modern scholarly views considering peace as the norm in determining relations between Muslims and non-Muslims are not, however, limited to individual scholars, although the above discussion attempts to highlight the prominent examples among them.[80] Huge collective efforts have recently been made by Muslim scholars from places as diverse as Asia and North America in the eighth, fourteenth and sixteenth conferences of the Egyptian-based Supreme Council for Islamic Affairs from the 1990s onwards. Looking at these three annual conferences collectively shows that an important turning point has been reached as to how modern Muslim scholarship evaluates the classical offensive theory of jihad, at least in its interpretative presentation as exemplified by classical and some modern exegetes, some of whom we have considered. …

In a remarkable reaction to Samuel Huntington's hypothesis set out in his *The Clash of Civilizations and the Remaking of World Order*, the eighth conference held in 1998 chose "Islam and the Future Dialogue between Civilisations" as the title for its four-day proceedings.[81] Scholars from more than seventy countries representing various international organisations, some from European countries, considered the proposition that dialogue and not war is the way to solve modern international problems.[82] Mufid Shihab, the then-Chancellor of Cairo University, stated that war in Islam is defensive and Muslims resort to it once all other peaceful means are exhausted.[83] In a bid to explain the present-day attitude of Muslims towards non-Muslims with special reference to the 11 September attacks in 2001,[84] the fourteenth conference in 2003 directed a special focus on explaining the modern applications of jihad, its objectives and various rulings, and how it differs in meaning from other terms such as "fighting" (*qital*), "violence" (*unf*) and "terrorism" (*irhab*). Out of the fifty-two published research papers, around seventeen of them were dedicated to jihad alone. The scholars, who came from fifty-six countries, collectively agreed that peace was the underlying principle between Muslims and non-Muslims and that war was permitted only in self-defence.[85] It is a measure that could be likened to surgery carried out only when medicine is of no avail.[86] Some 153 scholars from all five continents attended the sixteenth conference in 2004 in which a special focus was given to terrorism from a Qur'anic perspective, the ethics of war in Islam, present-day attitudes in international relations between Muslims and non-Muslims, and tolerance as understood from the Qur'an and the Sunnah. It is clear from the almost seventy-five papers presented that war was considered by those present as an exception in relations between Muslims and non-Muslims.[87]

It is notable that the proceedings of these three conferences have received scant attention in modern Western scholarship, even though some of the papers were published in English. Moreover, while many of the participating scholars occupy leading positions among Muslim communities in the West, it is still rare to find a Western academic being fully involved in such serious collective discussions. In our view, this is a reason why authors such as Qutb and his like-minded followers are widely discussed, and their views are sometimes mistakenly or intentionally represented as "mainstream" views of Islam. The absence of moderate voices, in their individual as well as collective forms, in modern Western scholarship adds to the blurred atmosphere. In addition, it should not be forgotten that some media outlets in the West have their own biases, shown by the way they selectively highlight extremist views of jihad by Qutb and others.

Moreover, whether individual or collective, the modern views surveyed above are given by trained theologians and scholars well-versed in their fields, who have received solid theological training at reputable seminaries such as the Azhar University. While their views sometimes stand in total contrast to the classical interpretative theory, they apply convincing approaches in their criticisms. ...[88]

NOTES

1. International Committee of the Red Cross (ICRC), "What Is International Humanitarian Law?" (2004). Available https://www.icrc.org/eng/assets/files/other/what_is_ihl.pdf (last accessed 9 December 2017).
2. Ibid, 1.
3. Ibid.
4. ICRC, "IHL and Human Rights Law" (2010). Available https://www.icrc.org/eng/war-and-law/ihl-other-legal-regmies/ihl-human-rights/overview-ihl-and-human-rights.htm (last accessed 9 December 2017).
5. Ibid.
6. Ibid.
7. Ibid.
8. Ibid.
9. Patrick Knäble, "The Relationship between International Humanitarian Law and International Human Rights Law in Situations of Armed Conflict", *The New Zealand Postgraduate Law e-Journal* 4 (2007): 1.
10. Ibid, 2.
11. Ibid. See references provided there.
12. Ibid. See references provided there.
13. Ibid. See references provided there.
14. Ibid, 2; 6. See references provided there.
15. Ibid. See references provided there.
16. Ibid, 30. See references provided there.
17. Ibid. See references provided there.
18. François Bugnion, "Just Wars, Wars of Aggression and International Humanitarian Law", *International Review of the Red Cross* 847(84) (2002): 5.
19. Seth Lazar, "War" in *The Stanford Encyclopaedia of Philosophy*. Summer Edition, Edward N. Zalta (ed.) (2016). Available http://plato.stanford.edu/archives/sum2016/entries/war (last accessed 9 December 2017).
20. Ibid.
21. Ibid.
22. Ibid.
23. Ibid.
24. ICRC, "The Geneva Conventions of 1949 and their Additional Protocols" (2014). Available https://www.icrc.org/en/document/geneva-conventions-1949-additional-protocols (last accessed 9 December 2017).
25. *ICCPR*, art. 20.

26. Office of the High Commissioner for Human Rights (OHCHR), "General Comment No. 11: Prohibition of Propaganda for War and Inciting National, Racial or Religious Hatred (Art. 20)". 29 July 1983, [2]. Available http://www.ohchr.org/Documents/Issues/Opinion/CCPRGeneralCommentNo11.pdf (last accessed 9 December 2017).
27. Abdullahi Ahmed An-Na'im, *Toward an Islamic Reformation: Civil Liberties, Human Rights, and International Law* (Syracuse, NY: Syracuse University Press, 1996), 142.
28. An-Na'im, *Toward an Islamic Reformation*, 142.
29. Ahmad Atif Ahmad, "The Evolution of Just War Theory in Islamic Law: Texts, History, and the Purpose of 'Reading'", *American Foreign Policy Interests* 28 (2006): 108.
30. An-Na'im, *Toward an Islamic Reformation*, 142.
31. Ibid, 143.
32. Hamid Mavani, "Tension between the Qur'an and the Hadith: The Case of Offensive Jihad", *Journal of Shi'a Islamic Studies* IV(4) (2011): 399.
33. Ibid, 412, note 10.
34. Armand Abdel, "Dar al-Islam", *Encyclopaedia of Islam*, 2nd edn, Peri Bearman et al. (eds.), (Brill Online, 2013). Available http://referenceworks.brillonline.com.ezp.lib.unimelb.edu.au/entries/encyclopaedia-of-islam-2/dar-al-islam-SIM_1703 (last accessed 11 December 2017).
35. Manoucher Parvin and Maurie Sommer, "Dar al-Islam: The Evolution of Muslim Territoriality and its Implications for Conflict Resolution in the Middle East", *International Journal of Middle East Studies* 11(1) (1980): 3.
36. Ibid, 3.
37. Ibid, 3.
38. An-Na'im, *Toward an Islamic Reformation*, 150.
39. Ibid.
40. Ibid, 144–5.
41. Ibid, 145.
42. Ibid, 144.
43. Ibid, 145.
44. Said Mahmoudi, "The Islamic Perception of the Use of Force in the Contemporary World", *Journal of the History of International Law* 7 (2005): 60.
45. Karima Bennoune, "As-Salamu Alaykum? Humanitarian Law in Islamic Jurisprudence", *Michigan Journal of International Law* 15 (1994): 617.
46. Mahmoudi, "The Islamic Perception of the Use of Force", 57.
47. Bennoune, "As-Salamu Alaykum?", 609, with reference to Mustansir Mir, "Jihad in Islam", in *The Jihad and its Times*, Hadia Dajani-Shakeel & Ronald Messier (eds.) (Ann Arbor: University of Michigan Press, 1991), 123.
48. An-Na'im, *Toward an Islamic Reformation*, 149.
49. Ibid, 148.
50. Ibid, 142–3.
51. Ibid, 149.
52. Ibid, 149–50.
53. Bennoune, "As-Salamu Alaykum?", 635.
54. Ibid, 628.
55. Ibid, 624.
56. Ibid, 623.
57. Mahmoudi, "The Islamic Perception of the Use of Force", 59.
58. Bennoune, "As-Salamu Alaykum?", 632–3.
59. al-Bukhari, *Sahih al-Bukhari*, Kitab al-'Itq, No. 2545.
60. Bennoune, "As-Salamu Alaykum?", 632.
61. An-Na'im, *Toward an Islamic Reformation*, 151.
62. Mahmoudi, "The Islamic Perception of the Use of Force", 57.
63. Ibid.

64. Bennoune,"As-Salamu Alaykum?", 617, citing K. Ahmad, "Islam's Contributions to International Political Thought", in *L'Islam dans les relations internationals* (Aix-en-Provence: Édisud, 1986), 64; see also Bennoune, "As-Salamu Alaykum?", 636–7.
65. See *Charter of the Organization of Islamic Cooperation* (2008), Preamble [4]. Available http://www.oicun.org/2/24/20140324031549266.html (last accessed 9 December 2017).
66. Manisuli Ssenyonjo, "Jihad Re-Examined: Islamic Law and International Law", *Santa Clara Journal of International Law* 10(1) (2012): 33.
67. An-Na'im, *Toward an Islamic Reformation*, 143.
68. Ibid, 150.
69. Onder Bakircioglu , *Islam and Warfare: Context and Compatibility with International Law* (Abingdon, Oxon; New York: Routledge, 2014), 172.
70. Ibid. However, this is not always the case when it comes to certain aspects of international human rights law.
71. Bakircioglu, *Islam and Warfare*, 172.
72. Ibid, 173.
73. Muhammad Abu Zahrah, *Al 'Alaqat al-Dawliyyah fi al-Islam* (Cairo: Dar al-Fikr al-Arabi, 1415/1995), 50–55; 89–94; idem, *Al-Mujtama' al-Insani fi Zill al-Islam* (Jeddah: Al-Dar al-Su'udiyyah li al-Nashr wa al-Tawzi', 2nd edn, 1401/1981), 152, 155; idem, *Concept of War in Islam*, trans. Muhammad al-Hady and Taha Omar, rev. & ed. Shawki Sukkary (Cairo: Ministry of Waqfs, Supreme Council for Islamic Affairs, 1987), p. 31; idem, "Al-Jihad", in *Kitab al-Mu'tamar al Rabi' li-Majma' al-Buhuth al-Islamiyyah* (Cairo: Majma' al-Buhuth al Islamiyyah, 1388/1968), pp. 79–91.
74. Muhammad Sa'id Ramadan al-Buti, *Al-Jihad fi al-Islam: Kayf Nafhamuh? Wa Kayf Numarisuh?* (Damascus: Dar al-Fikr, 2nd abridged edn, 1424/2003), 227–31.
75. The first edition of al-Buti's book was published in 1997.
76. Ibid, 231.
77. Wahbah al-Zuhayli, *Al-Alaqat al-Dawliyyah fi al-Islam: Muqaranah bi al-Qanun al-Dawli al Hadith* (Beirut: Mu'assasat al-Risalah, 1401/1981), 94 f.
78. Al-Zuhayli, *Athar al Harb*, 131.
79. Ibid, 131, n. 3.
80. For the views of other scholars who maintain the same view, see for example 'Abd al-Wahhab Khallaf, *Al-Siyasah al-Shar'iyyah aw Nizam al-Dawlah al-Islamiyyah fi al-Shu'un al-Dusturiyyah wa al-Kharijiyyah wa al-Maliyyah* (Beirut: Mu'assasat al-Risalah, n.d.), 76–80; 'Abd al Halim Mahmud, *Al-Jihad fi al-Islam* (Cairo: Dar al-Ma'arif, 2nd edn, 1988), 21; Maher Hathout, *Jihad vs. Terrorism*, ed. Samer Hathout (Los Angeles: Multimedia Vera International, 2002), 67; Esposito, *What Everyone*, 120; Abou El Fadl, *The Great Theft*, 223; Bernard K. Freamon, "Martyrdom, Suicide, and the Islamic Law of War: A Short Legal History", *Fordham International Law Journal*, 27(1) (2003): 315 f.; Sherman A. Jackson, "Jihad and the Modern World", *Journal of Islamic Law and Culture*, 7(1) (2002): 25; Sayyid Sabiq, *Fiqh al-Sunnah* (Cairo: Al-Fathli al-I'lam al' Arabi, n.d.), vol. 3, p. 16; Shaheen Sardar Ali and Javaid Rehman, "The Concept of Jihad in Islamic International Law", *Journal of Conflict and Security Law*, 10(3) (2005): 321–43, citation at p. 335.
81. Samuel P. Huntington, *The Clash of Civilizations and the Remaking of World Order* (New York, NY: Simon & Schuster, 1996).
82. Mahmud Hamdi Zaqzuq, "Muqaddimah" in *Islam and the Future Dialogue between Civilizations, Researches and Facts. The Eighth General Conference of the Supreme Council for Islamic Affairs* (Cairo, n.p., 1418/1998), 5.
83. Mufid Shihab, "Al-Qanun al-Dawli wa al-Shar i'ah al-Isla miyyah", in *Islam and the Future Dialogue*, 337 f.
84. Mahmud Hamdi Zaqzuq, "Taqdim" in *The Truth about Islam in a Changing World, Researches and Proceedings. The Fourteenth General Conference of the Supreme Council for Islamic Affairs* (Cairo: Matabi' al-Ahram al-Tujariyyah, 1424/2003), 3.
85. See for example Sufi Hasan Abu Talib, "Al-Kifah al-Mashru' li alShu'ub", in *The Truth about Islam*, 679 f; al-Najjar, "Tahdid al-Mafahim fi Majal al Sira' al-Bashari", 795.

86. Abu Salim Muhammad 'Abd al-Rahim, "Al-Jihad" in *The Truth about Islam*, 752.
87. See for example 'Abbas al-Jarari, "Mu'adalat al-Silm wa al Harb fi Manzur al-Islam" in *Tolerance in the Islamic Civilization, Researches and Facts. The Sixteenth General Conference of the Supreme Council for Islamic Affairs* (Cairo: Matabi' al-Ahram al-Tujariyyah, 1425/2004), 1, 192 f; Jamal al-Din Mahmud, "Al-Jihad wa Akhlaqiyyat al Harb fi al-Isla m", in *Tolerance in the Islamic Civilization*, 848.
88. Mahmud, "Al-Jihad wa Akhlaqiyyat al-Harb", 848.

Conclusion

This book has shown that there is significant interest in the international human rights discourse among Muslim scholars, the governments of Muslim-majority states, civil society and, increasingly, amongst ordinary Muslims. However, discussions of "rights" among Muslims is not just a recent phenomenon. Rights have a long history in Islamic tradition. Since the early period of Islam, Muslim jurists have been interested in the rights of human beings and their connection to God. Legal and moral frameworks were established in the early Muslim community to safeguard certain rights, such as the rights of children (who were recognised as particularly vulnerable in society), the right to freedom of religion for religious minorities (who were not to be forced to convert to Islam), and the protection of non-combatants in situations of armed conflict. Steps were also taken to rectify injustices that were occurring in pre-Islamic society, such as the lack of agency and legal capacity experienced by women, the killing of female infants, and the practice of marrying unlimited numbers of wives. Notably, these rights and protections are not foreign to the international human rights discourse.

The discourse on rights in Islamic thought has always been explicitly grounded in religious terms. Human rights in Islam come from a religious-moral framework where God is the giver of rights and has rights Himself (*huquq Allah*), and human beings, while having rights (*huquq adamiy)*, also have duties and obligations. This conceptual architecture does not make Islam's discourse on rights incompatible with international human rights law. As I have argued, it is reductive to conclude that human rights are secular in nature and have no connection to religious traditions or ethical or moral value systems. There is support within many religious traditions for the notion of human rights because, at its heart, the human rights discourse is about affirming and safeguarding humankind's inherent human dignity, and this idea has roots in many cultures and religious traditions. Even within the discourse on rights that emerged out of Western philosophical and legal thought, religious elements can be found if it is traced back to its roots in natural law theory. It was only subsequently that human rights were stripped of all religious language, as the international community sought to secure universal political support for a set of norms that would prevent atrocities of the kind that occurred during the Second World War from ever happening again.

Since human rights norms have historically sat comfortably within a religious framework, there is no reason why they cannot be framed in such a way again, nor is there any reason why they cannot be upheld in a state governed by Islamic precepts. Recent research has suggested that the idea that there is only one ideal type of relationship between religion and the state is problematic. Even those states that are emphatically "secular" in nature are having difficulty protecting some human rights, particularly in the area of religious freedom. Ensuring that the public sphere is strictly free of religion and all religious expression is confined to the private sphere has only served to protect some people's rights at the expense of others.

Indeed, the balancing act of protecting all peoples' rights and freedoms equally is something that all states struggle with. Instead of focusing on "secularism" as an ideal model, governments should focus on freedom of religion for all and state neutrality when it comes to matters of religion. These are certainly challenges for contemporary Muslim-majority states, but not conceptually unachievable, and there are precedents from Islamic tradition that can be used to support these principles of governance. The fact that most Muslim-majority states today are not democratic is also problematic for the promotion and protection of human rights. Yet Islam itself is not necessarily opposed to democracy, and there is no one model of governance prescribed by the Qur'an or Islamic tradition. Instead, Islamic tradition affirms that governance should be about ensuring justice and fairness, and preventing chaos, division, hatred, enmity, and injustice. If Muslim-majority states applied these principles in reality, there would be no incompatibility between Islamic governance and human rights norms.

Several chapters of this book have looked at state practice when it comes to human rights. It is clear that Muslim-majority states are not disengaged from the international human rights system. They are clearly interacting with human rights standards and the UN's special mechanisms and treaty monitoring systems, although not always in a way that the international community is comfortable with. Muslim-majority states have put in place reservations against many key articles of human rights treaties, qualifying their obligations with respect to those rights. Some of their specific objections include equality within marriage and the family, divorce, adoption, and religious freedom, along with more general reservations that claim the right to implement particular articles in line with the Shari'a. Another development has been the drafting of alternative human rights instruments. These declarations or treaties claim to represent a more indigenous Muslim conception of human rights. They attempt to frame human rights in an explicitly "Islamic" way, recognising the role of God in granting rights and the duties of people towards God and the state, and they incorporate (to a varying degree) elements of Islamic tradition about rights. While these instruments clearly fall short of international standards when it comes to many substantive human rights and lack mechanisms (and political will) for enforcement, they show that Muslim-majority states are taking part in the discourse on Islam and human rights and actively grappling with the relationship between Islamic law and human rights standards.

In the second part of the book I have looked at a number of specific rights from the perspective of both international human rights norms and Islamic tradition. As I have shown, there are many points of intersection between the two, as well as a number of resources within Islamic tradition that can be used to support international human rights standards. Many of these resources come from the Qur'an itself, including texts that affirm the right to life (Q. 17:33); the right to freedom of expression (Q. 55:1–4); the prohibition on religious compulsion (Q 2:256); and affirmations of equality between men and women (Q. 4:124 and others). There are also a number of incompatibilities, such as the explicit rules of inheritance prescribed by the Qur'an that do not grant males and females equal shares; the permissibility of polygyny; the notion of offensive jihad; traditional rules regarding the care and custody of children; and the criminalisation of blasphemy and apostasy. In some instances, contextualising verses from the Qur'an or hadith of the Prophet may help to resolve the tensions. For instance, the classical doctrine of offensive jihad was developed by early Muslim jurists in response to particular sociocultural conditions that no longer exist today (such as the acceptance of the idea of military conquests). If we recognise the relevance of the revelation or practice to that original context and the circumstances of our present context, then it may be possible to achieve the underlying message of that teaching in a new and contextually relevant way today, or even to set it aside as no longer relevant. In other cases the incompatibility might remain, despite efforts to reconcile Islamic and international human rights law.

While there is a great deal of potential for harmonisation between international human rights standards and Islamic law, we should also keep in mind some of the challenges such harmonisation faces. Among these challenges I would include the authoritarian nature of many Muslim-majority states, which leaves relatively little freedom—most importantly intellectual freedom—for many Muslims in these states. This lack of freedom to explore, challenge, critique, and bring forward new ideas is a significant obstacle for developing an Islamic discourse around human rights. In addition, authoritarian regimes are likely to resist greater support for human rights, particularly when they relate to personal freedom, intellectual freedom, freedom of expression, and the like.

A second challenge is the way Islamic educational institutions address human rights discourses. In most traditional Islamic institutions of higher learning, there is relatively little emphasis on modern discourses like human rights. This means the religious leadership emerging in Muslim-majority countries is often unfamiliar with the discourse on Islam and human rights. While there are attempts at reform in traditional Islamic education in at least some Muslim contexts, Muslims have a long way to go in terms of bringing traditional Islamic education into the contemporary context as far as teaching and researching human rights are concerned.

The third challenge comes from the kind of human rights activism which rejects religious values and ideas when discussing human rights issues. This anti-religious, militantly secular approach to human rights is likely to have difficulty in finding a comfortable place in Muslim societies, which are still very much religiously based. Pushing their particular ideas and approaches on to Muslims, who tend to be very suspicious of secular discourses, will most likely do a disservice to the project of human rights in Muslim societies.

These challenges and many others, despite their existence, should not be seen as insurmountable. They do exist to different degrees in various parts of the Muslim world. While in many Muslim-majority countries these problems are significant, Muslim-minority contexts, particularly in the West, tend to give more room for Muslims to explore ideas associated with human rights in a more scholarly, critical fashion. In fact, we are seeing a number of works on Islam and human rights coming from these contexts, particularly in North America and Europe. These works will make their mark on Muslims around the world and will contribute significantly to enriching Muslim discourses on human rights, hopefully also leading to ways of reconciliation between international human rights law and Islamic law. This book is a modest contribution to this very vibrant and highly relevant discourse on Islam and human rights.

Bibliography

Aaronson, Susan Ariel and Jean Pierre Chauffour, "The Wedding of Trade and Human Rights: Marriage of Convenience or Permanent Match?" (2011) *WTO* 15 February, 2011. Available https://www.wto.org/english/res_e/publications_e/wtr11_forum_e/wtr11_15feb11_e.htm#feedback.

Abdel, Armand, "Dār al-islām" in Peri Bearman, Th. Bianquis, C.E. Bosworth, E. van Donzel and W.P. Heinrichs (eds.), *Encyclopaedia of Islam*, 2nd edn (2013) Brill Online. Available http://referenceworks.brillonline.com.ezp.lib.unimelb.edu.au/entries/encyclopaedia-of-islam-2/dar-al-islam-SIM_1703.

Abu Dawud, *Sunan Abi Dawud*. Available https://sunnah.com/abudawud.

African Charter on Human and Peoples Rights. Doc CAB/LEG/67/3 rev. 5, 21 I.L.M. 58 (1982). Available http://www.achpr.org/instruments/achpr/#a25.

Ahmad, Ahmad Atif, "The Evolution of Just War Theory in Islamic Law: Texts, History, and the Purpose of 'Reading'" (2006) 28 *American Foreign Policy Interests*, 107–15.

Ahmad, Nehaluddin, "Comment: Women's Testimony in Islamic Law and Misconceptions. A Critical Analysis" (2011) 6 *Religion and Human Rights*, 13–23.

Ahmad, Nehaluddin, "Modern Debate on the Socio-Political Rights of Muslim Women" (2012) 1 *Asia-Pacific Journal on Human Rights and the Law*, 42–64.

Ahmed, Jibran, "Dorm Debate Led to Death in Pakistan 'Blasphemy Killing' – Witnesses" (2017) *Reuters* 14 April, 2017. Available http://in.reuters.com/article/pakistan-blasphemy-idINKBN17G1DI.

al-Ahsan, Abdullah, "Law, Religion and Human Dignity in the Muslim World Today: An Examination of OIC's Cairo Declaration of Human Rights" (2008–09) 24(2) *Journal of Law and Religion*, 569–97.

al-Buti, Muhammad Sa'id Ramadan, *Al-Jihad fi al-Islam: Kayf Nafhamuh? Wa Kayf Numarisuh?* (Damascus: Dar al-Fikr, 2nd abridged edn, 1424/2003).

al-Hibri, Azizah, "Islam, Law, and Custom: Redefining Muslim Women's Rights" (1997) 12(1) *American University International Law Review*, 1–44.

al-Jarari, 'Abbas, "Mu'adalat al-Silm wa al Harb fi Manzur al-Isla m" in *Tolerance in the Islamic Civilization, Researches and Facts. The Sixteenth General Conference of the Supreme Council for Islamic Affairs* (Cairo: Matabi' al-Ahram al-Tujariyyah, 1425/2004).

al-Mujtama', *al-Insani fi Zill al-Islam* (Jeddah: Al-Dar al-Su'udiyyah li al-Nashr wa al-Tawz i', 2nd ed., 1401/1981).

Al-Mutairi, Mansour Z., "Necessity in Islamic Law" (1997). Thesis submitted to the University of Edinburgh for the Degree of Doctor of Philosophy. January.

al-Rahim, Abu Salim Muhammad 'Abd, "Al-Jihad", in *The Truth about Islam in a Changing World, Researches and Proceedings. The Fourteenth General Conference of the Supreme Council for Islamic Affairs* (Cairo: Matabi' al-Ahram al-Tujariyyah, 1424/2003).

al-Zuhayli, Wahbah, *Al'Alaqat al-Dawliyyah fi al-Islam: Muqaranah bi al-Qanun al-Dawli al Hadith* (Beirut: Mu'assasat al-Risalah, 1401/1981).

Ali, Kecia, *Marriage and Slavery in Early Islam* (Cambridge, MA: Harvard University Press, 2010).

Ali, Shaheen Sardar, "The Conceptual Foundations of Human Rights: A Comparative Perspective" (1997) 3(2) *European Public Law*, 261–82.

Ali, Shaheen Sardar, *Conceptualising Islamic Law, CEDAW and Women's Human Rights in Plural Legal Settings: A Comparative Analysis of Application of CEDAW in Bangladesh, India and Pakistan* (New Delhi: UNIFEM, 2006).

Ali, Shaheen Sardar and Rehman, Javaid, "The Concept of Jihad in Islamic International Law" (2005) 10(3) *Journal of Conflict and Security* Law, 321–343.

"Al-Jihad" in *Kitab al-Mu'tamar al Rabi' li-Majma' al-Buhuth al-Islamiyyah* (Cairo: Majma' al-Buhuth al Islamiyyah, 1388/1968).

Altıok, Özlem, "Muslim Family Laws and CEDAW: A Factsheet" (2015). Available https://www.socwomen.org/wp-content/uploads/Muslim-Family-Laws.pdf.

American Declaration of the Rights and Duties of Man. 2 May, 1948. Available https://www.cidh.oas.org/Basicos/English/Basic2.american%20Declaration.htm.

Amin, Elsayed M. A., *Reclaiming Jihad: A Qur'anic Critique of Terrorism* (Markfield, UK: The Islamic Foundation, 2014).

Amnesty International, "Death Penalty Only for 'Most Serious Crimes'" (2011) Available https://www.amnesty.org.hk/en/our-work/abolish-death-penalty/death-penalty-only-for-most-serious-crimes.

An-Na'im, Abdullahi A., "The Rights of Women and International Law in the Muslim Context" (1987–1988) 9 *Whittier Law Review*, 491–516.

An-Na'im, Abdullahi A., *Toward an Islamic Reformation: Civil Liberties, Human Rights, and International Law* (Syracuse, NY: Syracuse University Press, 1996).

An-Na'im, Abdullahi A., "Human Rights in the Arab World: A Regional Perspective" (2001) 23(3) *Human Rights Quarterly*, 701–32.

An-Na'im, Abdullahi A., ""Sharia and Positive Legislation: Is an Islamic State Possible or Viable?" (1998) 5(1) Yearbook of Islamic and Middle Eastern Law Online, 29 ff.

An-Na'im, Abdullahi A., "The Interdependence of Religion, Secularism, and Human Rights: Prospects for Islamic Societies" (2005) 11(1) *Common Knowledge*, 56–80.

Anthony, Dorothea, "Indivisibility of Human Rights: A Theoretical Critique" (2010) Thesis submitted to the University of Technology, Sydney in Fulfilment of the Requirements for 76040 Research Thesis. Available https://www.uts.edu.au/sites/default/files/law-form-dorothea-anthony.pdf.

Arkoun, Mohammad, *Rethinking Islam: Common Questions, Uncommon Answers* (Boulder: Westview Press, 1994).

Armstrong, Karen, *Muhammad: A Biography of the Prophet* (San Francisco: Harper, 1992).

Azzam, Salem, "Universal Islamic Declaration of Human Rights" (1998) 2(3) *International Journal of Human Rights*, 102–12.

Baderin, Mashood A., "Establishing Areas of Common Ground between Islamic Law and International Human Rights" (2001) 5(2) *The International Journal of Human Rights*, 72–113.

Baderin, Mashood A., "Human Rights and Islamic Law: The Myth of Discord" (2005) 2 *European Human Rights Law Review*, 165–85.

Baderin, Mashood A., *International Human Rights and Islamic Law* (Oxford: Oxford University Press, 2005).

Baderin, Mashood A., "Islam and the Realization of Human Rights in the Muslim World" (2007) 4(1) *Muslim World Journal of Human Rights*, 1–25.

Baderin, Mashood A., "The Role of Islam in Human Rights and Development in Muslim States" in *Religion, Human Rights and International Law: A Critical Examination of Islamic State Practices*, Javaid Rehman and Susan C. Breau (eds.) (Leiden: Martinus Nijhoff Publishers, 2007), 321–58.

Baderin, Mashood A. and Manisuli Ssenyonjo, "Development of International Human Rights Law before and after the UDHR" in *International Human Rights Law: Six Decades after the UDHR and Beyond*, Mashood A. Baderin and Manisuli Ssenyonjo (eds.) (Farnham: Ashgate Publishing, 2010).

Baha'i International Community, "Situation of Baha'is in Iran" (2016). Available https://www.bic.org/focus-areas/situation-iranian-bahais/current-situation#wqtEuzeyWPvSWdf7.97.

Bakircioglu, Onder, *Islam and Warfare: Context and Compatibility with International Law* (Abingdon, Oxon; New York: Routledge, 2014).

Barlas, Asma, "Muslim Women and Sexual Oppression: Reading Liberation from the Quran" (2001) 10 *Macalester International*, 117–46.

Barlas, Asma, *"Believing Women" in Islam: Unreading Patriarchal Interpretations of the Qur'an* (Houston, TX: University of Texas Press, 2002).

Barlas, Asma, "Amina Wadud's Hermeneutics of the Qur'an: Women Reading Sacred Texts" in *Modern Muslim Intellectuals and the Qur'an*, Suah Taji-Farouki (ed.) (Oxford: Oxford University Press, 2004), 97–124.

Barlas, Asma, "The Qur'an, Sexual Equality, and Feminism" (2004) Speech presented at the University of Toronto, 12 January 2004. Available http://www.asmabarlas.com/TALKS/20040112_UToronto.pdf.

Barlas, Asma, "Does the Qur'an Support Gender Equality? Or, Do I Have the Autonomy to Answer this Question?" (2006) Paper delivered at a workshop on Islam and Autonomy at the University of Groningen, 24 November 2006. Available http://www.asmabarlas.com/TALKS/Groningen_Keynote.pdf.

Bayhaqi, Abu Bakr al-, *al-Sunan al-Kubra*, Muhammad ʿAta (ed.) (Beirut: Dar al-Kutub al-ʿIlmiyya, 1424/2003).

Bays, Daniel H., "A Tradition of State Dominance" in *God and Caesar in China: Policy Implications of Church–State Tensions*, Jason Kindopp and Carol Lee Hamrin (eds.) (Washington DC: Brookings Institution Press, 2004).

BBC Persian, "Ḥasan Yūsifī Ishkivarī Āzād Shud", 6 February, 2005. Available http://www.bbc.co.uk/persian/iran/story/2005/02/050206_a_eshkevari.shtml.

Bennoune, Karima, "As-Salamu Alaykum? Humanitarian Law in Islamic Jurisprudence" (1994) 15 *Michigan Journal of International Law*, 605–43.

Bentley, Kristina Anne, "Can There Be Any Universal Children's Rights?" (2005) 9(1) *International Journal of Human Rights*, 107–23.

Berman, Harold J. , *Faith and Order: The Reconciliation of Law and Religion* (Grand Rapids, MI; Cambridge, UK: Wm. B. Eerdmans Publishing, 1993).

Betton, John, "Human Rights, Globalism and Cultural Values: Universality and the Nation State" (2007) 4(3) *International Journal of the Humanities*, 1–6.

Bielefeldt, Heiner, "Muslim Voices in the Human Rights Debate" (1995) 17(4) *Human Rights Quarterly*, 587–617.

Bielefeldt, Heiner, "'Western' versus 'Islamic' Human Rights Conceptions?: A Critique of Cultural Essentialism in the Discussion on Human Rights" (2000) 28(1) *Political Theory*, 90–121.

Bristow, William, "Enlightenment" in *Stanford Encyclopaedia of Philosophy* (2011) (Summer Edition), Edward N. Zalta, (ed.). Available http://plato.stanford.edu/entries/enlightenment.

Brown, David, "Democratization and the Renegotiation of Ethnicity" in *Towards Illiberal Democracy in Pacific Asia*, Daniel A. Bell, David Brown, Kanishka Jayasuriya and David Martin Jones (eds.) (New York: St. Martin's Press, 1995).

Bugnion, François, "Just Wars, Wars of Aggression and International Humanitarian Law" (2002) 847 (84) *International Review of the Red Cross*, 1–26.

Bukhari, Muhammad b. Isma'il al-, *Sahih al-Bukhari*. Translation of Sahih Bukhari. Available http://www.islamicity.com/mosque/sunnah/bukhari/084.sbt.html.

Calfano, Brian Robert and Emile Sahliyeh, "Determining Democracy in the Organization of the Islamic Conference" (2008) 89(3) *Social Science Quarterly*, 751–64.

Chaudhry, Serena, "Millions Pushed into Child Labor in Pakistan" (2012) *Reuters* 7 February 2012. Available http://www.reuters.com/article/us-pakistan-childlabour-idUSTRE8160LA20120207.

Cole, Wade M, "Does Respect for Human Rights Vary across 'Civilizations'? A Statistical Re-examination" (2013) 54(4) *International Journal of Comparative Sociology*, 345–81.

Committee on Economic, Social and Cultural Rights, "General Comment No. 16 (2005) The Equal Right of Men and Women to the Enjoyment of all Economic, Social and Cultural Rights (Art. 3 of the International Covenant on Economic, Social and Cultural Rights)". 11 August, 2005. UN Doc E/C.12/2005/4.

Committee on Economic, Social and Cultural Rights, "Concluding observations of the Committee on Economic, Social and Cultural Rights: Mauritius". 8 June 2010. UN Doc E/C.12/MUS/CO/4.

Committee on Economic, Social and Cultural Rights, "Concluding Observations of the Committee on Economic, Social and Cultural Rights: Lebanon". 24 October 2016. UN Doc E/C.12/LBN/CO/2.

Committee on the Elimination of All forms of Discrimination against Women, "General Recommendation No. 21: Equality in Marriage and Family Relations". 1994. UN Doc A/49/38.

Committee on the Elimination of All forms of Discrimination against Women, "General Recommendation No. 23: Political and Public Life"

(1997). UN Doc A/52/38. Available http://www.un.org/womenwatch/daw/cedaw/recommendations/recomm.htm#recom12.

Committee on the Elimination of All forms of Discrimination against Women, "Consideration of State Party Reports, Combined Initial and Second Periodic Report of Malaysia". 2005. UN Doc CEDAW/C/MYS/1-2.

Committee on the Elimination of All forms of Discrimination against Women, "Written Replies from the Government of Tunisia to the List of Issues and Questions (CEDAW/C/TUN/Q/6) with regard to the Consideration of the Combined Fifth and Sixth Periodic Reports (CEDAW/C/TUN/5-6) Tunisia". 18 August, 2010. UN Doc CEDAW/C/TUN/Q/6/Add.1.

Committee on the Elimination of All forms of Discrimination against Women, "Concluding Observations of the Committee on the Elimination of Discrimination against Women: Tunisia". 5 November, 2010. UN Doc CEDAW/C/TUN/CO/6.

Committee on the Elimination of All forms of Discrimination against Women, "Replies of Pakistan to the List of Issues to be Taken Up in Connection with the Consideration of its Fourth Periodic Report". 27 November 2012. UN Doc CEDAW/C/PAK/Q4/Add.1.

Committee on the Elimination of All forms of Discrimination against Women, "Concluding Observations on the Fourth Periodic Report of Pakistan, Adopted by the Committee at its Fifty-Fourth Session (11 February–1 March 2013)". 27 March, 2013. UN Doc CEDAW/C/PAK/CO/4.

Committee on the Elimination of All forms of Discrimination against Women, "Concluding Observations on the Initial Report of Qatar". 10 March, 2014. UN Doc CEDAW/C/QAT/CO/1.

Committee on the Elimination of All forms of Discrimination against Women and Committee on the Rights of the Child, "Joint General Recommendation No. 31 of the Committee on the Elimination of Discrimination against Women/General Comment No. 18 of the Committee on the Rights of the Child on Harmful Practices". UN Doc CEDAW/C/GC/31-CRC/C/GC/18. 14 November, 2014.

Committee on the Elimination of All forms of Discrimination against Women, "Concluding Observations on the Eighth Periodic Report of Bangladesh". 18 November, 2016. UN Doc CEDAW/C/BGD/CO/8.

Committee on the Rights of the Child, "Concluding Observations on the Fourth Periodic Report of Yemen". 25 February, 2014. UN Doc CRC/C/YEM/CO/4.

Committee on the Rights of the Child, "Concluding Observations on the Combined Third and Fourth Periodic Reports of the Islamic Republic of Iran". 14 March, 2016. UN Doc CRC/C/IRN/CO/3-4.

Committee on the Rights of the Child, "Consideration of Reports Submitted by States Parties under Article 44 of the Convention. Concluding Observations: Pakistan". 27 October 2003. UN Doc CRC/C/15/Add.217.

Committee on the Rights of the Child, "Consideration of Reports Submitted by States Parties under Article 44 of the Convention. Concluding Observations: Bahrain". 3 August, 2011. UN Doc CRC/C/BHR/CO/2-3.

Committee on the Rights of the Child, "Consideration of Reports Submitted by States Parties under Article 44 of the Convention. Concluding Observations: Maldives". 14 March, 2016. UN Doc CRC/C/MDV/CO/4-5.

Committee on the Rights of the Child, "Consideration of Reports Submitted by States Parties under Article 44 of the Convention. Concluding Observations: Saudi Arabia". 25 October, 2016. UN Doc CRC/C/SAU/CO/3-4.

Committee on the Rights of the Child, "General Comment No. 5, General Measures of Implementation of the Convention on the Rights of the Child (Arts. 4, 42 and 44, Para. 6)". 27 November, 2003. UN Doc CRC/GC/2003/5.

Committee on the Rights of the Child, "General Comment No. 14 (2013) on the Right of the Child to Have his or her Best Interests Taken as a Primary Consideration (Art. 3, Para. 1)". 29 May, 2013. UN Doc CRC/C/GC/14.

Corley, Felix, *Religion in the Soviet Union: An Archival Reader* (Basingstoke, UK: Palgrave Macmillan, 1996).

Council of Europe, "The Margin of Appreciation" (undated). Available https://www.coe.int/t/dghl/cooperation/lisbonnetwork/themis/echr/paper2_en.asp.

Dalacoura, Katerina, *Islam, Liberalism and Human Rights: Implications for International Relations* (London; New York: I.B. Tauris, 1998).

Dallmayr, Fred, "Whither Democracy? Religion, Politics and Islam" (2011) 37(4) *Philosophy and Social Criticism*, 437–48.

Danish Institute for Human Rights, "The OIC's Permanent Independent Human Rights Commission: An Early Assessment" (2015). 2015/3 *Matters of Concern Human Rights Research Papers*. Available http://www.humanrights.dk/sites/humanrights.dk/files/working_papers/2015%20matters_of_concern_kayaoglu_2015.pdf.

De Mesquita, Bruce Bueno, George W. Downs, Alistair Smith, and Feryal Marie Cherif, "Thinking Inside the Box: A Closer Look at Democracy and Human Rights" (2005) 49(3) *International Studies Quarterly*, 439–57.

Decherf, Dominique, "French Views of Religious Freedom" The Brookings Institution, 1 July 2001. Available http://www.brookings.edu/research/articles/2001/07/france-decherf.

Donnelly, Jack, "Human Rights and Human Dignity: An Analytic Critique of Non-Western Conceptions of Human Rights" (1982) 76(2) *The American Political Science Review*, 303–16.

Donnelly, Jack, "Cultural Relativism and Universal Human Rights" (1984) 6(4) *Human Rights Quarterly*, 400–19.

Donner, Fred M., *Muhammad and the Believers: At the Origins of Islam* (Cambridge, MA: Belknap Press, 2010).

Donoho, Douglas Lee, "Relativism versus Universalism in Human Rights: The Search for Meaningful Standards" (1990–91)27 *Stanford Journal of International Law* 345–91.

El-Awa, M.S., *Punishment in Islamic Law: A Comparative Study* (Indianapolis: American Trust Publications, 1982).

El Fadl, Khaled Abou, *Islam and the Challenge of Democracy* (Princeton, NJ: Princeton University Press, 2004).

El Fadl, Khaled Abou, "In Recognition of Women" (2011). Available http://www.scholarofthehouse.org/inreofwobykh.html.

El Fadl, Khaled Abou, *Reasoning with God* (Lanham, MA: Rowman & Littlefield, 2014).

Danish Institute for Human Rights, "The OIC's Permanent Independent Human Rights Commission: An Early Assessment" (2015). 2015/3 *Matters of Concern Human Rights Research Papers*. Available http://www.humanrights.dk/sites/humanrights.dk/files/working_papers/2015%20matters_of_concern_kayaoglu_2015.pdf.

El Fegiery, Moataz Ahmed, "Islamic Law and Freedom of Religion: The Case of Apostasy and its Legal Implications in Egypt" (2013) 10(1) *Muslim World Journal of Human Rights*, 1–26.

Eshkevari, Hasan Yousefi, *Asnādi Dādgāhi Kunfirānsi Birlīn-Muqaddami (Qismati Duvvum)* (2011). Available http://yousefieshkevari.com/?p=1791.

Esposito, John L. *What Everyone Needs to Know About Islam* (Oxford: Oxford University Press, 2002).

Esposito, John L., and Natana J. DeLong-Bas, *Women in Muslim Family Law*, 2nd edn (Syracuse, NY: Syracuse University Press, 2001).

European Council for Fatwa and Research, "Permissibility of Conventional Mortgage under Necessity". Resolution Adopted at its Fourth Ordinary Session, 27–31 October 1999. Available http://eshaykh.com/halal_haram/permissibility-of-conventional-mortgage-under-necessity.

Fadel, Mohammad H., "Public Reason as a Strategy for Principled Reconciliation: The Case of Islamic Law and International Human Rights Law" (2007) 8(1) *Chicago Journal of International Law*, 1–20.

Fernandez, Norman, "Opinion: Subashini Case—Worrying Implications for Non-Muslim Spouse" (2007) *The Malaysian Bar* 30 March, 2007. Available http://www.malaysianbar.org.my/members_opinions_and_comments/opinion_subashini_case_worrying_implications_for_non_muslim_spouse.html.

Fisch, M.S., "Islam and Authoritarianism" (2002) 55(1) *World Politics*, 4–37.

Fox, Jonathan, "World Separation of Religion and State into the 21st Century" (2006) 39(5) *Comparative Political Studies*, 537–69.

Fox, Jonathan, "State Religious Exclusivity and Human Rights" (2008) 54 *Political Studies*, 928–48.

Freamon, Bernard K., "Martyrdom, Suicide, and the Islamic Law of War: A Short Legal History" (2003) 27(1) *Fordham International Law Journal*, 299–369.

Freedom of Religion and Belief Program Egyptian Initiative for Personal Rights, "Freedom of Religion and Belief in Egypt Quarterly Report" (2009). Available https://eipr.org/en/publications/freedom-religion-and-belief-egypt-quarterly-report-oct-dec-2009.

Freeman, Marsha A., "Reservations to CEDAW: An Analysis for UNICEF" (2009). Available http://www.unicef.org/gender/files/Reservations_to_CEDAW-an_Analysis_for_UNICEF.pdf.

Freeman, Michael, "The Problem of Secularism in Human Rights Theory" (2004) 26 *Human Rights Quarterly*, 375–400.

Gaffney-Rhys, Ruth, "A Comparison of Child Marriage and Polygamy from a Human Rights Perspective: Are the Arguments Equally Cogent?" (2012) 34(1) *Journal of Social Welfare & Family Law*, 49–61.

Girlsnotbrides, "Child Marriage around the World: Indonesia" (2016). Available http://www.girlsnotbrides.org/child-marriage/indonesia.

Goolam, Nazeem MI, "The Cartoon Controversy: A Note on Freedom of Expression, Hate Speech and Blasphemy" (2006) 39(2) *The Comparative and International Law Journal of Southern Africa*, 333–50.

Government of Maldives, *Constitution of the Republic of Maldives 2008*. Available http://www.presidencymaldives.gov.mv/Documents/ConstitutionOfMaldives.pdf.ir.

Government of Pakistan, "Hudood Laws". Available http://www.pakistani.org/pakistan/legislation/hudood.html.

Government of Pakistan *The Offence of Zina (Enforcement of Hudood) Ordinance, 1979*. Ordinance No. VII of 1979. 9 February 1979. Available http://www.pakistani.org/pakistan/legislation/zia_po_1979/ord7_1979.html.

Guo, Changgang and Fengmei Zhang, "Religion and Social Stability: China's Religious Policies in the Age of Reform" (2015) 36(11) *Third World Quarterly*, 2183–95.

Gyan, Kwame, "The Duty (Responsibility) of the Individual in the African Charter on Human and Peoples' Rights as It Relates to International Human Rights" (2000-2002) 21 *University of Ghana Law Journal*, 156–91.

Hakeem, Farrukh B., M.R. Haberfeld, and Arvind Verma, *Policing Muslim Communities: Comparative International Context* (New York: Springer, 2012).

Haleem, M.A.S. Abdel, *The Qur'an*. M.A.S. Abdel Haleem (trans.) (Oxford: Oxford University Press, 2005).

Hallaq, Wael B., *A History of Islamic Legal Theories: An Introduction to Sunni Uṣul al-Fiqh* (Cambridge: Cambridge University Press, 1997).

Hallaq, Wael B., *The Origins and Evolution of Islamic Law* (Cambridge: Cambridge University Press, 2005).

Hashemi, Kamran, "Religious Legal Traditions, Muslim States and the Convention on the Rights of the Child: An Essay on the Relevant UN Documentation" (2007) 29(1) *Human Rights Quarterly*, 194–227.

Hassan, Riffat, "On Human Rights and the Qur'anic Perspective" in *Human Rights in Religious Traditions*, Arlene Swidler (ed.) (New York: Pilgrim Press, 1982).

Hassan, Rifatt, "Muslim Women and Post-Patriarchal Islam" in *After Patriarchy: Feminist Transformations of the World's Religions*, Paula M. Cooey, William R. Eakin and Jay B. McDaniel (eds.) (Maryknoll, NY: Orbis Books, 1991).

Hastings, J. (ed.) *Encyclopaedia of Religion and Ethics* Vol. II (Edinburgh: T&T Clarke, 1909).

Hathout, Maher, *Jihad vs. Terrorism* (Los Angeles: Multimedia Vera International, 2002).

Hevener, Natalie Kaufman, *International Law and the Status of Women* (Boulder, CO: Westview Press, 1983).

Hille, Rolf, "Human Rights and Islam—Is the 'Clash of Civilizations' Already Pre-Programmed?" (2006) 30(4) *Evangelical Review of Theology*, 352–61.

Hoffmann, Abdul Hadi, "Muslims in Germany: The Struggle for Integration" in *Islam and the Question of Minorities*, Tamara Sonn (ed.) (Atlanta: Scholars Press, 1996).

Hourani, A., *Minorities in the Arab World* (Oxford: Oxford University Press, 1947).

Human Rights Committee, "Concluding Observations of the Human Rights Committee: Jordan". 18 November, 2010. UN Doc CCPR/C/JOR/CO/4.

Human Rights Committee, "Concluding Observations of the Human Rights Committee: Islamic Republic of Iran". 29 November, 2011. UN Doc CCPR/C/IRN/CO/3.

Human Rights Committee, "Concluding Observations of the Human Rights Committee: Yemen". 23 April, 2012. UN Doc CCPR/C/YEM/CO/5.

Human Rights Committee, "Concluding Observations on the Initial Report of Indonesia". 21 August, 2013. UN Doc CCPR/C/IDN/CO/1.

Human Rights Committee, "Concluding Observations on the Second Periodic Report of Tajikistan". 22 August, 2013. UN Doc CCPR/C/TJK/CO/2.

Human Rights Committee, "Concluding Observations on the Fifth Periodic Report of Iraq". 3 December, 2015. UN Doc CCPR/C/IRQ/CO/5.

Human Rights Committee, "Concluding Observations on the Third Periodic Report of Kuwait". 11 August 2016. UN Doc CCPR/C/KWT/CO/3.

Human Rights Committee, "General Comment No. 17: Article 24 (Rights of the Child)". 29 September, 1989.

Human Rights Committee, "General Comment No. 19: Article 23 (The Family)". 27 July, 1990.

Human Rights Committee, "General Comment No. 22: The Right to Freedom of Thought, Conscience and Religion (Article 18)". 30 July, 1993. UN Doc CCPR/C/21/Rev.1/Add.4.

Human Rights Committee, "General Comment No. 28: Article 3 (The Equality of Rights between Men and Women)". 29 March, 2000. UN Doc CCPR/C/21/Rev.1/Add.10.

Human Rights Committee, "General Comment No. 34 (Article 19: Freedoms of Opinion and Expression)". 21 July, 2011. UN Doc CCPR/C/GC/34.

Human Rights Committee, "Human Rights Committee Considers Report of Sudan" (2014) *UN Media Release* 9 July, 2014. Available http://www.ohchr.org/EN/NewsEvents/Pages/DisplayNews.aspx?NewsID=14841&LangID=E.

Human Rights Committee, "List of Issues in Relation to the Third Periodic report of Kuwait". 21 April, 2016. UN Doc CCPR/C/KWT/Q/3/Add.1.

Human Rights Committee, "List of Issues in Relation to the Third Periodic Report of Kuwait. Addendum: Replies of Kuwait to the List of Issues". 21 April, 2016. UN Doc CCPR/C/KWT/Q/3/Ad.

Human Rights Council, "Annual Report of the United Nations High Commissioner for Human Rights and Reports of the Office of the High Commissioner and the Secretary-General: Study of the United Nations

High Commissioner for Human Rights Compiling Existing Legislations and Jurisprudence Concerning Defamation of and Contempt for Religions". 5 September, 2008. UN Doc A/HRC/9/25.

Human Rights Council, "Question of the Death Penalty: Report of the Secretary-General". 30 June, 2014. UN Doc A/HRC/27/23.

Human Rights Watch, "Summary and Recommendations" in 9 (7(E)) *Iran: Religious and Ethnic Minorities: Discrimination in Law and Practice* (1997). Available https://www.hrw.org/reports/1997/iran/Iran-01.htm.

Human Rights Watch, "The Legal Framework" in 9 (7(E)) *Iran: Religious and Ethnic Minorities: Discrimination in Law and Practice* (1997). Available https://www.hrw.org/legacy/reports/1997/iran/Iran-04.htm#P143_18379.

Human Rights Watch, "Saudi Arabia: Poet Sentenced to Death for Apostasy Reverses Earlier Ruling of 4 Years, 800 Lashes" (2015). Available https://www.hrw.org/news/2015/11/23/saudi-arabia-poet-sentenced-death-apostasy.

Huntington, Samuel P., "The Clash of Civilizations?" (1993) 72(3) *Foreign Affairs*, 22–49.

Ibn Asakir Abu al-Qasim, *Tarikh Madinat Dimashq*, ed. Amr al-Amrawi (Cairo: Dar al-Fikr, 1415/1995).

Ibn Hanabal, Ahmad, *Musnad*, Shu'ayb al-Arna'uṭ and Adil Murshid et al. (eds.) (Beirut: Mu'assasat al-Risala, 1421/2001).

Ibn Majah, *Sunan Ibn Majah*. Available https://sunnah.com/ibnmajah/.

Ignatieff, Michael, "Human Rights as Idolatry" in *Human Rights as Politics and Idolatry*, Amy Gutman (ed.) (Princeton: Princeton University Press, 2001).

International Centre for Not-For-Profit-Law, "NGO Law Monitor: League of Arab States" (2016). Available http://www.icnl.org/research/monitor/las.html.

International Committee of the Red Cross, "What Is International Humanitarian Law?" (2004). Available https://www.icrc.org/eng/assets/files/other/what_is_ihl.pdf.

International Committee of the Red Cross, "IHL and Human Rights Law" (2010). Available https://www.icrc.org/eng/war-and-law/ihl-other-legal-regmies/ihl-human-rights/overview-ihl-and-human-rights.htm.

International Committee of the Red Cross, "The Geneva Conventions of 1949 and their Additional Protocols" (2014). Available https://www.icrc.org/en/document/geneva-conventions-1949-additional-protocols.

International Council on Human Rights Policy, "Taking Duties Seriously: Individual Duties in International Human Rights Law" (undated). Available http://www.ichrp.org/files/reports/10/103_report_en.pdf.

International Justice Resource Center, "Overview of the Human Rights Framework" (undated). Available http://www.ijrcenter.org/ihr-reading-room/overview-of-the-human-rights-framework/.

Iran Human Rights Documentation Centre, "Apostasy in the Islamic Republic of Iran" (2014). Available www.iranhrdc.org/english/publications/reports/1000000512-apostasy-in-the-islamic-republic-of-iran.html (last accessed 1 March 2018).

Iran Human Rights Documentation Center, "Witness Statement of Ali Afshari" (2008). Available http://www.iranhrdc.org/english/publications/witness-testimony/3175-witness-statement-ali-afshari.html#.U3Fo5oFdXyI.

Ishaque, Shabnam and Muhammad Mustafa Khan, "The Best Interests of the Child: A Prevailing Consideration within Islamic Principles and a Governing Principle in Child Custody Cases in Pakistan" (2015) 29 *International Journal of Law, Policy and the Family*, 78–96.

Ishay, Micheline, "What Are Human Rights? Six Historical Controversies" (2004) 3(3) *Journal of Human Rights*, 359–71.

Islam, Mahmuda, "CEDAW and Bangladesh: A Study to Explore the Possibilities of Full Implementation of CEDAW in Bangladesh" in *Conceptualising Islamic Law, CEDAW and Women's Human Rights in Plural Legal Settings: A Comparative Analysis of Application of CEDAW in Bangladesh, India and Pakistan*, Shaheen Sardar Ali (ed.) (New Delhi: UNIFEM—South Asia Regional Office, 2006).

Islamic Republic of Iran, *Islamic Penal Code of 2013 of the Islamic Republic of Iran*. Book 1 (English translation). Available http://www.iranhrdc.org/english/human-rights-documents/iranian-codes/1000000455-english-translation-of-books-1-and-2-of-the-new-islamic-penal-code.html#1.

Jackson, Sherman A., "Jihad and the Modern World" (2002) 7(1) *Journal of Islamic Law and Culture*, 1–26.

Jamal, Zara, "To Be a Woman in Pakistan: Six Stories of Abuse, Shame and Survival" (2012). Available http://www.theatlantic.com/international/archive/2012/04/to-be-a-woman-in-pakistan-six-stories-of-abuse-shame-and-survival/255585.

Kamali, Mohammad Hashim, "Freedom of Religion in Islamic Law" (1992) 21 *Capital University Law Review*, 63–81.

Kamali, Mohammad Hashim, "Fundamental Rights of the Individual: An Analysis of Haqq (Right) in Islamic Law" (1993) 10(3) *American Journal of Social Sciences*, 340–66.

Kamali, Mohammad Hashim, *Freedom of Expression in Islam* (Kuala Lumpur: Berita Publishing, 1994).

Kamali, Mohammad Hashim, *Islamic Law in Malaysia: Issues and Developments* (Kuala Lumpur: Ilmiah Publishers, 2000).

Kashefi, Mahmoud "Max", "The 'Arab Spring' and its Theoretical Significance: Samuel Huntington's 'The Clash of Civilizations' Revisited" (2013) 39(1) *International Review of Modern Sociology*, 29–51.

Kayaoğlu, Turan, "It's Time to Revise the Cairo Declaration of Human Rights in Islam" (2012). Available http://www.brookings.edu/research/opinions/2012/04/23-cairo-kayaoglu.

Kayaoğlu, Turan, *The OIC's Permanent Independent Human Rights Commission: An Early Assessment* (Copenhagen: The Danish Institute for Human Rights, 2015), 4–8. Available http://www.humanrights.dk/sites/humanrights.dk/files/working_papers/2015%20matters_of_concern_kayaoglu_2015.pdf.

Khallaf, 'Abd al-Wahhab, *Al-Siyasah al-Shar'iyyah aw Nizam al-Dawlah al-Islamiyyah fi al-Shu'un al-Dusturiyyah wa al-Kharijiyyah wa al-Maliyyah* (Beirut: Mu'assasatal-Risalah, n.d.).

Khan, M. Ilyas, "Why Is a Pakistani Bill to Protect Women Unpopular" (2016). Available http://www.bbc.com/news/world-asia-35811180.

Khir, Bustami Mohamed, "The Right of Women to No-Fault Divorce in Islam and its Application by British Muslims" 17(3) *Islam and Christian–Muslim Relations*, 295–306.

Kindopp, Jason, "Fragmented Yet Defiant: Protestant Resilience under Chinese Communist Party Rule" in *God and Caesar in China: Policy Implications of Church–State Tensions*, Jason Kindopp and Carol Lee Hamrin (eds.) (Washington DC: Brookings Institution Press, 2004).

Kindopp, Jason, "Policy Dilemmas in China's Church–State Relations: An Introduction" in *God and Caesar in China: Policy Implications of Church–State Tensions*, Jason Kindopp and Carol Lee Hamrin (eds.) (Washington DC: Brookings Institution Press, 2004).

Knäble, Patrick, "The Relationship between International Humanitarian Law and International Human Rights Law in Situations of Armed Conflict" (2007) 4 *The New Zealand Postgraduate Law e-Journal*, 1–31.

Koraytem, Tabet, "Arab Islamic Developments on Human Rights" (2001) 16(3) *Arab Law Quarterly*, 255–62.

Krivenko, Ekaterina Yahyaoui, *Women, Islam and International Law within the Context of the Convention on the Elimination of All Forms of Discrimination against Women* (Leiden: Martinus Nijhoff Publishers, 2009).

Kutty, Faisal, "Islamic Law, Adoptions and Kafalah" (2012) *Jurist*. Available http://www.jurist.org/forum/2012/11/faisal-kutty-adoption-kafalah.php.

Langlaude, Sylvie, "Children and Religion under Article 14 UNCRC: A Critical Analysis" (2008) 16 *International Journal of Children's Rights*, 475–504.

Lau, Martin, "Human Rights, Natural Justice and Pakistan's Shariat Courts" in *Religion, Human Rights and International Law: A Critical Examination of Islamic State Practices*, Javaid Rehman and Susan C. Breau (eds.) (Leiden: Martinus Nijhoff Publishers, 2007), 359–78.

Lazar, Seth, "War" in *The Stanford Encyclopaedia of Philosophy* (Summer edn) (2016), Edward N. Zalta (ed.). Available http://plato.stanford.edu/archives/sum2016/entries/war.

League of Arab States, *Arab Charter on Human Rights*. 22 May 2004. Reprinted in 12 *Int'l Hum. Rts. Rep*. 893 (2005). Available http://hrlibrary.umn.edu/instree/loas2005.html.

Leblanc, L.J., "Reservations to the Convention on the Rights of the Child: A Macroscopic View of State Practice" (1996) 4 *International Journal of Children's Rights*, 357–81

Lentz, Susan A., "Revisiting the Rule of Thumb: An Overview of the History of Wife Abuse" (1999) 10(2) *Women & Criminal Justice*, 9–27.

Levin Institute, "Origins of Human Rights", (undated). Available http://www.globalization101.org/human-rights-vs-natural-rights.

Li, Xiaorong, "A Cultural Critique of Cultural Relativism" (2007) 66(1) *American Journal of Economics and Sociology*, 151–71.

Luehrmann, Sonja, *Secularism Soviet Style: Teaching Atheism and Religion in a Volga Republic* (Bloomington, IN: Indiana University Press, 2011).

Machado, Michel, "Muslims in France: Jacobinism Confronts Islamism" in *Islam and the Question of Minorities*, Tamara Sonn (ed.) (Atlanta: Scholars Press, 1996).

Mahmoudi, Said, "The Islamic Perception of the Use of Force in the Contemporary World" (2005) 7 *Journal of the History of International Law*, 55–68.

Mahmud, 'Abd al Halim, *Al-Jihad fi al-Islam* (Cairo: Dar al-Ma'arif, 2nd edn, 1988).

Mahmud, Jamal al-Din, "Al-Jihad wa Akhlaqiyyat al Harb fi al-Islam" in *Tolerance in the Islamic Civilization, Researches and Facts. The Sixteenth General Conference of the Supreme Council for Islamic Affairs* (Cairo: Matabi' al-Ahram al-Tujariyyah, 1425/2004).

Maneli, Mieczyslaw, *Juridical Positivism and Human Rights* (New York: Hippocrene Books, 1981).

Marshall, Paul, "Exporting Blasphemy Restrictions: The Organization of the Islamic Conference and the United Nations" (2011) 9(2) *The Review of Faith & International Affairs*, 57–63.

Mavani, Hamid, "Tension between the Qur'an and the Hadith: The Case of Offensive Jihad" (2011) IV(4) *Journal of Shi'a Islamic Studies*, 397–414.

Mayer, Ann Elizabeth, "The Islam and Human Rights Nexus: Shifting Dimensions" (2007) 4(1) *Muslim World Journal of Human Rights*, Article 4.

Mayer, Ann Elizabeth, *Islam and Human Rights: Tradition and Politics* (Boulder, CO: Westview Press, 2012).

Mernissi, Fatema, *The Veil and the Male Elite: A Feminist Interpretation of Women's Rights in Islam* (New York: Addison-Wesley, 1996).

Midlarsky, M.I. "Democracy and Islam: Implications for Civilizational Conflict and the Democratic Peace" (1998) 42(3) *International Studies Quarterly*, 458–511.

Mir, Mustansir, "Jihad in Islam" in *The Jihad and its Times*, Hadia Dajani-Shakeel and Ronald Messier (eds.) (Ann Arbor: University of Michigan Press, 1991).

Mir-Hosseini, Ziba, "The Politics and Hermeneutics of Hijab in Iran: From Confinement to Choice" (2007) 4(1) *Muslim World Journal of Human Rights*, 1–17.

Mokhtari, Shadi, "Human Rights and Power amid Protest and Change in the Arab World" (2015) 36(6) *Third World Quarterly*, 1207–21.

Monsma, Stephen V. and Soper, Christopher J., *The Challenge of Pluralism: Church and State in Five Democracies* (Lanham, MD: Rowman & Littlefield Publishers, 2008).

Monshipouri, M. and Kaufman, C., "The OIC, Children's Rights and Islam" (2015) *The Danish Institute for Human Rights*. Available https://www.humanrights.dk/publications/oic-childrens-rights-islam (last accessed 1 March 2018).

Moosa, Ebrahim, "The Dilemma of Islamic Rights Schemes" (2000–2001) 15(1/2) *Journal of Law and Religion*, 184–215.

Morgan-Foster, Jason, "Third Generation Rights: What Islamic Law Can Teach the International Human Rights Movement" (2005) 8 *Yale Human Rights and Development Law Journal*, 67–116.

Morsink, Johannes, *The Universal Declaration of Human Rights: Origins, Drafting, and Intent* (Philadelphia: University of Pennsylvania Press, 1999).

Mosaffa, Nasrin, "Does the Covenant on the Rights of the Child in Islam Provide Adequate Protection for Children Affected by Armed Conflicts?" (2011) 8(1) *Muslim World Journal of Human Rights*, 1–18.

Muslim b. Hajjaj, *Sahih Muslim*. Available https://sunnah.com/muslim.

Nasir, J., *The Islamic Law of Personal Status* (Leiden: Brill, 1990).

National Imams Consultative Forum, "An Australian Muslim Perspective on Some Key Contemporary Concerns" (2015). Available http://nceis.unimelb.edu.au/__data/assets/pdf_file/0011/1467362/NICF-Statements.pdf.

Nobel Foundation, "Tawakkol Karman—Nobel Lecture". Available https://www.nobelprize.org/nobel_prizes/peace/laureates/2011/karman-lecture_en.html.

Norris, Pippa and Ronald Inglehart, "Islamic Culture and Democracy: Testing the 'Clash of Civilizations' Thesis" (2002) 1(3-4) *Comparative Sociology*, 235–264.

Office of the High Commissioner for Human Rights, "General Comment No. 11: Prohibition of Propaganda for War and Inciting National, Racial or Religious Hatred (Art. 20)". 29 July, 1983.

Office of the High Commissioner for Human Rights, "International Standards I3C – Freedom of Religion or Belief: Excerpts of Relevant Paragraphs of 25 Years Mandate Reporting Practice [Special Rapporteur on Freedom of Religion or Belief] (1986–2011)". UN Doc A/60/399. Available http://www.ohchr.org/EN/Issues/FreedomReligion/Pages/IstandardsI3c.aspx.

Office of the High Commissioner for Human Rights, "Rapporteur's Digest on Freedom of Religion or Belief: Excerpts of the Reports from 1986 to 2011 by the Special Rapporteur on Freedom of Religion or Belief Arranged by Topics of the Framework for Communications" (2011). Available http://www.ohchr.org/EN/Issues/FreedomReligion/Pages/FreedomReligionIndex.aspx.

Office of the High Commissioner for Human Rights, "Status of Ratification: Interactive Dashboard". Available http://indicators.ohchr.org.

Oh, Irene, *The Rights of God: Islam, Human Rights and Comparative Ethics* (Washington DC: Georgetown University Press, 2007).

OIC *Cairo Declaration on Human Rights in Islam.* 5 August 1990. UN GAOR, World Conf. on Human Rights, 4th Session, Agenda Item 5. UN Doc A/CONF.157/PC/62/Add.18 (1993) [English translation]. Available https://www1.umn.edu/humanrts/instree/cairodeclaration.html.

OIC *The Universal Islamic Declaration of Human Rights.* 21 Dhul Qaidah 1401/19 September, 1981. Available http://www.alhewar.com/ISLAMDECL.html.

Omran, Abdel Rahim, *Family Planning in the Legacy of Islam* (London: Routledge, 1992).

Orend, Brian, *Human Rights: Concept and Context* (Peterborough, ON: Broadview Press, 2002).

Organisation of Islamic Cooperation, "Resolutions on Islamic and Cultural Affairs Adopted by the Twenty-Second Islamic Conference of

Foreign Ministers, Casablanca, Kingdom of Morocco, 8–10 Rajab, 1415 H (10–12 December, 1994)". Available http://www.oic-oci.org/english/conf/fm/22/Resolution22-C.htm.

Organisation of Islamic Cooperation, *Covenant on the Rights of the Child in Islam* (2005). Doc OIC/9-IGGE/HRI/2004/Rep.Final. Available http://www.refworld.org/docid/44eaf0e4a.html.

Organisation of Islamic Cooperation, *Charter of the Organization of Islamic Cooperation* (2008). Available http://www.oicun.org/2/24/20140324031549266.html.

Palomino, Rafael, "Legal Dimensions of Secularism: Challenges and Problems" (2012) 4(2) *Contemporary Readings in Law and Social Justice*, 208–25.

Parvin, Manoucher and Maurie Sommer, "Dar al-Islam: The Evolution of Muslim Territoriality and its Implications for Conflict Resolution in the Middle East" (1980) 11(1) *International Journal of Middle East Studies*, 1–21.

Petrasek, David, "Taking Duties Seriously: Individual Duties in International Human Rights Law" (1999) *International Council on Human Rights Policy*. Available http://ichrp.org/files/reports/10/103_report_en.pdf (last accessed 1 March 2018).

Pocar, Fausto, "Some Thoughts on the Universal Declaration of Human Rights and the 'Generations' of Human Rights" (2015) 10 *Intercultural Human Rights Law Review*, 43–54.

Presidential Decree No. 1083. *Code of Muslim Personal Laws of the Philippines.* 4 February, 1977. Available http://www.lawphil.net/statutes/presdecs/pd1977/pd_1083_1977.html.

Prophet Muhammad's Last Sermon. Available http://www.themodernreligion.com/prophet/prophet-lastsermon.htm.

Qutb, Sayyid, *Ma'alim fi al-Tariq* (Beirut: Dar al-Shuruq, 1979).

Rafiq, Aayesha, "Child Custody in Classical Islamic Law and Laws of Contemporary Muslim World (An Analysis)" (2014) 4(5) *International Journal of Humanities and Social Science*, 267–77.

Rahman, Fazlur, *Islam and Modernity: Transformation of an Intellectual Tradition* (Chicago: University of Chicago Press, 1984).

Rahman, S.A., *Punishment of Apostasy in Islam*, 2nd edn (Lahore, Pakistan: Institute of Islamic Culture, 1978).

Rajabi-Ardeshiri, Masoud, "The Rights of the Child in the Islamic Context: The Challenges of the Local and the Global" (2009) 17 *International Journal of Children's Rights*, 475–89.

Rishmawi, Mervat, "The Revised Arab Charter on Human Rights: A Step Forward?" (2005) 5(2) *Human Rights Law Review*, 361–76.

Sabiq, Sayyid, *Fiqh al-Sunnah*, vol. 3 (Cairo: Al-Fathli al-I'lam al' Arabi, n.d.).

Saeed, Abdullah, *Islamic Thought: An Introduction* (Abingdon, UK: Routledge, 2006).

Saeed, Abdullah (ed.) *Islam and Human Rights* (Cheltenham, UK and Northampton, MA, USA: Edward Elgar Publishing, 2012),

Saeed, Abdullah, *Islam and Belief: At Home with Religious Freedom* (Palo Alto, CA: Zephyr Institute, 2014).

Saeed, Abdullah, "Limitations on Religious Freedom in Islam: The Witness of the Qur'an and Prophetic Traditions" (2014) *ABC Religion and Ethics* 23 May 2014. Available http://www.abc.net.au/religion/articles/2014/05/23/4010689.htm.

Saeed, Abdullah and Hassan Saeed, *Freedom of Religion and Apostasy in Islam* (Farnham: Ashgate Publishing, 2004).

Sarakhsi, Abu Bakr al-, *Kitab al-Usul* (Beirut: Dar al-Ma'arifa, n.d.).

Sarakhsi, Abu Bakr al-, *Sharh al-siyar al-kabir* (n.p.: al-Sharika al-Sharqiyya li-l-I'lanat 1971).

Saraqusti, Abu Muhammad Qasim b. Thabit al-, *Al-Dala'il fi gharib al-hadith*, ed. Muhammad al-Qannas (Riyadh: Maktabat al-Ubaykan, 1421AH).

Sayeh, Leila P. and Adriaen M. Morse, Jr, "Islam and the Treatment of Women: An Incomplete Understanding of Gradualism" (1995) 30 *Texas International Law Journal*, 311–334.

Schacht, Joseph, "Islamic Law in Contemporary States" (1959) 8(2) *American Journal of Comparative Law*, 133–47.

Scott, Rachel M., "Contextual Citizenship in Modern Islamic Thought" (2007) 18(1) *Islam and Muslim–Christian Relations*, 1–18.

Scott, Rachel M., "A Contextual Approach to Women's Rights in the Qur'an: Readings of 4:34" (2009) 99 *The Muslim World*, 60–85.

Shah, Niaz A., "Freedom of Religion: Koranic and Human Rights Perspectives" (2005) 1 & 2 *Asia-Pacific Journal on Human Rights and the Law*, 69–88.

Shah, Niaz A., "Women's Human Rights in the Koran: An Interpretive Approach" (2006) 28 *Human Rights Quarterly*, 868–903.

Social Watch, "The Arab Region: 30 Years of CEDAW" (2010). Available http://www.socialwatch.org/sites/default/files/B15ArabRegion2010_eng.pdf.

Sonn, Tamara (ed.) *Islam and the Question of Minorities* (Atlanta: Scholars Press, 1996).

Spiegel, Mickey, "Control and Containment in the Reform Era" in *God and Caesar in China: Policy Implications of Church–State Tensions*, Jason Kindopp and Carol Lee Hamrin (eds.) (Washington DC: Brookings Institution Press, 2004).

Ssenyonjo, Manisuli, "Jihad Re-Examined: Islamic Law and International Law" (2012) 10(1) *Santa Clara Journal of International Law*, 1–33.

Steiner, Henry J., Philip Alston and Ryan Goodman, *International Human Rights in Context: Law, Politics, Morals*, 3rd edn (Oxford: Oxford University Press, 2012).

Steiner, Kerstin, "Religion and Politics in Singapore—Matters of National Identity and Security? A Case Study of the Muslim Minority in a Secular State" (2011) 58 *Osaka University Law Review*, 107–34.

Stevenson. A, (ed.) *Oxford Dictionary of English*, 3rd edn (2010) Oxford: Oxford University Press.

Stoljar, Samuel J. *An Analysis of Rights* (Wiltshire, UK: Macmillan, 1984).

Stowasser, B.F., *Women in the Qur'an, Traditions, and Interpretation* (New York: Oxford University Press, 1994).

Sturges, Paul, "Limits to Freedom of Expression? Considerations Arising from the Danish Cartoons Affair" (2006) 32 *IFLA*, 181–8.

Sukkary, Shawki (rev & ed.), *Concept of War in Islam*. Trans. Muhammad al-Hady and Taha Omar (Cairo: Ministry of Waqfs, Supreme Council for Islamic Affairs, 1987).

Tabari, Abu Ja'far al-, *Jami ' al-bayan an tafsir ay al-Qur'an*, ed. Ahmad Shakir (Beirut: Mu'assasat al-Risala, 1420/2000).

Talib, Sufi Hasan Abu, "Al-Kifah al-Mashru' li alShu'ub" in *The Truth about Islam in a Changing World, Researches and Proceedings. The Fourteenth General Conference of the Supreme Council for Islamic Affairs* (Cairo: Matabi' al-Ahram al-Tujariyyah, 1424/2003).

Tamimi, Azzam, "Islam and Democracy from Tahtawi to Ghannouchi" (2007) 24(2) *Theory, Culture & Society*, 39–58.

Tharoor, Sashi, "Are Human Rights Universal?" (1999/2000) 16(4) *World Policy Journal*, 1–6.

Tirmidhi, Abu 'Isa Muhammad, *Jami' al-Tirmidhi*. Available at https://sunnah.com/urn/674690.

Tuckness, Alex, "Locke's Political Philosophy" in *The Stanford Encyclopedia of Philosophy* (Spring edn) (2016), Edward N. Zalta (ed.). Available http://plato.stanford.edu/entries/locke-political/#LawNat.

UNICEF, "Child Marriage and the Law" (2008). *Legislative Reform Initiative Paper Series*. Available http://www.unicef.org/policyanalysis/files/Child_Marriage_and_the_Law(1).pdf.

United Nations, "The Foundation of International Human Rights Law" (undated). Available http://www.un.org/en/sections/universal-declaration/foundation-international-human-rights-law/index.html.

United Nations, *Charter of the United Nations*. 24 October, 1945. 1 UNTS XVI. Available http://www.refworld.org/docid/3ae6b3930.htm.

United Nations, "International Human Rights Law: A Short History" (2009) vol. XLVI (1 & 2) *UN Chronicle*. Available https://unchronicle.un.org/article/international-human-rights-law-short-history.

United Nations Economic and Social Council, "Implementation of the Declaration on the Elimination of All Forms of Intolerance and of Discrimination Based on Religion or Belief: Report submitted by Mr. Abdelfattah Amor, Special Rapporteur, in Accordance with Commission on Human Rights Resolution 1996/23". 30 December, 1996. UN Doc E/CN.4/1997/91.

United Nations General Assembly, *Universal Declaration of Human Rights*, 10 December 1948. Available http://www.refworld.org/docid/3ae6b3712c.html.

United Nations General Assembly, *International Covenant on Civil and Political Rights*. 16 December, 1966. Available http://www.refworld.org/docid/3ae6b3aa0.html.

United Nations General Assembly, *International Covenant on Economic, Social and Cultural Rights*. 16 December, 1966. Available http://www.refworld.org/docid/3ae6b
36c0.html.

United Nations General Assembly, *Convention on the Elimination of All Forms of Discrimination against Women*. 18 December, 1979. Available http://www.refworld.org/docid/3ae6b3970.html?.

United Nations General Assembly, *Convention on the Rights of the Child*. 20 November, 1989. Available http://www.refworld.org/docid/3ae6b38f0.html.

United Nations General Assembly, "Report of the Special Rapporteur of the Commission on Human Rights on Freedom of Religion or Belief, Asma Jahangir". 30 September, 2005. UN Doc A/60/399.

United Nations General Assembly, "Report of the Special Rapporteur on Freedom of Religion or Belief, Heiner Bielefeldt". 20 December, 2011. UN Doc A/HRC/19/60.

University of Michigan, "Interdependence and Indivisibility of Economic and Political Rights" (undated). Available http://humanrightshistory.umich.edu/problems/indivisibility.

University of Minnesota, "A Short History of Human Rights" (undated). Available http://www1.umn.edu/humanrts/edumat/hreduseries/hereandnow/Part-1/short-history.htm.

US National Archives, "The Declaration of Independence: A Transcription" (undated). Available http://www.archives.gov/exhibits/charters/declaration_transcript.html.

Van Bueren, Geraldine, *The Best Interests of the Child: International Co-operation on Child Abduction* (London: British Institute of Human Rights, n.d.).

Van der Ven, Johannes A., "From Natural Rights to Human Rights: A Cultural War in the Modern Era" (2013) 41(2) *Religion, State & Society*, 164–87.

Venkatraman, Bharath Anandi, "Islamic States and the United Nations Convention on the Elimination of All Forms of Discrimination against Women: Are the Sharia and the Convention Compatible?" (1994–1995) 44 *American University Law Review*, 1949–2027.

Wadud, Amina, *Qur'an and Woman: Rereading the Sacred Text from a Woman's Perspective* (New York: Oxford University Press, 1999).

Waltz, Susan, "Universal Human Rights: The Contribution of Muslim States" (2004) 26 *Human Rights Quarterly,* 799–844.

Waltz, Susan, "Universalizing Human Rights: The Role of Small States in the Construction of the Universal Declaration of Human Rights" (2001) 23(1) *Human Rights Quarterly*, 44–72.

Waltz, Susan, "Reclaiming and Rebuilding the History of the Universal Declaration of Human Rights" (2002) 23(3) *Third World Quarterly*, 437–48.

Warren, Christie S., "Lifting the Veil: Women and Islamic Law" (2008–2009) 15 *Cardozo Journal of Law & Gender*, 33–66.

Wong, Wing-wah Mary, "The Sunday Times Case: Freedom of Expression versus English Contempt-of-Court Law in the European Court of Human Rights" (1984) 17 *New York University Journal of International Law and Politics*, 35–76.

Yilmaz, Ihsan, "Towards a Muslim Secularism" (2012) 3(2) *Turkish Journal of Politics*, 41–52.

Yilmaz, Ihsan, "Pakistan Federal Shariat Court's Collective Ijtihad on Gender Equality, Women's Rights and the Right to Family Life" (2014) 25(2) *Islam and Christian–Muslim Relations*, 181–92.

Zahrah, Muhammad Abu al-, *'Alaqat al-Dawliyyah fi al-Islam* (Cairo: Dar al-Fikr al 'Arabi, 1415/1995).

Zaqzuq, Mahmud Hamdi, "Taqdim" in *The Truth about Islam in a Changing World, Researches and Proceedings. The Fourteenth General Conference of the Supreme Council for Islamic Affairs* (Cairo: Matabi' al-Ahram al-Tujariyyah, 1424/2003).

Zaretsky, Robert, "How French Secularism Became Fundamentalist". *Foreign Policy* 7 April, 2016. Available http://foreignpolicy.com/2016/04/07/the-battle-for-the-french-secular-soul-laicite-charlie-hebdo.

Index